I, Duryodhana...

Pradeep Govind

Om Books International

First published in 2019 by

Om Books International

Corporate & Editorial Office
A-12, Sector 64, Noida 201 301
Uttar Pradesh, India
Phone: +91 120 477 4100
Email: editorial@ombooks.com
Website: www.ombooksinternational.com

Sales Office
107, Ansari Road, Darya Ganj,
New Delhi 110 002, India
Phone: +91 11 4000 9000
Fax: +91 11 2327 8091
Email: sales@ombooks.com
Website: www.ombooks.com

ISBN: 978-93-5276-619-2

Printed in India

10 9 8 7 6 5 4 3 2 1

PRADEEP GOVIND is an NRI media marketing professional currently working in the Sultanate of Oman. He was the Project Director of the prestigious *Times of Oman* Literary Contest, a first of its kind literary project in the Middle East initiated and blueprinted by him with a view to offer emerging creative writers a platform to express themselves and benchmark their creative writing talent with the best in the region. His first book titled *The 'Capillary' Effect & Other Short Stories* was published on Amazon in 2013. One of the stories in the book titled 'Unto Thy Neighbour' was awarded an Honourable Mention for Literary Excellence in the Top 25 out of 1114 entries in the International Short Story Contest conducted by noted writer Lorian Hemmingway, the granddaughter of the legendary Ernest Hemmingway.

Pradeep is also an enthusiastic lyricist and musician and has released his own English music album on the HMV label in 1995 where he not only penned the lyrics, but composed the songs and performed the vocals as well. He also scripted the music video for one of the songs in it titled 'It Could've Been Me'. He also does guest columns and articles for the *Times of Oman*—Oman's leading English newspaper publication.

Acknowledgements

My heartfelt appreciation and thanks to Suhail Mathur and the Book Bakers team for representing me as my literary agent. I wish them mega success in the days ahead in their worthy endeavour of unearthing the rich hidden creative writing talent in India. I would also like to thank Ajay Mago, Publisher, Om Books International and his team for their enthusiasm and faith in this work.

Special thanks to M.S. Neelakandan for connecting me with my literary agent and also for his support and motivation.

Finally and most importantly, my humble salutations, reverence and gratitude to Bhagwan Shri Veda Vyasa, for providing me with a mega canvas for my work.

This book is a literary work of perception and claims no absolute conformance to any of the several narratives of Vyasa's *Mahabharata* as recounted over the ages.

Who's to judge, who's to blame,
Who's to know who sparked the flame?
Who's to know who was right or wrong
When history sings just the victor's song?

Dedicated to the 'sages'.

Prologue

The curtains are coming down as I struggle through laboured breaths. I, Duryodhana, am dying. But I must hold on. The muddy grass mingled with royal blood, hurts my naked thighs, the thighs that bore the proud slaps of a thousand victories, now waiting in fragments for the birds of prey. The birds, they have been floating in circles in the crimson sky in patient servitude. They dare not descend while I still breathe. I must not hold them for too long and yet wait they must, for the feast that they'll make of me must be served in joy. Know they must the heart they would peck belonged to the victor. Know they must that the eyes they would gouge never looked down in shame and the head they would perch upon never bowed but to friendship. Patience, my friends, for you shall soon be served your heart's fill. Ashwatthama won't be long. Ashwatthama, my one true friend in this moment of truth… Ashwatthama, lonely and misunderstood…perhaps I honoured him too late.

Dusk has set in and the fireflies romance in the darkness above me. The battle dust has settled down. The air is getting cold and the pain intense. The frogs of the lake croak their hymns for the dying, and I've heard them for too long. The freshness is gone from the heaven's flowers that rained on me. The blood has stopped streaming to the lake. There is no blood left. Yet I hold on, hold on by the power of hatred. The birds...have they left feeling denied? Or did the stench of my rotting flesh turn them away? Alas...alas, my friends, why do you desert me in this twilight hour of solitude? Why do you deny me these last moments of my generosity? No, please, let it not be said that I, Duryodhana, disappointed. Ashwatthama, where are you? What keeps you so long? You will not let me down. You will win the war for me, for you love me truly. 'Love me truly?' They all loved me truly–Grandsire Bheeshma, the Acharyas, and even Radheya...one and only Radheya, but they loved Yudhishthira too. Yudhishthira, the mighty Emperor who resorted to falsehood to kill your father and Guru...all for a piece of land... Yudhishthira, the master of exalted sacrifices who coveted his brother's wife and pawned her in a game of dice...and yet the paragon of virtues, loved by all. But not you, Ashwatthama...you'll never forgive him. You'll return with news of victory...and until then, I shall hold my soul within the nine gates of what is left of this body...*and then I will die happy in the favourable arms of history.*

The pain is unbearable. Life is ebbing away. Mother, I'm tired. Mother, my sweet mother, how I long for the comfort of your soft lap. How I long for your gentle fingers caressing my hair. But no, you should not see me this way. I, Duryodhana, who once placed my feet over royal heads across the land of Bharata, now wait for the birds to descend on me for supper. But mother, you refused to see me then. Why would you see me now? Now, when the world has lost its charm, and there's nothing left to celebrate except the news of the death of the Kaunteyas. Kaunteyas, the sons of Kunti, born of many fathers. Kunti, my aunt...yes, she loved me too. The sweetness of her pudding still lingers in the palate of my soul. I recall her always taking my side against that gluttonous bully, her very own Bheema. She knew in the depths of her heart that I was the one who was wronged. Yet she spoke nothing when it mattered. She weakened in stealth, the will of Radheya– and made him a Kaunteya at her convenience. Radheya, my shadow and my shield, my glorious victory and yet my most shameful defeat, dear Radheya, born a bastard and now dead, truthfully a bastard.

The open jaws of death wait in readiness to devour me. My vision blurs. I see a yellow tinge in the mist and it's getting closer. I fail to see clearly for the dew drops linger in my eyes and my hands refuse to move. The yellow is next to me now. I feel the touch of silk on my face, wiping the dew. Gentle fingers caress my hair. Who can this be? My eyes fail me. Is that you, Bhanumati? Poor Bhanumati, who lives in fear of the night, for, that's when the frightful dream comes calling. No. I'll know your touch even in death. You must be getting the pyre ready to follow me, your lord, in death...even if it leads you to the lowest hell...for that's where traditions have thought you to find your highest heaven. This is not you. Then is that you, Ashwatthama? No, it cannot be. These are not your battle-scarred fingers either. Who, then, could you be my friend? Who could you be, so foolish in your generous affection for Duryodhana, who wronged the world in the eyes of the sages, and that too in his fallen moment of shame? Why are you silent? What do I make of your soft laughter? Yes, now I know who you are. That laughter could belong to only one. But why have you come back to me at this moment? Do you wish hell upon yourself by offering meaningless solace to the one you proclaimed to the world as the embodiment of unrighteousness? Have you not time and again spurned my promise of friendship? Tell me, what is your new trick? Haven't you tried them all and have I not graciously allowed them upon myself? Is there any trick left? What is it that you seek of me now? That soft laughter again. But wait...what is that silent drop that just fell on my face? Why does my pain seem to ease? Why is a sudden calm filling my heart? My eyes are clearing up...and again a drop! Yes, I'm right...it's you Vaasudeva...smiling as always...but these drops are from your lotus petal eyes!

1

I have died once before, so has Uncle Shakuni told me. The battle was different. I had lost my race with Yudhishthira to arrive first on this planet and so was sentenced to death in my mother's womb, and the murderer...my very own mother. My mother, the great Gandhari, the pious queen of Dhritarashtra, the blind King of Hastinapur.

My mother, the cheerful Princess of Gandhara, whose hand was offered to the blind Dhritarashtra to bear his progeny and live 'happily ever after'. My mother, refused to see the world, the view of which was denied to her lord, and blindfolded herself to take her rightful share in his destiny. My mother's devotion to Lord of Kailash was unmatched. And yet, on hearing of the birth of Yudhishthira to Aunt Kunti in the forests, my mother, the gentle Gandhari, beat me in her womb a hundred times in frustration and forced me out. I was born a lump of lifeless flesh, so had Uncle Shakuni told me. Uncle Shakuni of Gandhara, the doting brother, watched in impotence as his favourite sister was given away in marriage to the blind king. How could the proposal that came from the mighty Bheeshma of Hastinapur for his blind nephew be spurned? Bheeshma, was the past master in warfare, learned in the knowledge of the divine missiles. Bheeshma, the disciple of Bhargava whom even the Gods feared to displease, the great Bheeshma, the son of Ganga, renounced his claim to the throne of Hastinapur and undertook the great vow of celibacy to please the carnal appetite of his king and father, the famed Shantanu.

I was given life by the great sage Krishna Dwaipayana, also known to the world as Veda Vyasa or simply Vyasa for his accomplishment of compiling the vedas and other esoteric scriptures. The all-knowing Vyasa was born of sage Parashara and my great grandmother, the beautiful Satyavati through a clandestine union that remains an 'unquestioned privilege' of the sages. That was before Satyavati married my great grandfather Shantanu. Satyavati was the adopted daughter of a chieftain of a community of fishermen, and Shantanu, the glorious monarch of Hastinapur had been infatuated with her. But her father's insistence that she would be offered to him in marriage only on the condition that the child born of them would succeed the throne, left him despondent. How could he take away what rightfully belonged to his son Devarata? How could he deny justice to Devarata, his valiant and virtuous son born of River Goddess Ganga. The king's despondency affected his reign and this was not lost on the empathising Devarata, who took upon himself the task of uniting Satyavati with his father. He renounced his claim to the throne and took the oath of celibacy thereby ensuring there would be no claimants to the throne from his lineage. He thus cleared the way for his father to marry Satyavati and earned the name "Bheeshma", the keeper of the terrible oath. His duty as a son towards fulfilling his father's infatuation seemed to weigh more heavily on him than his duty towards his land and subjects. He kept his vow astutely and Vichitravirya, the son of Satyavati and Shantanu ascended the throne after Shantanu. Bheeshma arranged Vichitravirya's marriage with Ambika and Ambalika, the princesses of Kashi. He had forcefully abducted Amba, Ambika and Ambalika, the princesses of Kashi and brought them to Hastinapur for Vichitravirya. However, Amba was released to her will when she disclosed that she had already given her heart to King Salva of Saubha. Ambika and Ambalika were married to Vichitravirya who, however, did not live long enough to leave an heir to the throne. Queen Mother Satyavati summoned her son Vyasa begotten from Parashara, and requested him to impregnate the queens to continue the lineage, which he obliged (in the truthful spirit of the sages). Thus was born my father, the blind Dhritarashtra to Ambika and my uncle, the pale-skinned Pandu to Ambalika. But Vyasa's foresight prompted him to extend his 'sagely' services to the chief maid of the queens as well, and from that union was born Vidura. Vidura, who was to be the embodiment of knowledge...held the wisdom of the world between his ears... the wisdom that stalled the coronation of my father. My father's blindness was stated to be the reason. My helpless father had no choice. Uncle Pandu ascended the throne. My father veiled his disappointment, as he loved his younger brother deeply. King Pandu conquered many a frontier and his fame spread to the four quarters of the earth.

Then came the curse.

Uncle Pandu was cursed by Sage Kindama that he would lose his life at the very moment of a conjugal union. His crime was he had shot a fatal arrow at the sage and his wife who were blissfully copulating in the deep woods. While hunting for sport, he had observed some movements behind the bushes and mistaken the couple for spotted deer in the deceptive foliage.

He had shot his arrow, piercing through the sage and his wife who were on the threshold of ecstasy. The sage pronounced his curse and breathed his last.

The curse made Uncle Pandu lose all interest in kingship. Did his capabilities as a ruler and administrator revolve around his carnal life? I do not know. He was probably keeping in line with the tradition of his grandfather Shantanu. He left for the forests with his queens, Aunt Kunti and Aunt Madri, to live with 'the sages'. He entrusted the lordship of Hastinapur to my blind father. My father became the king and discharged his duties with the Grandsire to guide him and Vidura, who was appointed the Chief Minister. If the king's blindness was acceptable to everyone including Vidura at that time, why was it an issue earlier? But my father proclaimed that he served only as a representative of his brother Pandu. Why? I do not know. My father, the eldest prince, well-versed in scriptures and administrative knowledge, should have ascended the throne in the first place and Uncle Pandu should have administered the kingdom as his representative. Why this senseless and illogical reversal? I do not know...perhaps the hidden hand of destiny was weaving its web for me.

Then came the news of Yudhishthira's birth to Kunti in the forests. However, Uncle Pandu was still alive and hearty with the 'sages' in the forests. Was Kindama's curse an empty one? That cannot be. There were some stories floating around about Aunt Kunti's knowledge of certain incantations to propitiate any deity of her choice and bear that deity's child in her womb through a celestial union that would leave no bearing on her 'pristine and unsullied' chastity. It was claimed that Yudhishthira was born by the grace of Dharma, the Deity of Justice. I never cared to investigate the authenticity of the matter in my entire life as I considered it unbecoming of my stature. Yudhishthira was the son of Aunt Kunti, whom I honoured as my own mother, and hence was to be seen as the son of Pandu. I firmly believed that the birth and death of a person was not half as important as that of the life that he led. Dear Radheya would have borne testimony to that. The news of Yudhishthira's birth reached my mother who was carrying me in her womb. Then came those blows of desperation as I was forced out. And, I, Duryodhana, the future King of Hastinapur, lay lifeless...an unshapely mass of flesh.

I was sprinkled with holy water, chopped to a hundred and one pieces, and placed in many earthern pots by Maharishi Vyasa. He had to make true his boon to the Queen that she would mother a hundred sons. Of course, my mother's request to the sage for a daughter was honoured too and hence a hundred and one pots. The first pot was opened a year later and a bonny young baby sprang to life, and that was I, Duryodhana. The second pot was uncovered the next day and my handsome brother Dushasana who was but a part of me came to life. In the next ninety-eight days, the remaining pots were opened and my brothers who were all but a part of me were welcomed to our planet. The last pot was opened on the ninety-ninth day, and that was my lovely dove-eyed sister Dushala.

I'm told that I brayed like an ass when I came to life. There were several other mysterious omens at my birth like the howling of jackals and untimely rainstorms, all indicative of peril for Hastinapur. It was Vidura who came up with the suggestion of doing away with me...so had Uncle Shakuni told me. Vidura advised my father to put me to death, as he feared that the presages that accompanied my birth were inauspicious and that my life spelt doom for the entire Kshatriya race. Vidura, the 'wise' minister of Hastinapur, the 'embodiment of virtue and knowledge', instructed my father to put me to death while I was still a newborn but my father refused to oblige. "Your Majesty, paternal affection should never come in the way of a king's duty." This was the advice given by Vidura and the other 'wise and learned' men of the court. My father, stubborn as he was, decided to keep me alive because his heart gave him the 'ill advice' of not administering injustice on an innocent infant. He would rather prefer to incur the wrath of the Gods. Poor fool, how was he to know that he would be accountable to history in the future? How was he to know that the voices of his forefathers would haunt his dreams in the days to come?

Thus, I, Duryodhana, was allowed to live...and I, Duryodhana, the future king, was expected to have reverence for these 'wise and learned' men...so what if they wanted me butchered even before I tasted my mother's milk? They were 'wise and learned' men. Their wisdom was not to be questioned. These were the 'wise and learned' men whom my father, blind as he was, depended on to administer the welfare of Hastinapur...my Hastinapur.

2

I charmed Hastinapur. I was the favourite of everybody…well almost everybody except the 'wise and learned' Vidura. The Grandsire never tired of narrating to me the glorious tales of my heroic forefathers and of Hastinapur while I listened, perched on his lap. Acharya Kripa never missed an opportunity to share his wisdom through his moral lessons. Dushasana and I fought for our turns to get our scalp massaged by mother. I would always give in, for he was my little brother. Perhaps that laid the foundation for his hero worship and undying loyalty towards me. Something that he never regretted even when his heart was plucked out and his blood feasted upon, years later. Uncle Shakuni could never bear to be separated from me. He left his own son Uluka back at Gandhara and came to stay with me. Considering the blindness of my parents, he took upon the responsibility of grooming me. He would enchant me with stories of valour and value as he drowsed me to sleep on his chest.

My father insisted I attend the royal court whenever possible even when I was a child to understand statecraft. He used to place me on his lap while he dispensed justice and passed resolutions with his stamp of sovereignty. He would grip me with his strong left arm, never letting me go, and stroke my face as he discussed serious matters of administration with Grandsire Bheeshma, Vidura and the others.

"Son, Hastinapur must be above everything else...," he would say, feeling my soft face with his rough fingers, "One day this sacred land, this beautiful Hastinapur which is the home of divinities, where rain has never failed the harvest and subjects have no wants as their rulers never sway from the path of virtue, will be all yours and will look up to you to carry forward the torch of its glorious traditions."

And my heart would swell with pride as I would sit on his lap, listening attentively while playing with his long grey beard, intertwining my fingers in it, and all through this, I could feel Vidura's silent contemptuous stare on me...as if I were a worm on His Majesty's raiment.

"Never mind that son of a maid." Uncle Shakuni would say, "You are the future of Hastinapur. You are going to be the undisputed monarch. You must not let these trivial issues bother you. A day will come when Vidura will wait on you and take your orders." If he thought that I found comfort in his words, how mistaken was he? Then Dushasana would come to me with some new game and I would be gone to the banks of the Ganges where we princes played and enjoyed the sunshine. All my worries would soon be forgotten in those endless, innocent games. Those were the happy days in Hastinapur.

Then one morning arrived the Kaunteyas at the court of Hastinapur...five of them along with Aunt Kunti. Aunt Kunti– I was seeing her for the first time, although I had heard much about her. The last I had heard was she was living with the 'sages' in the forests. Uncle Pandu was no more. Sage Kindama's curse had come true. It was on a pleasant morning in spring. The clear waters of the melting Himalayas whispered from the brooks and the air was filled with fragrance of the flowers that had blossomed to welcome Kama–the God of Love. Uncle Pandu had just opened his eyes from his prayers when he saw Aunt Madri, drenched and voluptuous, emerging from the river after her morning ablutions. Nature took over discretion. He forced himself upon her despite her gentle resistance and the result was instant death. A guilt-laden Aunt Madri held her beauty responsible for the tragedy and immolated herself in the funeral pyre of her lord. So here was Aunt Kunti with five children born of 'celestial unions' with the Gods. Yudhishthira, the eldest, born by the grace of Dharma–God of Justice, Bheema, the second, who I understand was born on the same day I was, by the grace of Vayu–Wind God, Arjuna, born of the union with Indra–Rain God and also the King of Heavens, and the twins, Nakula and Sahadeva, born of the celestial physicians, the Ashwini twins, to Aunt Madri, who was also taught the 'sacred incantation' by Aunt Kunti.

Aunt Kunti, fragile, beautiful and regal even in the white raiment meant for widows was welcomed by my mother, as she would have been by her own sister. I was asked to offer my greetings to her by prostrating at her feet, and when I did, Aunt Kunti knelt down, held me in her arms and kissed me. She then looked at Bheema and said, "Look, Bheema, this is your brother Duryodhana and he is of the same age as you are. Did I not promise you that you will have company to play with in Hastinapur?"

Bheema, the big, wolf-bellied Bheema, who was believed to have broken a rock that he fell on as an infant and yet remained unscathed, looked at me from head to toe twice over and said to Aunt Kunti, "Mother, you say he is my age, but he is too tiny and frail for me. How can I play with him?"

There was laughter all around as I, Duryodhana, the shining star of Hastinapur, the future monarch, stood in silence, humiliated. I turned to the Grandsire for support, but there on his lap was Arjuna, enchanting him with his charm. And Kulaguru Kripacharya held Nakula and Sahadeva in his arms and was lost in an animated conversation with them...and then I saw my father, the blind King, holding Yudhishthira in his lap and talking to him while Yudhishthira intertwined his fingers in my father's beard...to play with, which was the sole privilege of mine.

Vidura then took to the centre of the court. He announced the arrival of the Kaunteyas and introduced them one by one to the noblemen of the court of my Hastinapur. They were received with huge cheer. There was excitement all over as I watched in silence. The Kaunteyas had charmed everyone. The citizens of Hastinapur thronged the royal court to get a glimpse of the sons of Pandu. Suddenly I felt I was in an alien place. I could feel the occasional glances of Vidura who seemed to relish my discomfort. I felt lonely. I, Duryodhana, who would turn heads in admiration wherever I walked, was suddenly ignored like an insignificant shadow. My eyes welled up with tears, much against my pride. I knew that a few more moments and I would burst. Just then, I felt a hand on my shoulder. I turned around. It was Uncle Shakuni. His eyes were moist too as he looked into mine.

3

Life had changed overnight in Hastinapur.

Mother asked me to offer my seat at the head of the table, we brothers dined on, to Yudhishthira. "He is the eldest and it is but proper that he occupies that seat," she said. Father never called me to attend the royal court as before. I had once strayed there and I was asked by Vidura to run along and play with the other children outside as they were discussing some important law reforms. Father remained silent. I looked at the Grandsire and all he did was shake his head in a gesture of supporting Vidura. I, Duryodhana, the Crown Prince who basked in the company of the exalted decision-makers of my Hastinapur was suddenly looked upon as a source of nuisance. I, Duryodhana, was asked to run along and play with the other boys. Suddenly the tutelage of statecraft was felt unnecessary for me. Humiliated, I left the hall. At the door, I saw Yudhishthira entering. What was he doing there? With a smirk, he walked past me towards the elders and was offered a seat by the side of my father. I could not stay there a moment longer. Tears of rage filled my eyes as I ran to Uncle Shakuni and climbed on to his lap, buried my face and wept uncontrollably.

"That's enough, child, now stop crying. These old men are just ensuring that the Kaunteyas feel at home. The Kaunteyas are your cousins, after all. Don't read anything more into this.

It does not befit the Crown Prince of Hastinapur to cry like a little girl. You are the future of Hastinapur. Nothing will stand between you and your Hastinapur–not while this uncle of yours is alive. So come on now, stop crying," he said as he wiped the tears off my face with the satin edge of his raiment, and once again, my heart swelled and my spirits soared at the thought of my Hastinapur.

Soon I was into my first summer with the Kaunteyas. The games continued in the royal orchards. Yudhishthira, I noticed, never took part in the games and preferred to watch from the side. Uncle Shakuni once prompted me to invite Yudhishthira to join us brothers in the games, but he turned down the invitation. I was not exactly unhappy about that, as I preferred it that way.

"Fool, can't you see, you are missing the big picture," said Uncle Shakuni, "He's not joining the games because he wants to portray himself as mature beyond his age. Believe me, in the long run, this is where he may edge you out. Not through his maturity, but his portrayal of it."

"What do you expect me to do if he doesn't want to join?" I asked.

"Then play his game." said Uncle Shakuni, lowering his tone.

"His game? But I never see him play."

"He's playing all along...and he's playing the real game. Watch his every gesture, listen to his every word, observe him closely how he conducts himself, especially in front of the Grandsire and Vidura, and you'll know his game. Someday in the future, Vidura may decide to present Yudhishthira's case to His Majesty and the wise men of the court. You, on the other hand, my poor nephew, may have to spend the rest of your life watching in servitude from the sidelines as he rules over Hastinapur, your Hastinapur, and then it will be too late for you to learn the game."

I listened, trying to absorb what I heard. He came closer and knelt by my side. Putting his arm around my shoulder, he whispered, "It's all about the game...the faster you learn it, the better for you."

The early seeds were sown...and Uncle Shakuni watched them germinate over the years with his careful nourishment.

4

The summer had peaked early. Fears and tears came calling every morning. The thought of my father's regal, ruby studded crown sitting comfortably on Yudhishthira's head gave me sleepless nights and stressful days. The presence of the Kaunteyas denied me the energy of life. No one seemed to understand, or to rephrase, no one seemed to care. Well, except one, I began to spend more time with Uncle Shakuni. I had lost my interest in the games while I worked on developing my passion for 'the game' under Uncle Shakuni's guidance. But even now, while I lie waiting for the birds, let me tell you, I was never as natural a player as Yudhishthira. Perhaps it was this shortcoming of mine that would charter the preferred course for history to guide generations till the end of time.

Then one morning, while Uncle Shakuni was refurbishing my 'game' skills, there was a loud noise from the orchard by the riverbank. We rushed to find Bheema lying under the mango tree, his body soiled with wet mud. There was sound of laughter from the treetop, and as I looked up, I saw there perched on the branches, Dushasana along with few of my other brothers.

"Brother, you missed the fall of the summer. Poor Bheema wanted to climb the tree along with us, but the branch couldn't take his weight." He said amidst laughter as his teeth bit into a juicy mango.

Bheema's eyes were now a fiery red. His chest began to heave like ocean waves in the wind. Then with a beastly roar, he charged at the tree and shook it violently. Before I could react, my brothers fell down one after the other like dry autumn leaves. When the last one, my dearest Dushasana hit the ground, he picked him by the neck, as if he were a squirrel, and dived into the river only to surface on the other side. And when he emerged on the other side, he still had Dushasana in his firm grip as my brother looked like a washed and spun cloth in Bheema's arm. I watched helplessly along with Uncle Shakuni, as he once again dived and this time to emerge on our side of the river. He came out of the river and threw Dushasana on the ground. We rushed to his side and Uncle Shakuni raised him and held him in his lap as he passed out. Soon the attendants came to our help and carried Dushasana indoors. I seethed with rage. I looked around for that beast and there I saw him sitting with Arjuna, Nakula and Sahadeva, enjoying a mango as if nothing had happened. I picked up the knife that hung in Uncle Shakuni's scabbard and headed towards Bheema's direction, but before I could take a few steps, Uncle Shakuni caught hold of me and dragged me back.

"Fool, do you wish to get killed? That monster could make mincemeat of you."

"The world is too small for the two of us." I said, trying to wriggle out of his grip.

"Yes, but if I let go of you now, he'll be the one standing at the end of it."

"But I prefer death to a life like this."

"Son, trust this uncle of yours. Your time will come. Until then learn to veil your thoughts. Hide the hatred in your heart with a smile on your lips. Conceal the firmness in your resolve with sweetness in your words, and when the time is right, strike back. That is the way of the winners."

"So you want me to watch in silence while he humiliates my brothers and I wait for my 'time' to arrive?"

"No. Now just do as I say. Invite him to lunch with us tomorrow."

"What? After all this, you want me to invite that glutton to lunch with us?"

"Dear nephew of mine, learn to cultivate the virtue of patience. Just listen and obey your uncle. It will all be for your good."

I agreed reluctantly. Bheema did not need much coaxing. His face took an amorous expression as he eyed the lavish spread before him the next afternoon. Soon he feasted as if he had never seen food before. As we brothers gathered to resume our games after lunch, we found Bheema lying on the ground in a state of deep slumber. As I tried to wake him, Uncle Shakuni came from behind. "Don't bother, son, he won't get up for long," he said as he held out his open palm carrying some seeds.

"These seeds that I mixed in his pudding will ensure that he doesn't awaken for a while. Now is your chance. You can never take him on when he is awake."

I cringed at the suggestion. "Uncle, I could never think of doing what you suggest. I am the Prince of Hastinapur. I am a Kshatriya prince. I prefer the shame of defeat to victory by deceit."

"Very well, then. Soon Yudhishthira, Arjuna and the elders are going to come looking for Bheema. What is the explanation you are going to give them?"

My mind was drawing a blank.

Uncle Shakuni turned to Dushasana, "Come help me lift this giant. Let us tie him up and throw him in the river. Your brother can remain here with his lofty ideals."

Dushasana was eager to oblige as the experience of the previous afternoon was still fresh in his mind. As they lifted the sleeping Bheema, Uncle Shakuni once again looked at me. "So you don't want to be a part of this?"

Soon I was helping them tie up Bheema. We lifted him and flung him into the river. The echo of the loud splash reverberated in my heart. This was not the way I had wanted to even scores. We saw Bheema's face submerge into the depths of the cool waters.

Uncle Shakuni's face lit up with a strange expression of pride and achievement. "Now, dear Crown Prince, that should give you some relief."

I remained silent.

The news of Bheema missing was all over Hastinapur. Aunt Kunti was inconsolable. Mother remained by her side, comforting her. Vidura repeatedly questioned me as to when I saw Bheema last. I repeated my lines that were well-rehearsed –"I don't know. The last I saw of him was when he lunched with us." Yet every time Vidura questioned me, my answer did not seem convincing enough to him as his eyebrows lifted suspiciously while he fixed his gaze on me.

For seven days and nights, my guilt-laden heart found no peace. Vidura's suspicious gaze and Aunt Kunti's wailing haunted my dreams. My fear and guilt drove me even closer to Uncle Shakuni whose calming presence was what I needed the most to get the load off my chest. Whatever little comfort I felt was from his reassurances that it was only an act of avenging the humiliation of my dear little brother, and that it fell within my rights and duties as a Kshatriya prince.

Then came the news that Bheema was back. He had miraculously escaped from the deep waters. How? I will never know. In the depth of my heart, I felt a subtle sense of relief as this was not the way I wanted to settle our score. Uncle Shakuni was speechless with disbelief but only for a few moments. Soon he was back at his 'game'. Turning around to me, he said, "That is great news. Come, son, let us go and welcome him." Reluctantly I followed him. In my mother's chamber, Bheema was indulging in all the attention he was getting from her and Aunt Kunti. The Kaunteyas were all looking relieved. However, the moment I stepped in, their faces took on a grim expression. Uncle Shakuni held Bheema in his arms and put on a brilliant display of affection and concern. However, I stayed put. A false facade was never one of my strengths. The moment Bheema's eyes met mine, the now familiar heaving of his chest began. Then from the corner of my eye, I caught Yudhishthira signalling Bheema to remain quiet. It seemed less like a pacifying gesture and more like an assurance...an assurance that his time to get even will eventually arrive.

5

The Grandsire found us a new teacher for weapon craft–Acharya Drona, the son of sage Bharadwaja and brother-in-law of Kripacharya. Acharya Drona, like the Grandsire, was also a student of the great Bhargava and a master in warfare and the usage of divine missiles. His fame as our preceptor spread far and wide and soon our allies and neighbouring kingdoms began to send their princes to Hastinapur to be tutored under him, and he accepted them as his students with the permission of my father. Today, as I lie here with death waiting on me, his dear son Ashwatthama is the only thread that lies between defeat and me.

None of us princes knew the hidden agenda behind Acharya Drona entering our lives. As days under Acharya Drona progressed, I found him spending more time with Arjuna. Arjuna was no doubt an excellent archer. But that did not mean there were no others to match his skills. I had heard the Acharya had promised Arjuna he would make him the greatest archer in the world. One hot afternoon, during our training in the forest, we found our hunting dog running towards us with its mouth open and jaws bridged by seven darts. We were amazed at this fantastic show of skill. Arjuna gaped in awe, as if it was something beyond him. We instructed the dog to lead us to the person who did this.

The dog led us to the interior forest where we came across a tribal youth. The youth, with his dark lithe physique and long wavy hair tied with a scarf, on seeing Acharya Drona rushed and fell at his feet. To everyone's surprise, in front of us, there stood a stone image of the Acharya bearing a garland strung by wild flowers. The youth identified himself as the Nishada Prince, Ekalavya, son of Hiranyadhanusa, a Nishada chieftain who was one of the commanders in the army of the mighty Jarasandha, the Emperor of Magadha. He had approached the Acharya once before, requesting him to accept him as his disciple. The Acharya had turned him down saying that the privilege of learning from the Acharya belonged only to the princes of the royal family (and all along, I had maintained that knowledge should never be a victim of casteism). Ekalavya did not allow this to discourage him. He had already accepted Acharya Drona as his Guru in his mind and had sculpted a statue of the Acharya and worshipped it ritualistically every day before commencing his archery training.

Arjuna turned to the Acharya and said, "Master, you promised to make me the best archer in the world, but you have gone back on your word."

Acharya put his arm around the sulking Arjuna and said, "Your master's word shall never go false, Arjuna. Now cheer up."

Turning to Ekalavya, he continued, "Ekalavya, you have acknowledged me as your Guru without my consent. I'm willing to overlook that transgression. But you will have to pay me my tutor's fee. If you don't, then the knowledge you gain will be stained with deceit. That is something I don't want my students to live with."

Ekalavya bowed down to the Acharya. "Acharya, to you I dedicate all my future exploits in archery. Mention your fee and I will gladly offer it at your feet."

The Acharya's face became stern. "Ekalavya, think carefully before you commit, for what I ask may not be pleasing to your ears."

Ekalavya looked into the Acharya's eyes, "Master, what you will ask for will be within the sphere of your Dharma. It would be my highest privilege to honour it."

The Acharya avoided Ekalavya's eyes. He turned and fixed his gaze on Arjuna, as his face wore a grim look. All of us watched in silence and the only noise that could be heard was the bubbling of the brook deep in the woods. The Acharya then addressed Ekalavya without shifting his gaze from Arjuna, "Ekalavya, I want the thumb of your right hand as my tutor's fee."

All of us were shocked. The initial shock on Arjuna's face was replaced by a smug smile. Ekalavya remained silent with a look of pain in his eyes.

The Acharya turned to him, "You don't seem pleased."

"Yes, Master, but not because of the fee you have asked. I'm pained that it took so much of hesitation from you to ask something that you could have commanded from me." Thus saying, Ekalavya removed the knife tucked in his waistband, and slashed his thumb. Wriggling with pain, he lifted the piece of flesh, wrapped it in a leaf and offered it at the feet of the Acharya who was gratified. We watched in horror as drops of blood from his thumb fell on the earth. Little did we realise that these were the early drops of the deluge of blood this very land would witness, as time would unfold at its deceptive leisure.

Days later, when I got some time alone with the Acharya, I asked him, "Master, what would you have done if the Nishada Prince had refused to part with his thumb?"

"He would never have refused. He is intelligent enough to know that if he hadn't parted with his thumb, I was capable of taking his severed head instead as my fee," replied the Acharya in the most casual tone.

That was the most unexpected reply from the Acharya. I gathered the courage to ask him for the justification in asking the thumb as his fee. After all, was that the only way to make Arjuna the greatest archer in the world? The Acharya was initially taken aback at my bluntness. Then he smiled and said, "Son, this forthrightness of yours is what endears you to me. Now, coming to your question...what would you do when a harmless dog disturbs you with its barking?"

I gave it a thought and then replied, "I'd shoo it away with a stick...or maybe hurl a small stone at it."

"Yes, of course, that would be the appropriate thing to do," said the Acharya. "Now look what that Nishada Prince did to that dog. Shooting seven darts into the mouth of that harmless mongrel just because he could and there would be no one to answer to...someone with that attitude...can you imagine what a menace to society he would become once he attained mastery in the science of battle? The highest dharma of a true warrior is to protect the weak and uphold justice. Power is something to be used for constructive and progressive purposes. It is not something to be abused. So now do you understand why I asked for his thumb?"

I was not sure if I was entirely convinced. Perhaps I had not understood the Acharya well enough.

6

The royal arena stood grand in the centre of the city. The flag of my Hastinapur waved ferociously over its gallery tower reflecting the excitement of its citizens. This was the day they had been waiting eagerly for. We, the princes of Hastinapur, were assembled in the arena. At a distance, in the enclosure meant for royalty were seated my mother, Aunt Kunti, the Grandsire and Uncle Shakuni along with my father, the King, who was flanked on either side of his throne by Vidura and Kripacharya. If love, pride, anxiety and insecurity could converge in a single expression, I saw it on all their faces that day. It was the day Acharya Drona was to show them what fine heroes he had moulded out of their princes. It was a day of exhibition and we the princes of Hastinapur were to display the measure of our skills with weapons to the citizens of Hastinapur to give them the confidence that their future was in safe hands. And more importantly for the Acharya, it was meant to be a day of reckoning. He had to provide proof that his tutelage had given the world its greatest archer ever.

And as it turned out, the day had much more to offer.

Towards evening, it was evident that the exhibition was just an excuse for the Acharya to showcase Arjuna's skill and prowess in archery. Arjuna had the audience spellbound with his dexterity and accuracy. His feats brought the crowd to its feet, and their deafening cheers brought tears of joy in Aunt Kunti's eyes as the Grandsire and Vidura looked on, their faces beaming with pride. Acharya Drona then proudly proclaimed to the cheering crowd, "Behold citizens of Hastinapur, the foremost archer in the modern world, your very own prince–Arjuna".

There were loud roars of celebration from the crowd. The noise was suddenly drowned by the booming twang of a bow that came from the main gate of the arena.

A sudden silence followed by low murmurs filled the arena. All attention turned towards the gate. There at the entrance stood a tall handsome youth, with broad shoulders, muscular arms that came down till his knees and effulgence like the midday sun piercing through the dense foliage of a monsoon forest. Holding a bow that seemed like it was a part of him, long hair combed behind his ears, displaying his shiny earrings, his metal armour holding tightly to his lithe frame, quiver of arrows hanging over his right shoulder, he got us wondering if he was some God from the heavens.

He walked up to the Acharya in slow, measured and sure-footed strides as he confidently surveyed the arena. He had a majestic aura as he stood his ground next to Acharya Drona and Arjuna. He bowed respectfully to the king and then turned and addressed the Acharya, "Acharya, it is improper to make proclamations without doing proper research." So saying, he went on to replicate Arjuna's feats with effortless ease, much to the embarrassment of the Acharya and the royal assembly.

This was just what the crowd wanted. The atmosphere was charged. The youth now turned to Arjuna and addressed him, "Arjuna, I, Vasusena, who takes pride in being known as

Radheya– the son of Radha, and disciple of the great Bhargava challenge you in the presence of His Majesty to engage me in single combat."

Arjuna, humiliated and eager to prove a point, looked at the Acharya for approval. At that very moment, there was a commotion in the royal enclosure. Aunt Kunti had fainted and had to be carried away. Probably the thought of her dear son entering into a single combat was too much for her.

Kripacharya stood up to speak. Pointing to Arjuna, he said, "This is Arjuna, a Prince of the Lunar Dynasty and the son of Kunti and King Pandu. Now please identify yourself as single combat can be only amongst equals in stature."

Radheya stood silent and the entire arena echoed his silence. After a few agonising moments, I decided to break the embarrassing silence. I stood up as I always did for what I felt was right. "Acharya, of what significance could that be? Anyway, look at him. Can we not tell that a lion can never come from a deer's womb? This man, whoever he is, comes from a noble family. I have no doubt about this. Even then if you insist on royalty as a prerequisite, then so be it."

I walked up to Radheya and placing my arm over his shoulder, announced to everyone present, "I, hereby, proclaim Radheya as the King of Anga which comes under my jurisdiction." I looked at my father who seemed pleased with my gesture. However, the Grandsire and Vidura did not look too happy. I summoned the royal priests and hurried them to perform a quick coronation ceremony with chanting of sacred hymns and sprinkling of holy water over Radheya's head as I removed my crown and placed it over Radheya's head. This was greeted by a tumultuous applause from the audience.

Radheya, eyes moistened, held my arms as he spoke to me in an emotion-laden voice, "My Lord, what have I done to deserve this generosity? What can I offer in return?"

I placed my hand on his shoulder, looked him in the eye and spoke, "Give me if you must, your friendship. I seek nothing else." So saying, I embraced this lion of a man.

In a choking voice he said, "To you, my King, I dedicate my future. The world shall refer to you and me for generations when it speaks of friendship."

Somehow, his words had a reassuring effect on me. They were the balm that I needed to soothe the burning wounds left by the Kaunteyas in my heart.

He then turned to Dronacharya and said defiantly, "So now, Acharya, this should settle your concern. Is there any other precondition you wish Arjuna to hide behind?"

Arjuna was furious. The duel was now a certainty and this was going to be the moment of truth. Acharya Drona had no choice but to withdraw, and Arjuna and Radheya stood facing each other, ready to fight. My excitement knew no bounds. My heart was beating fast.

Suddenly, an old man appeared at the gate. He came running towards Radheya. Radheya fell at his feet. The old man was Adhiratha, who had been my father's charioteer years before. Adhiratha lifted Radheya, embraced him and showered him with kisses. He said, "My son, I came running when I heard of your coronation. Your mother and I are so happy for you."

Suddenly Bheema got up and mocked loudly, "So you are the son of a charioteer after all, and you want to engage a royal prince of Hastinapur in single combat? A kingdom earned out of someone's charity does not make one a king. Royalty has to be in the lineage and blood. Go, attend the horses in the royal stables. That's where you belong, you son of a charioteer."

I turned to Bheema and said, "Ha, Bheema, well spoken. Need I tell you about the various stories circulating about the birth of you Kaunteyas?"

I knew I had overstepped the line. I was beyond caring. Aunt Kunti was not present anyway. I looked at the royal enclosure. The expression on the elders' faces showed they were unhappy with my comment. However, Uncle Shakuni gave me an approving nod, and that was enough for me. Bheema's chest began to heave once again. Then suddenly, before we realised, the sun had set in the western skies and its crimson rays were soon absorbed into the twilight darkness. Kripacharya looked relieved as he got up to announce it a day as the spectators gradually dispersed admist excited murmurs.

I offered Radheya to come along with me in my chariot. Arjuna glared at us with sheer contempt in his eyes. That this day in the life of Hastinapur that had promised to be written in his name had to be spoilt thus would give him sleepless nights. I also noticed for the first time a look of uneasiness and insecurity on Yudhishthira's face. The impact of the advent of Radheya in our lives was too strong to be ignored. As I rode back with Radheya, a strange peace filled my heart. It felt like I was reunited with some missing part of me. What was it in this lion of a man that influenced me to this extent? In his silence, I had found a feeling of reassurance that I could never get from the endless sermons and gamecraft lessons of Uncle Shakuni.

7

It was now the time for us princes to offer our fee to Acharya Drona for his tutorship. The Acharya declined all the riches that we offered him. We then asked him what it was that he expected as his fee. It was then that he revealed his true intention. He declared that he wanted Drupada, the King of Panchala to be brought before him as a prisoner. I gathered that Drupada and the Acharya were good friends during their youth and they learnt under the same Guru. When they had completed their education and were parting ways, they promised to remain best of friends till the end of time. Drupada went on to become the Lord of Panchala. Acharya Drona became a householder. As a Brahmin householder, the Acharya found it difficult to make ends meet and went through extreme poverty. The sight of his son Ashwatthama being mocked by other children for not knowing the taste of milk was too much for him to bear. He then decided to approach his friend Drupada for help. However, when the Acharya approached Drupada at his court, he encountered an arrogant Drupada whom he had never known earlier. The mighty king had become drunk with arrogance. He not only denied his friendship with the Acharya but also ridiculed him. He reminded the Acharya that friendship should be only amongst equals. The Acharya bore the insult in the true silent spirit of Brahmins and left the court with a steely determination to seek vengeance. He approached the great sage Bhargava and mastered the use of weapons from him, and then made his way into the royal household of Hastinapur as a teacher. And now, it was time to pay back for his insult.

I was only too happy to fulfil Acharya's desire, even though I knew he was always partial to Arjuna. I gathered my army and along with my brothers laid siege on Panchala. However, Drupada's army seemed too strong and more than a match for us and we had to retreat. For some reason, the Kaunteyas stayed back and did not join us. Those were perhaps the early signs that fighting under my banner was not acceptable to them. The Kaunteyas went separately and announced their intention to attack Drupada. Drupada, personally came out leading his army. While the other Kaunteyas engaged with the army, Arjuna somehow managed to get his chariot close to Drupada and seizing the right opportunity, accosted him by jumping on to his chariot, taking him by surprise. The mission was accomplished. Drupada was captured. If Arjuna had fought along with us, the credit for this would have perhaps had to be shared with us. This may have been the reason the Kaunteyas preferred to fight independently.

Drupada was brought before the Acharya who magnanimously embraced him and said, "Dear old friend, I will take half of your kingdom and return the rest to you. From now on, the territory of Ahichchhatra will belong to me. This will make us equals and ensure that we will be friends like before."

Drupada swallowed the Acharya's bitter sarcasm along with his pride. With a superhuman effort, he managed to veil his humiliation and asked for the Acharya's forgiveness for his earlier indiscretion. The Acharya indulged in his own magnanimity, released Drupada, and sent him back to Panchala with all the royal honours.

It was a decision that would cost him dearly.

8

As days passed by, I found the Acharya spending more time with Arjuna. I gathered from reliable sources that he had even imparted the knowledge of the incantations to invoke the Brahmastra and Brahmashirastra to Arjuna. These were divine missiles with the potency of rendering the entire world lifeless. His partiality towards Arjuna was not lost on his own son, Ashwatthama. This esoteric knowledge that he imparted to Arjuna was something he denied even to his own son. The Acharya felt that Ashwatthama had neither the discipline nor the mastery of emotional restraint to covet this knowledge. The father and son had several arguments over this. Over a period, this worked in my favour as I found Ashwatthama's friendship and loyalty leaning towards me. Meanwhile, Bheema and I, on the advice of the Acharya, had enrolled ourselves to study the art of mace fighting under the tutorship of Balarama of Dwaraka, the highly respected Warrior Prince of the Yadava race, who was also the cousin of the Kaunteyas. His father Vasudeva was the brother of Aunt Kunti. Although Bheema was heavier and perhaps stronger, I was more agile, skilful and faster in picking up the subtleties of the art of mace fighting, and it was no surprise I became Balarama's favourite student—something that he had no hesitation in declaring openly on the completion of our training.

Meanwhile, the pressure mounted on my father to announce his heir apparent. He spent sleepless nights as his mind knew no rest. He often called on me to check if I was in good health and spirits. He and Uncle Shakuni repeatedly advised me to mingle more with the citizens and acquaint with their problems instead of spending time hunting in the forests with my brothers and Radheya. They wanted me to endear myself to the citizens of Hastinapur. Otherwise, someday that would work against me, and in favour of Yudhishthira, in the race to the throne. I argued with them. Why should I justify myself to my own people? I knew I was dear to them. Putting up a false facade...and that too with the citizens of my own Hastinapur was something I would never relish. And where was the question of any race? I, Duryodhana, the eldest son of the king had the undisputed right to the throne.

The crafty Vidura, however, had other thoughts.

Very often, I would walk into the middle of a conversation between him and the Kaunteyas, and the hushed voices would immediately become completely silent. I couldn't care less. Then one day, in the royal court, came a group of people. They were the representatives of some of our provinces, appointed by Chief Minister Vidura during the reign of Uncle Pandu. Vidura introduced them to my father and asked them to speak up.

The oldest one amongst them came forward and with folded palms spoke, "Your Majesty, we have come to you with a concern that is perhaps on the mind of every citizen in Hastinapur."

My father was disturbed. There was a moment of silence. On Vidura's prompting, the man continued, "Your Majesty, the Kingdom of Hastinapur is awaiting the announcement of its Crown Prince."

I could sense my father's discomfort even though he did his best to conceal it as he spoke. He said, "I don't see why this is a matter of grave concern? At the appropriate time, when the planets are allied favourably, the proclamation of my eldest son Duryodhana as the Crown Prince shall take place. There is no need for the citizens of Hastinapur to be anxious on this front."

My face lit up on hearing those words. Radheya smiled at me proudly from across the hall. There were sudden murmurs as a wave of uneasiness swept across the royal court. A look of worry took over Grandsire Bheeshma and the other elders present in the court. Vidura had a smirk on his face. It seemed to me that he was anticipating this and was perhaps stage-managing the whole thing. He addressed the King, "Your Majesty, what you say does not address the concern of the citizens...instead, what you say is precisely their concern."

The King said, "What do you mean, Vidura? Please make yourself clear."

Vidura continued, "Your Majesty, as you have proclaimed in the past, you are a representative of King Pandu, and it is but right that when the time arrives, you should coronate Pandu's eldest son as his successor and the Crown Prince."

No sooner than he had said this, than the group of men echoed his statement in unison.

I clenched my fist and silently gritted my teeth at the audacity of this wily man to host such a charade. He was very careful to avoid my gaze. My father became restless. He said, "What you say is true, Vidura...I did proclaim that I was

Pandu's representative, but that was when he was still alive and in the forest. Had he returned, I would have gladly abdicated the throne for him. But unfortunately, he never returned."

Vidura interrupted, "But his sons have, Your Majesty, and it is only appropriate that the eldest of them become the heir apparent."

The King looked helpless and seemed trapped in the web of his minister's logic. I turned around and looked at Uncle Shakuni. He seemed lost in deep thought as he softly stroked his beard. Then I saw Vidura signalling our army commander. The commander stepped forward and sought permission to speak.

He said, "Your Majesty, the reports that I have been hearing from my sources reveal that there could be an insurgency if anybody other than Yudhishthira is made the Crown Prince."

Suddenly, the Grandsire rose up from his seat and proclaimed, "Let those who wish to rebel remember that I, the son of Ganga, will allow no such thing in this land as long as I live in flesh and blood." Turning to the commander, he continued, "Who are those citizens who dare to plot against the king?"

The Commander replied, "The rebellion, if it happens, will not be against the King, your Excellency, but against his decision...and that is the birthright of every law abiding citizen of Hastinapur. And as the Commander of our army, it will be my duty to protect their rights."

The Grandsire was silent. He turned to look at my father. Beads of perspiration appeared on his forehead. Only silence echoed. All eyes were turned towards my father. As I turned to look at each one of them, they made sure that they avoided my gaze.

With great difficulty, the King finally spoke, trying hard to conceal the emotion in his voice, "Very well, if that's what the subjects want, let the astrologers be consulted for the appropriate time when the stars are favourably aligned for the coronation of Yudhishthira as the Crown Prince of Hastinapur."

The citizens took leave after proclaiming the glory of the King. The Grandsire looked thoughtful while Acharya Drona and Kripacharya maintained silence. Uncle Shakuni kept stroking his beard while Radheya held my hand in a reassuring gesture. My father got up to retire to his chamber. He shoved away Vidura's hand as he tried to help him get on to his feet.

9

With the issue of succession now settled, the Kaunteyas along with Aunt Kunti had decided to travel across the kingdom and spend time intermingling with the citizens and learning about their lives and problems directly. I must say this was a great initiative from Yudhishthira. I was sure it was Vidura's brain that was working behind this.

The 'Pashupati' festival in Varnavrat, one of our village provinces, was a great attraction for tourists and pilgrims, not just within Hastinapur but among neighbouring kingdoms as well. The beautiful village located in a clearing surrounded by forests on all sides was one of my favourite retreats. The Kaunteyas, after consulting with the elders and on advice from my father decided to spend some time in Varnavrat to experience the Pashupati festival. One of our aides, Purochana, who was an architect, was assigned the responsibility of constructing a temporary palace for the Kaunteyas to stay.

The Kaunteyas took our leave. I was relieved for the time being as I did not have to bear the humiliating agony of their presence, every day. Surprisingly, the Kaunteyas stayed at Varnavrat for almost a year, indulging in daily hunting and other sport. Uncle Shakuni had deployed some of his trusted men to spy on them and periodically update us on their activities. One of them brought us news that there was a visitor at the palace every evening and that he had once seen the same person with Vidura. This aroused our suspicion. However, we remained silent, yet alert.

Then one morning, we heard the unexpected news that the Kaunteyas along with Aunt Kunti and Purochana had perished in a big fire that broke out in the palace. Hastinapur was engulfed in grief. The Grandsire went into a stupor. My father was inconsolable. He was enveloped with guilt as he felt his brother's children were his responsibility. He ordered for the sacred rites for the dead to be performed with the charred remains of the Kaunteyas and Aunt Kunti. The whole kingdom went into mourning. I was also, surprisingly, feeling a little empty. The sudden absence of the prime objects of my hatred from my life seemed to leave an unexplainable void. My dear Radheya also seemed to reflect my thoughts. Arjuna's death seemed to have taken away the very purpose of his existence. Destiny had snatched away his prized target, denying him the indulgence of the duel for which he lived and breathed. Hastinapur wore a deserted look. The markets were closed for trading for a very long time. The sages and balladeers who frequented our royal court were now seen less. Messages of condolence poured in from our allies across the four quarters. However, in the midst of all this grief, I noticed that only one person carried on with his work as usual, and this was something that I found unusual. It was Vidura. After the initial shock and grief, he surprisingly recovered fast and resumed with his ministerial duties and obligations. I found this strange considering his special fondness for the Kaunteyas, especially Yudhishthira. I was not the only one who felt that way. Vidura's stoic calmness did not escape Uncle Shakuni as well. We discussed this over a game of dice.

Just then, one of Uncle Shakuni's spies entered. His demeanour indicated that all was not well.

"Your Majesty, I, along with my team have been mingling with the citizens of Varnavrat for the last few days and there is a rumour that you and Prince Duryodhana are behind the death of the Kaunteyas."

I looked at him in disbelief.

"Who dare speak such things?" I roared, "I will send him to the abode of Yama."

Uncle Shakuni signalled me to quieten down and asked his spy to continue.

"The talk is that you had instructed Purochana to make a palace of wax and other inflammable material for the Kaunteyas and torch it while they were asleep."

Uncle Shakuni smiled and said, "Now that is some imagination. Palaces and houses are made of stones and mud. I have never heard of one made of wax, leave alone anyone living in it. Again, if this was the case, what was the need to wait for one year to execute this plan? And if Purochana did execute this, how was it that he himself fell victim to the fire? This was nothing but an accident...but I can sense there is a propaganda operating here."

He dismissed his spy and returned to the square board.

"Son, nothing is over yet...it has just begun," he said.

"What?" I asked curiously, while still trying to control my rage.

"You may not have seen the last of the Kaunteyas as yet. The real game...it has just begun," he said, gently stroking his beard as he stared hard at the board.

10

Months passed by. On Uncle Shakuni's advice, I went around visiting the various provinces in the jurisdiction of Hastinapur, mingling with the people, getting to know more about their lives, their needs and their aspirations. Rumours were still floating around about the mysterious death of the Kaunteyas. Uncle Shakuni tried to trace the origin of these rumours without much success. He warned me to be alert to any attempt of insurgency. However, as long as Grandsire Bheeshma was with us, this was something I never lost my sleep on.

Then one evening, I was summoned to my father's apartment along with Radheya. Mother was there along with him.

My father said, "Son, we have received an invitation from our friend and ally Chitrangada. His daughter, the fair Bhanumati, has come of age and he has requested the honour of your participation in her swayamvara."

Chitrangada was the King of the Kalinga, a neighbouring kingdom to the southeast of Hastinapur. He ruled from his capital Rajapura where the swayamvara was to be held. The swayamvara is a ceremony where a princess who has come of age is allowed to choose her future lord from an assembly of eligible kings and princes invited from all quarters by her father. The suitors are introduced to her along with a narrative of their credentials and the princess makes her choice by garlanding the one she feels worthy of her...a privilege that was denied to my mother.

I was not really prepared for this. I said, "Father, I feel it is too early for me to be fettered by matrimony. Besides, my focus now is purely on gaining proficiency in administrative matters. I am afraid, matrimony will be a distraction."

A faint appreciating smile appeared on my father's lips. He said, "Who ever told you that? It has been in our traditions that the queen always plays a part in important decision-making processes. Your mother will agree."

My mother was silent, though I could sense her restraining an urge to say something.

My father continued, "Son, you should also remember that Chitrangada has been a faithful and loyal ally of ours. Your absence from the swayamvara would be an insult to him. It is not wise to make enemies out of friends. This is also a part of statecraft and diplomacy."

I was in two minds.

I said, "Father, what if Bhanumati rejects me and chooses someone else? You know me. I do not take kindly to rejections. I will not bear such shame. I would rather not go and be insulted."

My father continued, "I am sure the swayamvara is just a cosmetic formality. Chitrangada surely knows the cost he would have to incur by insulting a Kuru prince. The father and daughter would have already discussed and decided on you. But the traditions demand that the swayamvara be held. So he is just going along with it. Besides, why would any intelligent maiden look beyond you? You need not entertain any fear of rejection."

I felt an arm on my shoulder. It was Radheya, "Congratulations in advance, my friend."

I looked at him with scepticism. "Not so early," I said.

Radheya addressed my father, "Your Majesty, as the ruler of Anga, I have also received an invitation to participate in this swayamvara. If your Majesty permits, I will accompany the prince to the swayamvara. He will return with the Princess of Kalinga. This is my assurance."

My mother interrupted, "Well spoken, Radheya. my Son has no reason to worry as long as you are with him. But remember...this is not about your friendship. This is about the right of a maiden to choose her lord." She continued, turning in my direction, "Hastinapur would not want to accept as its daughter-in-law, someone who has not come of her own free will. It happened once before when your Grandsire Bheeshma forcefully brought the daughters of King of Kashi for your grandfather, King Vichitravirya and you know the consequences. He was not destined to live long with them. We don't want that happening again."

"I understand, Mother," I said, as I took leave along with Radheya.

11

Rajapura wore a bright and festive look. We were welcomed at the gates of the city with all the royal honours and accommodated in the best of mansions. The citizens thronged in thousands to catch a glimpse of the heroes of the land of Bharata as their chariots rode along the streets decorated with the best of seasonal flowers. Notable among the heroes were Prince Rukmi of Vidharba, King Shishupala of Chedi and the mighty Jarasandha, the Emperor of Magadha which was one of the most economically prosperous kingdoms in the region along with Panchala and, of course, my Hastinapur. The three of them were allies and I had heard that Rukmi's sister Rukmini, the princess of Vidharba was to be given in marriage to Shishupala to strengthen their alliance. This was on the advice of Jarasandha who was a close friend and advisor to both Rukmi and Shishupala.

Chitrangada was a gracious host. He had us all seated in the best of seats. When I looked around at this ensemble of royalty, these tigers among men, I realised that my father might have been wrong in assuming I would be the chosen one. It was very evident that not one of these mighty men assembled here was worth antagonising. So this was a proper and fair ceremony after all. I was seated in the middle of the right side of the hall and Radheya took his seat next to mine. Women of the royal family of Kalingas thronged the balcony as they tried to catch a glimpse of the arrayed suitors. I realised that many of them had their gaze fixed on the handsome Radheya and he also seemed to be aware of the effect he was exercising on them. The pride and confidence that emanated from his personality was not lost on the various kings and princes as well.

Then, to the sound of music and sacred chanting, she appeared from an inner chamber, accompanied by a maid and some eunuch bodyguards. Bhanumati bowed with folded palms before Chitrangada who blessed her. He brought his daughter forward and introduced her to all. She was beautiful and yet she walked with a gait that had no shades of feminine timidity. The moment I saw her, I realised that she was the one for me. She would be a worthy queen for my Hastinapur. As Chitrangada introduced all the suitors, describing their individual lineage, achievements, credentials, prowess, and so on, her eyes scanned the various heroes across the hall. Her gaze finally rested on Radheya. I realised she had made her choice. But the humility of rejection was more than made up by the joy of knowing her choice of my friend.

As the King gave her the permission to go ahead and garland the hero of her choice, she walked past each one of us with a small gesture of greeting with folded palms that appeared to be more of an apology for rejecting us. As she walked past me and headed towards the direction of Radheya, he suddenly rose from his seat and said, "Halt in your steps, O Princess."

A loud murmur echoed across the hall.

"O fair maiden, you have unwittingly committed an error of judgement for which you cannot be grudged. It is your age and your apparent lack of awareness that has led you to overlook my friend, the mighty Prince Duryodhana of the Lunar race. Duryodhana, who is the heir to the throne of Hastinapur, the student of Drona, unmatched in the use of the mace, has the mighty Bheeshma, Drona, and myself Radheya, all disciples of Bhargava, to fight under his banner and wait for his orders. The fact that he is here today because he has thought of you as worthy to be his consort should be viewed as the greatest honour bestowed on you and the Kalingas. But you have, out of ignorance, overlooked him. However, this is something that his magnanimity would be happy to forgive if you retrace your steps and place your garland around his neck which is its rightful place."

Bhanumati stood quiet as the hall erupted with shouts of protests. Chitrangada watched in helplessness as Radheya drew an arrow from his quiver and placed it on his bow. Then with a voice booming like thunder, he addressed Chirangada, "O King, I, Radheya, the King of Anga, am claiming your daughter for my dear friend, master and the Crown Prince of Hastinapur, Duryodhana."

Turning to the gathering, he continued, "Let he who dares to raise objection to this challenge me to combat and stake his claim to the Princess of Kalinga."

"So you are Radheya...the son of the charioteer who challenged the mighty Arjuna?" roared a voice from across the hall amidst the silence, "I have heard much about you and your prowess. Now let me see for myself if all that I've heard is true. You may take Bhanumati, but only after defeating me in single combat."

It was Jarasandha. He was no ordinary fighter. He was feared as much as he was respected across the four quarters and was responsible for forcing the eighteen tribes of Yadavas out of Mathura and seek refuge in the island of Dwaraka.

I stepped forward and with folded palms addressed the great emperor, "O mighty one, you are my father's friend and hence no less than a father to me. This is Radheya, the King of Anga, my friend and alter ego. If out of indiscretion he has offended you, I beg your forgiveness. For you, I shall gladly forego my claim to the hand of the daughter of Chitrangada."

A surprised Radheya took the cue, laid down his bow and saluted Jarasandha with folded palms.

Jarasandha spoke now in a more reconciliatory tone, "Duryodhana, you are a worthy son to a worthy father and I am pleased with your conduct. However, as a Kshatriya, I cannot let a challenge to my prowess pass by. Let this magnificent warrior who glows like Lord Surya himself defeat me in single combat and win the fair Bhanumati for you. If he fails, then I would have won Bhanumati whom I shall take as my daughter-in-law for she shall be my gift to you, for you have regarded me as you will, your own father."

Radheya stepped forward and addressed Jarasandha, "O mighty one, I, Radheya, seek your forgiveness for my impertinence. But if you must combat me, then I seek your blessings and approval."

Jarasandha was pleased. He gave his approval and with the formal permission of Chitrangada, there ensued a great combat between these two lions amongst men. Their dexterity and skill in usage of weapons was on display for all to see. After a while, age seemed to get the better of Jarasandha as fatigue overtook him. Soon Radheya was in a position of advantage and his victory was evident to all. Jarasandha conceded defeat.

He hugged Radheya and congratulated him. "Dear Radheya, I am pleased with your valour. Duryodhana is indeed fortunate to have a friend in you. May your friendship be spoken about till the end of time. I am pleased to gift you the province of Malini under Magadha's jurisdiction. Please accept it as a token of my appreciation of your valour." Turning to me, he continued,"Duryodhana, you may now take the fair Bhanumati with the blessings of Chitrangada."

Bhanumati stood silent with the garland in her hand. On Chitrangada's gesture, she stepped forward and placed the garland around my neck and there was loud blaring of musical instruments and celebratory rhythms accompanied by chants of sacred hymns.

I tried to read Bhanumati's mind behind her stoic expression but was unable to come to any conclusion. Chitrangada, now my father-in-law, gave us many gifts that we carried back to Hastinapur. The citizens of Rajapura came in thousands to give us a farewell. I stood tall in my gold-decked chariot with the serpent banner waving in the sweet breeze. Bhanumati stood by my side, displaying no emotion. At the head of my retinue was dear Radheya, regal as ever, conquering with a glance all that he proudly surveyed. He had reason to be proud for he had fulfilled his promise to my father.

It was now my turn to fulfil my mother's wish...to ensure that Bhanumati's free will was honoured and that she entered Hastinapur by her own choice. I spoke to Radheya about this and once again, he took this up as his own cause. With my approval, he spoke to Bhanumati privately while we broke the journey for some rest. He used his persuasive skills to convince her that our actions were in accordance to the dharma of a

Kshatriya and cited the example of the Grandsire, when he did the same to the princesses of Kashi. Once the ice thawed, it did not take me much time to bring Bhanumati under the spell of my charm and by the time we reached Hastinapur, she looked forward to the grand welcome that she subsequently received from my Hastinapur. Citizens came out in thousands to greet their future queen. Sweet melodious notes from the musicians and bards filled the air while sacred chants reverberated in the background. The Grandsire, my father and mother as well as other elders of the were all present to welcome the bride and we sought blessings from them. Tears flowed from the edge of the scarf that covered my mother's eyes as she stood next to my father while listening to her maids describe Bhanumati's beauty–from her tresses down to her toes. My mother blessed Bhanumati, "May you remain in blessed union with Duryodhana and his Hastinapur and bear worthy sires to carry forward the torch of its glory."

The days that followed serve as perhaps the sweetest memories of my life. Bhanumati brought in auspiciousness as Hastinapur flourished. The Gods were kind and the rains never failed the harvest. Trade flourished and the treasury was filled to the brim. Those were days of endless sport, feast and celebrations. Time flew in the company of Bhanumati, Radheya, Dushasana, Uncle Shakuni and his son Uluka. Soon I became the proud father of twins, a boy and a girl whom we named Lakshman and Lakshmanaa. The Kaunteyas almost eroded from my memory. The rumours floating around their death also faded. My father progressively delegated several responsibilities of governance to me and I fulfilled my obligations to his expectations. Whenever in doubt, I turned to the Grandsire or Kripacharya for guidance. At times, when I could not agree with their views, I sought the guidance of Uncle Shakuni and Radheya. Although I could not get rid of Vidura as that would have upset my father, I made sure that his role was reduced and he exercised no more control.

Then came the invitation from Panchala.

12

King Drupada, who was now an ally by virtue of his renewed 'friendship' with Acharya Drona, had announced the swayamvara of his daughter, Panchali, famed for her matchless beauty. Being the daughter of Drupada, she was called Draupadi. She was also known as Yagnaseni–she was believed to have been born out of the sacrificial fire. After the humiliation suffered at the hands of Acharya Drona, Drupada, like a true Kshatriya was single-minded in seeking vengeance, although he managed to conceal his thoughts. He then conducted a special ritual on the advice of sages to beget a son who would be responsible for the death of the Acharya and for a daughter who would strengthen the Kingdom of Panchala through an alliance by marrying the greatest warrior of the time. Out of the sacrificial fire emerged the fiery Drishtadyumna and the dusky Draupadi, who was also called Krishnaa because of her dark complexion. Drupada took them as his own children. His eldest son Shikhandi, the Crown Prince, was a famed warrior. There were stories floating around that Shikandi was actually born a woman and that she became a man after undergoing a sex change with the help of a Gandharva, a sub-celestial being. Shikhandi, however, showed absolutely no trace of femininity in his appearance or gait.

When the messenger from Panchala arrived with the invitation, Uncle Shakuni took the opportunity to coax us brothers to accept the invitation. He felt that a marriage alliance with the Panchalas would be the best thing to happen for Hastinapur. However, there was a problem. At the swayamvara, Drupada had offered a challenge to all the heroes of the land. At the centre of the royal amphitheatre of Drupada, on a raised platform, he had set up a uniquely designed bow that only the best of archers well-skilled and knowledgeable in the dynamics of the bow could lift and string. Next to it were placed five long and sharp arrows. Above this, he had constructed a revolving apparatus in the shape of a fish and below it was a vessel of water. He had laid down a condition that only he who could lift the bow, string it and shoot down the revolving fish by looking at its reflection in the vessel of water, would be considered worthy of Draupadi.

To me, this invitation was nothing but an insult in the garb of diplomacy. Uncle Shakuni, however, had other plans. He insisted that we should attend the swayamvara.

"I am not prepared to go and make a mockery of myself. It almost happened once before and if not for my Radheya, I would have been humiliated. Please do not ask me to go." I pleaded.

But Uncle Shakuni said, "Son, this could be a chance for you to repay Radheya. With Arjuna no more with us, this contest is something that perhaps only Radheya can win. However, he will refuse to go for this swayamvara if you do not go. So you must go and take him along. If Radheya wins Draupadi, that in itself will serve Hastinapur's alliance with the Panchalas, for Radheya has tied his destiny with that of Hastinapur."

It was a compelling argument that I couldn't ignore.

Bhanumati did not object to my going for the swayamvara when I mentioned to her that I was going for the sake of Radheya. I set forth to Kampilya, the capital of Drupada along with Radheya, Ashwatthama, Dushasana and my other brothers. Panchala was a prosperous kingdom and Drupada was a powerful and respected monarch. The grand amphitheatre in the north-east section of the city was an imposing structure that made a statement on Drupada's imperial stature. The citizens filled up the gallery as they came in hundreds to watch the swayamvara and get a glimpse of the foremost heroes of the land of Bharata gathered in an ensemble to seek the hand of their Panchala's princess. The royal invitees and prospective suitors, clothed in fine raiment and attended to by the best of slaves of the Panchalas, were seated in a special pavilion erected for them within the amphitheatre There were many illustrious sages present to witness the auspicious event. There was a grand display of cultural music and dance as a prelude to the main event. Drupada entered the amphitheatre to a resounding cheer from the citizens. Along with him was a group of priests chanting sacred hymns. They were followed by Shikhandi and Dhrishtadyumna and behind them, richly attired in a white elegant garment and holding a garland walked Draupadi with her attendants. There was a buzz around the theatre as the citizens gasped for breath, enchanted by the beauty of their dusky princess. I turned around and looked at Radheya. He seemed to be in a hypnotic trance. As I glanced around the pavilion, I saw the reaction that Draupadi evoked from the various heroes who had assembled there to seek her hand. There was Vatsaraja of Khoshala, Shishupala of Chedi,

Jarasandha from Magadha, Shalya, the King of Madra and many other heroes from all the quarters including a host of Yadava heroes from the island Kingdom of Dwaraka ruled by King Ugrasena. They were led by the mighty Balarama, my teacher, tall, well-built and handsome, looking regal in his rich blue silk attire. Next to him was his younger brother Vaasudeva, relatively dark in complexion and dressed in yellow silk. There was Satyaki, Kritavarama, Akrura, Uddhava–all from Dwaraka. They had their gaze riveted on Draupadi as their eyes feasted on her beauty. However, I noticed that the only one who did not seem that enamoured by Draupadi was Vaasudeva. He seemed strangely distracted. While others had their eyes feasting on Draupadi, Vaasudeva was gazing at a certain section of the gallery meant for the Brahmin guests.

Dhrishtadyumna came forward to welcome all the suitors. He then introduced all the invitees to the audience. The contest commenced. One by one, the suitors tried their hand at lifting the mighty bow but with no luck. Even the mighty Jarasandha had to humbly return unsuccessful. It was my turn, and the result was no different. I got back to my seat humiliated. I was seething with fury at the audacity of Drupada to host such a charade. I then felt an arm on my shoulder. It was Radheya. He was seeking my permission to give it a try. I nodded my approval and he got up and strode majestically like a lion with slow and measured steps towards the bow. All eyes were on him and he seemed to enjoy the attention. The audience seemed to expect something special as silence filled the amphitheatre. Radheya ran his hand gently over the carefully designed bow alloyed with timber and metal as he searched for the accurate spot. He suddenly gripped it tight and with a single hand, lifted it out of its holder to loud, deafening cheers from the crowd. He bent the bow and effortlessly strung it. He placed an arrow and looked into the vessel of water and carefully took aim. Just then, we heard a soft but assertive voice speak out. "I shall not wed the son of a charioteer."

It was Draupadi. Radheya immediately unstrung the bow and looked at the sky with a smirk as he retired to his seat. The humiliation was uncalled for. I got up from my seat fuming. "O King, by insulting Radheya, your daughter has insulted me and my Hastinapur. If Radheya's lineage is an issue, why was he invited to participate? You have brought shame on yourself and your kingdom by allowing this to happen." As my words reverberated across the amphitheatre, they were met with approval from most of the suitors and the audience. King Drupada was silent.

Dhrishtadyumna stepped forward and said, "O Prince of Hastinapur, on behalf of Panchala, I apologise to Radheya if he feels insulted. However, it has been the tradition of our land to always honour a woman's will and opinion when it comes to choosing her lord. Draupadi has just expressed her will and that will have to be honoured by His Majesty, not just as her father but also as the King. So please let this not come between the good relationships that our kingdoms enjoy as allies."

I was not pacified. I got up to leave amidst roars of protest but was stopped by Radheya. He said, "My friend, what Prince Dhrishtadyumna says is true. This is about me. Let this not become a reason for contention between the two kingdoms. I can live with any insult as long as I have your friendship. So please calm down. Let us wait and see if there's anyone capable of stringing this bow."

Just then, there was a voice from the crowd. It was an elderly Brahmin. He came forward and requested Dhrishtadyumna, "O Prince, does a Brahmin have permission to try his luck in this challenge?"

Drishtadyumna looked at Draupadi. He took her silence as her approval. There was mocking laughter all around. This swayamvara looked like it was becoming a big joke. The Kshatriya warriors gathered around teased Drishtadyumna, "Looks like your sister, Yagnaseni, will have to return to the sacrificial fire. You hold a contest which no Kshatriya can win, and bar the only one who came close to having a chance at winning. Now you allow the Brahmins to insult us by taking part in this charade."

"I beg to differ," said a voice from a corner. All eyes turned to the direction of the voice. It was Vaasudeva. He had a mocking smile on his lips as he spoke. "O heroes of this land, what cause is there to feel insulted if a Brahmin takes part in this contest? If he loses, there is no surprise as he is expected to. If he wins, there is nothing to feel slighted about as we know that Brahmins by virtue of their rigid austerities and penance are capable of great heroic acts that even the mightiest Kshatriyas are not. There are many examples of this. Need I remind you of the great Bhargava or even his disciple, the mighty Drona, the good friend of His Majesty? Even the Gods cannot match them in combat." He had a mischievous smile while mentioning Acharya Drona's name as he observed Drupada's reaction through the corner of his eye. He continued, "The question is whether the high-born Draupadi would be willing to compromise the comforts of the royal palace for that of a life in a Brahmin's household."

Draupadi smiled in silent affirmation. Dhrishtadyumna now addressed the Brahmin, "The matter is settled then. O Brahmin, you are welcome to try your luck with the bow. If you win, Panchali shall be yours."

The Brahmin said, "Your Highness, it is not for me but for my disciple."

He turned to a group of Brahmins and signalled one of them to come forward. The young Brahmin came forward and bowed down to Drupada. He was tall, dark with broad shoulders and had a lithe frame. He had powerful arms, which certainly did not seem to belong to a Brahmin who lived on alms received from performing sacrificial rituals. His features were that of a warrior. He saluted the bow with folded palms and then ran his palm across the bow, just the way Radheya did. He was trying to get a feel of the dynamics of its design. As he took a grip, he looked up at Draupadi who was watching in anxiety. He then turned his gaze to the pavilion in the direction of Vaasudeva and smiled. I wasn't sure why he did that. It was perhaps a gesture of gratitude. He then in a swooping movement, lifted the mighty bow and strung it evoking thunderous applause from the crowd. The Kshatriya princes who were watching were not humoured. The youth then placed an arrow on the bow and carefully took aim at the rotating fish above by looking at its reflection in the vessel of water placed below. In a flash, before it could catch the eye, the fish was down.

The amphitheatre erupted once again. Flowers were rained upon the youth as he stood there like a demigod. Draupadi gently walked up to him in the middle of sacred chants. She placed the garland around his neck as cheers and music of celebration reverberated in the air. I was not sure if Drupada was pleased over the developments. If he was not, he managed to conceal it. I turned to look at Radheya. He watched everything silently. The sense of injustice and denial that he experienced never showed on his face.

However, soon the amphitheatre was filled with agitation as all the monarchs and royal Kshatriyas assembled there were livid. Heated exchange of words followed about the propriety of allowing a Brahmin to contest. They felt that they were deliberately insulted by Drupada and threatened to kill him and his sons, and throw Draupadi into the fire. As they charged towards Drupada, the Brahmin youth stood in their way. They collectively attacked him but he single-handedly held them at bay with an unending stream of arrows that left his bow. It was a wonderful sight that thrilled everyone. Radheya, prompted by the other Kshatriya heroes now engaged the Brahmin youth. There ensued a fascinating combat and it seemed that the youth was getting the better of Radheya who was forced to acknowledge the youth's prowess, skill and dexterity. He was, however, softer in his approach than usual which was understandable, as no Kshatriya would like to invite the sin of hurting a Brahmin, leave alone killing him. Just then, Shalya, King of Madra, came forward to strike the youth. But he was startled by a sudden roar. He turned around to see a tall and well-built giant of a man, another Brahmin youth towering in front of him. He was lifted by the youth and thrown away a furlong. All this was applauded by the Brahmins in the gallery. I rushed to help Shalya and along with me were Shishupala, Jarasandha and others as we were about to launch a combined onslaught. On the other side were the two Brahmin youths,

Drupada, Dhrishtadyumna and Shikhandi ready to take us on. Suddenly a voice spoke out, "Stop this shameful fight, O great heroes."

It was Vaasudeva again.

"The sages are witness that Draupadi here has been won fairly in this contest and she had also approved of this young Brahmin. This wonderful youth has shown that he is no ordinary Brahmin but someone of the class of the great Bhargava himself. There is no shame in acknowledging the superiority of a Brahmin for after all, the Brahmins are the torchbearers of knowledge of all sciences known to man. Draupadi has indeed found a worthy suitor. Let us not be petty. Let us be magnanimous and celebrate this joyous occasion and congratulate King Drupada for the success of this swayamvara."

Somehow, when Vaasudeva spoke, the assembled heroes calmed down. They reluctantly withdrew their weapons in consent to what Vaasudeva said and peace prevailed. Drupada then gave the orders for the marriage rituals to commence. I stormed out of the place with Radheya and my brothers and soon we were on our way back to my Hastinapur. Throughout the journey, Radheya never spoke a word but I could feel the anguish of his heart and the humiliation gnawing at his soul and self-respect.

"Do not grieve, my friend. What you suffered today will be accounted for. This is my solemn promise to you," I said, placing my arm on his shoulder.

He just smiled dryly and turned his gaze towards the crimson sun that was slowly setting in the western horizon.

13

On the way back, we took a break in the forest to indulge in some hunting sport. I wanted to take Radheya's mind off from what happened at the swayamvara. When we reached Hastinapur a few days later, the city seemed to look very festive. There were floral decorations on display in the city and outside the houses. Musicians sang cheerfully on the streets. The mood was very celebratory. It got me curious. After the humiliation we suffered at Panchala, I wondered what the reason for celebrations at Hastinapur could be. When I reached the palace, I headed for my father's chamber, but as always, he was in a discussion with Vidura. I walked in along with Radheya and greeted both of them. My father said, "Son, we just got some auspicious news. Vidura here informs me that your brothers, the Kaunteyas and your Aunt Kunti are alive. The Brahmin youth who won Draupadi's hand was none other than your brother Arjuna."

The words hit me like Indra's thunderbolt. Radheya was also perplexed. It was now clear why he was not able to get the better of a simple Brahmin youth. Vidura was studying my reaction with a smug smile on his face. The news that his informers had brought him was that the Kaunteyas had escaped the fire through a tunnel that connected their palace at Varnavrat to the forest. But to my knowledge, there was no such tunnel in that palace when it was built. So this must have been something that they had themselves constructed during their one-year stay. The mysterious visitor who visited them every evening was probably the tunnel digger. So then, who were the five men and the old woman who perished in the fire along with Purochana? Now things were getting clearer. This was a master plan by the Kaunteyas to portray me as a villain among the people of Hastinapur. They had set fire to the palace themselves and made sure that one innocent woman and five innocent men were killed in the fire so that they could be mistaken for Aunt Kunti and her sons. They then settled among the common people of Hastinapur, disguised as Brahmins, and started the propaganda that I, Duryodhana, was responsible for setting the Varnavrat palace on fire in an attempted plot to murder them. Uncle Shakuni was right. We were seeing a vicious plan at work. The idea was to turn the public opinion against me. But somewhere in the core of my heart, I felt that the Kaunteyas by themselves were not capable of such a devious strategy that required devilish cunningness. Something told me that Vidura had a big role to play in all this, though I couldn't voice my opinion aloud.

As if all this was not enough, we also got news that Draupadi would be taking all the five brothers as her lords. This was something unheard of. A man sharing his rightfully wedded wife with his brothers? The reason for that, as I was given to understand, was that it was done on the advice of Aunt Kunti. Perhaps she knew the weaknesses of her sons. She knew in her mind that the bewitching Draupadi could become the cause of disunity and dissension amongst her sons. Hence, she felt it best that all of them share Draupadi. But how did King Drupada allow this moral transgression upon his daughter...that too, one born out of the sacrificial fire? Surely Draupadi would not have had to suffer this kind of humiliation had she chosen Radheya as her lord.

The Kaunteyas were now residing in Panchala enjoying the hospitality of Drupada. Vidura advised my father to invite them to return to Hastinapur, which was their rightful place. He advised my father that now, with Drupada as an ally, they have become more powerful and it would be in the best interest of everyone if the Kaunteyas were brought back at the earliest. My father also seemed to agree.

After Vidura left, I spoke my mind to my father. I told him in no uncertain terms that I would rather retire to the forest or kill myself than live in servitude under Yudhishthira's lordship. I told him to think of some way to ensure that the Kaunteyas remained in Panchala. Once again, I felt my Hastinapur slipping out of my hands, and this time I had no intention of letting that happen. No amount of pacification from my father could help. Finally he said, "Very well then, let us discuss this tomorrow in the court with your Grandsire Bheeshma, the Acharyas and other elders. I am sure they will arrive at the right decision that will be suitable to you as well."

The next day, the discussion went on endlessly. I stood by my decision. Vidura warned my father that now with Drupada as an ally and their cousins Balarama and Vaasudeva of Dwaraka as their well-wishers, the Kaunteyas have only become stronger. With the Panchalas and the Yadavas on their side, they have now become invincible even to the Gods. It was most prudent for Hastinapur to call them back for that would not only strengthen its alliances but also earn the respect from all quarters for following dharma. The other elders also echoed the same sentiment.

Frustration filled my entire being, as it seemed to me that I was once again cornered by the crafty Vidura and his arguments. Radheya then spoke out in an assertive voice, "Your Majesty, please do not let fear influence your decision in this regard. As long as I stand here with my bow, Hastinapur shall have no need to fear the Kaunteyas no matter who they have on their side. If Your Majesty so commands, we will attack the Kaunteyas and their allies straight away and I will personally ensure their destruction. Then there will be no further discussion on this subject. This is the approved way for Kshatriyas."

"Well spoken, Radheya, but your words seem to fly faster than your arrows. We heard about your combat with Arjuna at the swayamvara," said Vidura, his words filled with sarcasm.

Radheya retorted, "My fight there was with a Brahmin youth whose identity I knew not and hence I was not using all the faculties at my command. If it had not been in our traditions to respect and honour Brahmins, Arjuna would not have been alive today. He took shelter behind the guise of a Brahmin."

Then the Grandsire spoke to me, "Son, you must understand that this is your opportunity to rectify the bad name that the fire at Varnavrat has earned you...no matter what the truth behind it is. Let the citizens of Hastinapur know your magnanimity. Let's call back the Kaunteyas. That is the only way to let it be known to the world that whatever happened at Varnavrat was not your making as is being spoken about. As for their right to this kingdom, it is as much theirs as it is yours. Yudhishthira is elder to you and he has endeared himself to the citizens as well. It is my wish to see you and Yudhishthira live in peace with one another and be there for each other."

He then turned to my father and continued, "O King, this throne that you sit on is something I had abdicated in favour of peace in Hastinapur. Therefore, please place your trust in me implicitly that what I am about to propose to you will be in the best interest of Hastinapur. Please call back the Kaunteyas and let there be not the slightest trace of hostility or animosity from our side. They are your brother's sons after all and, therefore, no less than your own children. Offer them that half of Hastinapur that lies west to the Yamuna called Khandavaprastha. It is a stretch of dense forest and land that has potential to be developed into a fertile region. It has immense wealth hidden in its natural resources. I am sure that the Kaunteyas with their commitment and capabilities will be able to develop that into a land of abundance."

There was silence. For the first time, Vidura and I seemed to agree on something. We both felt it was wrong to partition Hastinapur, though, for different reasons. However, Dronacharya and Kripacharya also agreed with the Grandsire and impressed upon my father to move in that direction. My father made up his mind. It was decided that Vidura would personally go to Panchala as my father's emissary and request the permission of Drupada for the return of the Kaunteyas to Hastinapur along with Aunt Kunti and Draupadi.

14

The Kaunteyas received a warm reception on their return. The citizens came in thousands to see the princes and their common bride about whom they had heard much. My brothers Dushasana and Vikarna were personally assigned the responsibility of greeting them at the entrance of the city as they rode in. The elders of the Kuru clan were assembled at the royal palace to welcome the Kaunteyas. As much as I wanted to be left alone, Uncle Shakuni insisted that I be present there to offer my respects to Aunt Kunti and Yudhishthira, and extend a warm welcome to the brothers and Draupadi.

After paying their respects to the King and the elders, the Kaunteyas retired to rest for the night. The following day, my father summoned them to the royal assembly. The court was filled with the elders, the Acharyas, and prominent nobles and citizens of Hastinapur. The Kaunteyas arrived amidst loud cheers. After greeting the King and other elders, they took their seats.

My father then cleared his throat and addressed the Kaunteyas, "O sons of Kunti, words cannot express the joy of Hastinapur in having you all back with us, and none is happier than me and your Aunt Gandhari that the Gods have protected you. Not a day passed by without us shedding tears in your thoughts. There have been various loose talks and rumours in the kingdom about the fire at Varnavrat, to the extent that aspersions have been cast on my sons. Your disappearance also did not help much. I am not willing to dwell further into the reasons for your going into hiding. The past is past. However, the whole episode has opened a wound in Duryodhana's heart which, I am sure will heal with time...for, after all, you are all brothers. However, to prevent such unpleasant occurrences in the future, it is in the best interest of everyone here and the generations to come, that Hastinapur be partitioned and you be given your rightful share of it. This is the suggestion of your Grandsire Bheeshma, and I endorse it. The region of Khandavaprastha, on the west of River Yamuna is a vast area of forestland with fertile soil and the promise of progress if you brothers put in the effort. You have the permission to make use of all the resources available in Hastinapur for this. I look forward to you transforming it into a second 'Indraloka'. So proceed to Khandavaprastha. Your duty there awaits you. You have my blessings."

The Kaunteyas were silent. They looked at the Grandsire who nodded his approval. Vidura looked unhappy but he was helpless. Yudhishthira bowed down to the King in silent obedience and his brothers followed suit. They sought the blessings of the King and all the elders individually as they prepared to leave for Khandavaprastha.

15

The political map of my Hastinapur was thus redrawn and all I could do was watch in helplessness. The Kaunteyas departed for Khandavaprastha along with Draupadi and Aunt Kunti. I swore to myself that someday I would reclaim every bit of territory lost to the Kaunteyas. This was my sacred and solemn promise to my Hastinapur.

Years passed by uneventfully. My sister Dushala was married to Jayadratha, the son of the mighty Vradhakshatra and the Crown Prince of Sindhu. The marriage fortified our alliance with that kingdom. Radheya's father Athiratha found him a soulmate, Vrushali, a maiden of high virtue. She bore him nine sons. The eldest one Vrishasena grew up to be an excellent fighter, very much in the mould of his father. He was also very close to my son Lakshman. Bhanumati and Vrushali spent a lot of time together. My daughter was especially fond of Vrushali who was like a second mother to her. When she had a problem, she confided more in Vrushali than her own mother.

Meanwhile, the Kaunteyas had indeed converted Khandavaprastha to a land of plentiful bounty. They named their capital Indraprastha. There was no end to its grandeur recited by the visiting balladeers and sages. Yudhishthira had sent his four brothers in all directions with diplomatic missions for strengthening alliances with the various monarchs of the land of Bharata. The marriage of Arjuna to Subhadra, the step-sister of Balarama and Vaasudeva also strengthened their bond with the Yadavas of Dwaraka and their King Ugrasena. I remember that in my younger days, Balarama had wished to offer Subhadra's hand to me as I was his favourite student whom he regarded as the best. He even spoke his mind to me during one of my visits to Dwaraka. It was, therefore, surprising when we received news that she had been given away in marriage to Arjuna. The story was that Arjuna had forcefully abducted her on her way back from her prayers at the Raivataka Hills. Since the Yadavas were wary of his might and prowess as a warrior, they did not want to antagonise him. They decided it was best to overlook this audacity and settle the matter amicably and honourably by calling Arjuna back before he could reach Indraprastha and offering Subhadra to him with all the traditional fanfare and approval of the elders. I found it hard to believe this story as Balarama was a hero who valued his honour and self-esteem above everything else in this world. He would never have tamely submitted to such an insult to the entire Yadava clan. Uncle Shakuni too felt the same. He was of the opinion that Vaasudeva had a big role to play in this drama as everyone knew of his fondness for Arjuna.

Time marched on and my own Lakshmanaa had come of marriageable age. It was time for her to choose her lord from the various heroes of the land of Bharata. I had invitations sent out to all quarters inviting eligible suitors to attend the swayamvara of Lakshmanaa. The city was done up for the auspicious occasion. I had resting shelters constructed all the way from the outskirts leading to the city as many princes were expected to attend the ceremony. Special mansions were constructed to accommodate them. I was busy with the arrangements along with Radheya at the ceremony hall when we received news that my daughter Lakshmanaa had been abducted by an unidentified youth in a chariot while she was playing with her mates in the city garden. I was in a state of shock and disbelief. Who in all the worlds had the audacity to perform such an act? Surely he must be an adventurous fool to invite his death? I rushed to the palace. Bhanumati was inconsolable. Vrushali was by her side. I assured her that no harm would come to Lakshmanaa. Radheya immediately gave orders that the gates of the city be sealed and no one allowed to exit. The order was relayed at wind speed. Groups of men were sent out in different directions to trace the chariot. One of them returned with the news that the chariot had headed westward. Radheya himself set out with a small army on the swiftest of horses in the westward direction. They soon caught up with the youth. There ensued an excellent fight and the youth stood his ground against the mighty Radheya and his troop. He earned the admiration of his attackers. However, his youth and energy were no match for Radheya's skill and experience and he was soon captured. Given the situation, Radheya would have had no hesitation in severing the young man's head for the insult that he inflicted upon the Kauravas. But when the youth identified himself as the Yadava Prince Sambha, the son of Vaasudeva, Radheya decided that it was best that the decision in this regard be taken by the King, considering the friendly relations that we had with the Yadavas and their King Ugrasena.

Radheya took Sambha as a prisoner and brought him in chains to the royal court. The Grandsire admonished Sambha for his indiscretion. "It is a matter of shame that the son of Vaasudeva should behave in this manner. You have given a bad name to the entire clan of the Yadavas. Your father is highly respected for his knowledge of Dharma. Yet, you not only let him down but you also let down the fair name of your King Ugrasena and the Yadavas as well. If Hastinapur does not exact tribute from Dwarka, it is out of respect for your king and the relationship we have with the Yadavas and not out of fear. The Kurus and Yadavas are, after all, the descendants of the great Yayati."

Sambha was quiet.

Uncle Shakuni now spoke with a voice filled with sarcasm, "Perhaps it is not your fault. After all, abduction of maidens has never been a moral transgression for the Yadavas. Your father abducted the Princess of Vidharba whose hand was promised to Shishupala of Chedi. You Yadavas showered all honours on Arjuna who forcefully abducted your Aunt Subhadra. So your act perhaps finds its justification in the inspiration drawn from the various tales you grew up on."

Sambha retorted with a smirk, "Yes, many tales have inspired me, and not just pertaining to the Yadavas. Among them is the one about the daughter of Chitrangada of Kalinga and there is another tale about the three princesses of Kashi."

His verbal missiles had found their mark. The first one was aimed at me and the second was aimed at the Grandsire. I could not help admiring this youth's fearlessness and courage even in captivity, not to mention his handsome features and proud disposition. I would have been very happy to give away my daughter to this man if the circumstances were different. It was decided that he would be locked up in prison till someone from Dwaraka came to offer an explanation and apology to bail him out. Word was sent across to King Ugrasena of Dwaraka that Sambha was in our captivity.

No sooner than the news reached him, than Ugrasena sent Balarama along with Uddhava, a senior noble in his court, as his representatives to Hastinapur to resolve the issue. I was delighted at the news of Balarama's coming. We received him with all the honours. After the exchange of pleasantries, Balarama addressed my father and the other elders, "Your Majesty, King Ugrasena has expressed his regrets over the unfortunate incident. Know that Prince Sambha is the son of my brother, the high-souled Vaasudeva and his consort Jambavati, the daughter of the mighty Jambavan. His birth is an auspicious blessing of Lord Shankara himself. He is well-versed in scriptures as well as the science of arms. He is in every way a worthy suitor to Princess Lakshmanaa. It is our King's wish that you release him immediately and offer the fair hand of Lakshmanaa to him. Duryodhana has no need to worry about her well-being as in Dwaraka she will know no wants. If you do not accept my words, Hastinapur will have to face the consequences which may not be pleasant."

Although I regarded Balarama highly, he had crossed the line with the threat to my Hastinapur. That was uncalled for. It did not go down well with the elders. The Grandsire now spoke directly to Balarama. He said, "O Prince of Dwaraka, you must know that you Yadavas are today living in peace in Dwaraka by the grace of Hastinapur. You enjoy under the patronage of Hastinapur for the only reason that both the Kurus and the Yadavas are the descendants of the great Yayati. That is the only reason you enjoy the privileged alliance. We have overlooked the fact that your forefather Yadu was banished from Hastinapur and his descendants were to be ostracised as per the royal decree of the great Yayati. We valued your friendship out of the respect we carried for your King and for the famed wisdom of your brother Vaasudeva who is ever for peace. But this threat coming from your King who has been spared servitude only out of consideration and goodwill is not in good taste. You have come as a messenger and hence we will pardon your impertinence. You may go back and tell King Ugrasena that a shoe cannot be worn on the head and must ever remain at the feet for that is the right place for it. If he wishes the release of Sambha, he will have to fight for it. He may bring his entire army with all the famed Yadava heroes with him including the great Vaasudeva."

The Grandsire's words were applauded by others in the hall, especially Radheya.

Balarama was furious. He got up from his seat and roared, "Surely pride and arrogance have taken over the senses of the Kurus. I was wrong in thinking that wisdom would prevail in the court of Hastinapur where preside such esteemed and venerable people like you, Kripa, Drona and Vidura. Our King and the entire host of the Yadava heroes were thirsting for war and I pacified them with the intention of arriving at an honourable settlement out of my love for my pupil Duryodhana. Clearly, I was wrong and Vaasudeva was right as he always is. The intoxication of power has taken possession of your senses causing the loss of your discretion. Clearly a lesson on better judgement is in order here...and I do not need an army to teach you that lesson."

So saying, the mighty Balarama stormed out of the palace along with Uddhava. The elders were divided in their opinion about the whole episode. For once, I found the Grandsire and Radheya on the same side. They were prepared for battle. Others like Vidura, Acharya Drona and Kripacharya felt that it was not in the best interest of Hastinapur to antagonise the Yadavas...as long as they had Vaasudeva and Balarama on their side. I was in two minds. There was no doubt that Sambha had created an impression on me. Maybe he carried a little pride and arrogance that comes with youth, but that is something that we all relate to and identify with. My love and respect for Balarama was also another factor that weighed on my mind, but on the other hand, the insult to Hastinapur was something that I could never accept. Just then, I received a message from the inner chambers that Bhanumati wished to speak to me on something important.

I excused myself and went to her chamber. She looked at me and spoke hesitatingly, "My Lord, I feel that it is in the best interest of everyone that you release Sambha and offer Lakshmanaa to him. It will be difficult to find a suitor for her now that the news of her abduction must have spread all across. Besides, I spoke to her and she says that she also would not be able to accept anyone else as her Lord. She considers that it will be her good fortune in this birth to become the daughter-in-law of Vaasudeva. Let the Kurus and the Yadavas not fight over this."

I considered the matter carefully. However, I could not take a decision without consulting the elders first. I went back to the hall where the discussion was still raging. I shared aloud with everyone what Bhanumati felt about the matter. Her logic and argument appealed to everyone present including the Grandsire and my father. It was decided that we would immediately go to Balarama to pacify him and tell him about our decision. I headed out along with Radheya and Dushasana to bring back Balarama.

Balarama and Uddhava had meanwhile already started for Dwaraka. We finally caught up with them at the banks of Ganga. Balarama was striking hard at the ground with a plough where he stood and dragging the soil towards the Ganges. With each blow, the earth beneath shook causing tremors. Balarama's eyes were red with wrath and perhaps wine which was a weakness in him as he kept striking the earth. When he saw me, he spoke to Uddhava, "I will teach these arrogant fools a lesson. I will humble their pride. Today I shall bring down this city of Hastinapur and submerge it in this Ganga. Let her mighty son Bheeshma stop me if he can."

I approached him with folded palms, prostrated before him and begged his forgiveness. I told him about our decision. Balarama, as everyone knew, was as easy to placate as he was highly inflammable. Soon he calmed down, hugged me and said, "You must know that we Yadavas are well-wishers of the Kurus and consider the Kurus as our own. So it was very hurtful when your Grandsire Bheeshma spoke those words. However, you have pleased me with your humility and therefore I will not dignify the words of the senile old man by further hostility."

Sambha was thus released and Lakshmanaa offered to him in a grand ceremony in the presence of the foremost of renowned sages. The Yadavas led by Ugrasena and Vaasudeva came in large numbers. Sages from all over came to bless the couple. When it was time for farewell, I offered the Yadavas many gifts and chariots filled with precious stones as dowry which they were happy to accept. I had mixed emotions. On the one hand, was the sorrow of separation from my dear daughter and on the other, there was the joy of strengthening our alliance with Dwaraka. Bhanumati, however, was more composed. She would have no reason to worry on account of Lakshmanaa in Dwaraka as she was now under the care of the wise Vaasudeva.

16

Ever since my daughter's marriage to Sambha, there was one worry that troubled my father. He was not sure how this new alliance with Dwaraka would affect Hastinapur's relationship with Magadha. Not responding to the courtesy of our invitation to attend the marriage ceremony made it obvious that Jarasandha, the King of Magadha was not pleased. He was a sworn enemy of the Yadavas, especially Vaasudeva. This enmity traced its roots to Vaasudeva killing his own maternal uncle Kansa, the King of Mathura. Kansa had taken over Mathura from his father Ugrasena in a coup. He had Ugrasena hauled up in prison and took complete control of Mathura and its citizens. It was Vaasudeva who liberated Mathura from Kansa by killing him and reinstating Ugrasena as the King of Mathura. Jarasandha was the father-in-law of Kansa. He had married his daughters Asti and Prapti to Kansa. Furious over seeing his daughters widowed, Jarasandha set out to seek vengeance on Vaasudeva and the Yadavas. He relentlessly attacked Mathura, forcing the entire host of the Yadava tribes including the Vrishnis, Bhojas and Andhakas to move out of Mathura and relocate to the safe island of Dwaraka to the south-west.

My father's worry was put to rest when one day, we received news that Jarasandha was dead and his son Sahadeva had succeeded him to the throne of Magadha. Jarasandha was killed in a wrestling combat with Bheema. Jarasandha had a huge army and had conquered and brought many lands under his subjection. He had in his prisons, several monarchs who had dared to put up a resistance. He planned to make a mass human sacrifice of them to appease the three-eyed Rudra. Bheema together with Arjuna and Vaasudeva had visited his court in Magadha in the guise of Brahmins and challenged Jarasandha to choose any one of them for single combat with any weapon of his choice. This was an idea initiated by Vaasudeva. By their appearance, Jarasandha could make out that they were no ordinary Brahmins. When he demanded to know the truth, they disclosed their identities. Jarasandha was powerful and strong-armed. His might was well-known all over the world. It is the highest dharma of any Kshatriya to never shy away from a challenge to his prowess, but he felt it below his dignity to fight with Vaasudeva whom he viewed as a coward and had chased away from Mathura. Arjuna too, he felt, would be no match for him physically. In the true spirit and magnanimity of a Kshatriya, he chose to fight with Bheema whom he considered his equal and the weapons he chose were his strong, bare arms.

They fought for twenty-seven days, each matching the other strength for strength, skill for skill and blow for blow. However, towards the end, age got the better of Jarasandha and he was overpowered and killed in the combat. His son, Sahadeva was crowned the new King of Magadha under Vaasudeva's supervision, and the imprisoned kings were liberated and their respective kingdoms returned to them. As expected, with this strategy worked out by Vaasudeva, the Kaunteyas earned the gratitude and loyalty of all those brave monarchs whom they had liberated from captivity in one master stroke. Sahadeva himself became a loyal vassal of Yudhishthira. It was only later that I came to know the true purpose of this operation.

Yudhishthira had ambitions to perform the 'Rajasuya' sacrifice, which is one of the highest ritual sacrifices prescribed in the scriptures to be performed only by the best of kings to appease the Gods. However, this could be performed only by a king whose credentials and worthiness were unquestioned and who held the unchallenged status of an Emperor. The other mighty kingdoms of equal stature to Indraprastha were Hastinapur, Panchala and Magadha. The former two were bound to Indraprastha through familial ties and hence were expected to have no objection to Yudhishthira's claim to perform the Rajasuya. However, Magadha was different and as long as Jarasandha remained the lord, Yudhishthira's ambition would remain unfulfilled. Yudhishthira was counselled by Vaasudeva to avoid going to direct war with Magadha as Jarasandha had a vast army and it would result in needless bloodshed with very little chance of victory. Vaasudeva devised the strategy of going to Magadha in disguise with Bheema and Arjuna, and requesting Jarasandha for single combat knowing well that his ego would ensure he would reciprocate favourably. Everything happened as planned for the Kaunteyas. Now they had the entire army of Magadha with its new king at their disposal if neccessary.

17

Indraprastha was indeed everything that the balladeers had sung about. Its towers and minarets reached for the skies. The highways and streets were lined with shady trees and resting places for travellers. The various mansions, shops and markets that filled the streets were decked in floral decorations, competing with each other in grandeur and elegance. The fragrance from the fresh flowers of the beautiful gardens that interlaced the city filled the air. Citizens draped the best of perfumed silk raiment as they gathered on their terraces to get a glimpse of the visiting sages and royal dignitaries from all over to participate in Yudhishthira's Rajasuya which was to be presided by sage Vyasa himself. There was a full-strength delegation from Hastinapur including my father, the Grandsire and the other elders, the Acharyas, Uncle Shakuni, Radheya and, of course, me and my brothers. As much as I wanted to, I could not avoid the sacrifice as Yudhishthira had sent Nakula to Hastinapur to personally invite each one of us. Besides, I was also keen to behold the famed Maya Sabha of Indraprastha that I had heard so much about. It was a hall that was supposed to be filled with a lot of illusory effects. Being a keen student of magic and illusion myself, this was something I wished to experience. I also looked forward to meeting my son-in-law Sambha and also Balarama and Vaasudeva who had reached earlier than us.

We were welcomed by Yudhishthira personally and special care was taken to ensure that we were provided the best of accommodation and comfort. After paying his respects to the elders, Yudhishthira took the liberty of assigning us brothers and close relatives our special roles and responsibilities for the successful completion of the ceremony. Vaasudeva took up the responsibility of welcoming the Brahmins and washing their feet. Ashwatthama was assigned to take care of their comfort and needs. Dushasana was given charge of the food and refreshments. Arjuna was in charge of welcoming the guests. Bheema was assigned the control of expenses and finance. Nakula took care of the logistics while Sahadeva was asked to take care of the various sages who arrived for the ceremony. The vastly knowledgeable and experienced Grandsire Bheeshma and Acharya Drona took up the responsibilities of overseeing everything and ensuring that no details were left out. I was asked to receive on behalf of Yudhishthira, the gifts and tributes that poured in from the various kings who either came directly to attend the ceremony or sent their representatives.

The kings competed with each other with the gifts they brought in unlimited containers. Most of them who came could not even get a personal direct audience with Yudhishthira. But they never complained as they were made to feel welcome by someone from the Kuru family. They were all directed to the huge yards and storehouses of the treasury that I was in charge of, to offer their gifts. The rarest of precious gems from the north, the finest of gold embroidered silk from the east, the best of cows, horses and elephants, all poured into the treasury as the kings individually listed out their gifts and offerings to me while proclaiming their felicitations to Yudhishthira and

Indraprastha. It seemed that the entire world had placed its wealth and resources at Yudhishthira's feet...all this wealth that should have rightly belonged to my Hastinapur, if not for the act of partition. I could never forgive the Grandsire and my father for this. And to rub salt in the wound, I, Duryodhana, was assigned the role of the official receiver and caretaker of this wealth. It was not jealousy, as has been wrongly sung by the balladeers, but the feeling of injustice that gnawed my heart. With great effort, I managed to hide my disgust as I received the gifts and honours on behalf of Yudhishthira with all the grace befitting a prince of the Kuru family.

18

The Rajasuya sacrifice was completed successfully under the supervision of sage Vyasa. The royal dignitaries and guests were then invited to the royal hall and seated in special seats reserved for them. Yudhishthira, flanked by his brothers on either side was seated on the royal throne decked with costly gems and colourful feathers. Dhaumya, the royal preceptor of the Kaunteyas anointed him with sacred ash and sprinkled the holy sacrificial water over his head amidst recitation of sacred chants by the gathered sages. It was now time to honour the various dignitaries who had come to grace the occasion. However, Yudhishthira was in a dilemma as to who should receive the first honour. Murmurs on this had been going on in the inner circle for quite a few days now. Yudhishthira was yet to make up his mind. The hall was an ensemble of the best of heroes and sages who all seemed worthy of the first honour in terms of seniority, fame or prowess. It was difficult to offer the first honour to somebody without offending anyone's ego. It was a delicate situation for him that Uncle Shakuni and I quite relished.

But the clever fox that he was, Yudhishthira shifted the responsibility on to the Grandsire by seeking his guidance on the matter in the presence of everyone assembled there. By asking the Grandsire's opinion on who should receive the first honour, he cleverly took the Grandsire out of contention for this without making him feel slighted. Yudhishthira also knew that the Grandsire's choice would be acceptable to one and all as he was not only respected for his age and wisdom but also feared for his might and prowess.

All eyes were riveted on the Grandsire as he scanned the hall and his eyes finally rested on Vaasudeva seated across, looking elegant in his yellow silk raiment and wearing his trademark smile on his lips. It was an enchanting smile that seemed to give a different message each time you saw it. It was a smile that was hard to describe. It was an innocent smile and yet it was an all-knowing smile. It was a smile that seemed to confuse you with a thousand messages and emotions and yet a smile that reflected amazing clarity of thought. I had heard much about Vaasudeva's heroic exploits although I did not have the opportunity to get as close to him as I was with his elder brother. It was a matter of great comfort and happiness that my daughter was married to his son and I looked forward to our friendship growing in the coming years.

The Grandsire addressed Yudhishthira, "O King, you have successfully completed the Rajyasuya and your claim to supreme sovereignty has been accepted by all the great monarchs assembled here. The Gods have favoured you to perform this sacrifice. These lords assembled here have pledged their alliance and loyalty to you in full faith that you will never waver from righteousness and will always tread on the path of dharma. They have participated in this great and auspicious sacrifice in the knowledge that they will also benefit from it as your well-wishers. They are all worthy of the highest honour. You are also fortunate that this hall today has seen the holiest of sages of rigid vows and austerities come together and every one of them is worthy of receiving the highest honour. Your hall today resembles the vast sky lit with brilliant stars. However, all the stars that shine in the darkness of the night fade into oblivion in the presence of the midday sun. This hero from the Vrishni tribe whom you know as your cousin Vaasudeva and whom I know as the human manifestation of Lord Hari himself, who is the embodiment of truth, the ultimate object of every worship known to man, who is ever dear to the sages and ever engaged in doing good for the world...when he is here illuminating your august hall with his presence, can anyone else come forward to receive the first honour? If there's anyone in all the three worlds worthy of the first and foremost honour, it is Vaasudeva. So please offer your first honour to him."

The hall was quiet. No one spoke. Was everyone in agreement or was it out of fear and respect for the Grandsire? I will never know. Was it senility behind the Grandsire's rambling about Vaasudeva, or were there some elements of truth in it? Whatever may be the fact, I supported the Grandsire's choice since Vaasudeva was my Lakshmanaa's father-in-law now and I was happy to acknowledge his credentials for the honour.

On Yudhishthira's command, Sahadeva came forward to perform the first honours. He placed a garland of fresh forest flowers around Vaasudeva's neck, washed his feet with holy water and circled a tray of lit camphor around his face as a ritual of worship while sacred hymns were chanted in the background.

Suddenly a voice spoke out, "Fie on you, Yudhishthira, fie on you for insulting the entire Kshatriya race."

All eyes turned towards the direction of the voice. It was Shishupala, the King of Chedi. He stood up roaring like a wounded lion. "We monarchs came to this Rajasuya out of respect for you and not out of fear because we wrongly thought you were virtuous and knowledgeable in the aspects of Dharma. But alas, you have disappointed everyone here. You have chosen this Vaasudeva, born to a prison slave, who cannot even claim legitimate royalty by his birth over the galaxy of heroes here only to slight us. Listening to this old senile man born of a river, who hides his impotence in the false sheath of celibacy, you have broken all codes of Kshatriya honour."

The hall was stunned into silence. The audacity of this man drunk with arrogance was something this assemblage was unprepared for. Addressing the Grandsire as someone 'born of a river' was in the most derogatory sense, as a river always flowed from the higher to the lower and always welcomed anybody to come and take a dip in it. My hand went to my scabbard as I rose from my seat to sever the head of this insolent man when the Grandsire signalled me to remain calm. He had an excited look on his face as he took this verbal attack with a smile. The sages too looked excited as if they were waiting for this to happen. Yudhishthira was taken aback. The other Kaunteyas were enraged and so were the entire host of the Kuru and the Yadava heroes assembled there including Balarama. But they were all held back by Vaasudeva who never lost his smile. This was between him and Shishupala.

Shishupala was Vaasudeva's first cousin. He had a personal score to settle with Vaasudeva. Shishupala never forgot the fact that Vaasudeva was responsible for the death of Jarasandha who was his mentor. Shishupala now turned his attention from the Grandsire to Vaasudeva. He began a tirade of insults and accusations against him, calling him nothing but a cowherd who had no business to mingle with royalty. He accused him of being a coward who fled Mathura and relocated to Dwaraka out of fear of Jarasandha. He accused him of abducting Rukmini, the Princess of Vidharba and marrying her against her wishes. This was the real reason behind Shishupala's animosity as her brother Rukmi, the Crown Prince of Vidharba, had promised Rukmini's hand to him.

Sahadeva came forward and intervened. He lifted his right leg a foot above the ground and loudly proclaimed, "Vaasudeva is ever dear to us as we are to him. He has always been our guiding force. No one else is worthy of the first honour and let anyone who does not agree with me step forward and I will place my feet on his head."

The atmosphere became tensed as heated words were exchanged. As much as he wanted to avoid an unpleasant end to the grand sacrifice of Yudhishthira, the whole development culminated in Vaasudeva finally losing his patience and getting provoked to fight. Using his famed discus, known as the 'Sudarshana', in a flash, he severed Shishupala's head and that was the end of him. No one uttered a word. The Grandsire looked on with an all-knowing smile as though he just witnessed an event that he had foreseen. The sages uttered their blessings of that moment when Shishupala's head rolled off his shoulder. Just then, at that very moment, we felt a tremor as an untimely storm broke out dousing the golden-hued flame from the sacrificial alter pit outside the hall.

Yudhishthira's grand sacrifice thus came to an inauspicious end.

19

The guests left Indraprastha one by one after bidding farewell. Yudhishthira gifted them all many costly presents and honoured each one of them in accordance to their stature. The sages too left after receiving appropriate worship and offering their blessings to the Kaunteyas. Sage Vyasa, however, warned Yudhishthira to be prudent in everything he does for the next thirteen years as the omens that accompanied Shishupala's death did not augur too well for the Kaunteyas and in general for the entire race of Kshatriyas. He did not elaborate on this. Yudhishthira though disturbed, did his best not to show it in the presence of others. It was time for the Yadavas along with Vaasudeva to leave for Dwaraka. I did try to spend some time with Vaasudeva to get to know him better, but he was always preoccupied with Arjuna. My father too left for Hastinapur along with the other elders after blessing Yudhishthira. I however stayed back with Uncle Shakuni as I was yet to see the famed Maya Sabha. Yudhishthira had promised that he would arrange a tour of the Maya Sabha for me once the sacrificial ceremonies were over.

The Maya Sabha was a gift to Arjuna from a Danava named Maya. The Danavas were a class of sub-celestial beings with special illusory powers. Arjuna with the help of Vaasudeva had burnt down the entire forest of Khandava.

The forest located on the banks of the River Yamuna was the dwelling place for innumerable species of animals, birds, reptiles, rodents, various other life forms and also the rarest of trees, plants and herbs that served as the source for medicinal remedies for various ailments. Whenever there was a threat of a disease or epidemic in Hastinapur, the physicians always depended on the Khandava forest for remedial herbs. The forest also provided the best of teak and willow, which had contributed to the trade and economy, not to mention their use in architecture that was the trademark of my Hastinapur. The local tribes also depended on this forest for firewood, and other means of their livelihood. They lived off the fruits from trees of the forests and also the meat that they gathered from hunting. This rich forest was offered to the Kaunteyas during the partition of Hastinapur. It was completely burned down by Arjuna and Vaasudeva when they had gone camping on the banks of the Yamuna for recreation. In their enthusiasm to expand the city of Indraprastha, they completely overlooked the need for ecological preservation. They took special care to ensure that no inhabitant of the forest escaped the conflagration. However Maya, who also dwelled in the forest, was spared by Arjuna and as a favour for sparing his life, on the request of Vaasudeva, he constructed the special Maya Sabha for the Kaunteyas using his special architectural gifts. Maya had access to a secret location of rare and precious gems, stones and crystals that were in abundance on the banks of the pristine Vindu Lake on the Mainaika mountain ranges to the north of Kailash. He decorated the Sabha with these and embellished its grandeur using his special skills in illusion and visual imagery.

The Maya Sabha stood tall and magnificent, reaching out to the clouds. Its dazzling splendour put even the rays of the sun to shame. The exterior garden was lined with trees that would be found only in the bosom of the Himalayan ranges. Fragrance of fresh aromatic flowers of various colours and shapes filled the atmosphere. Golden columns supported the voluminous interiors, the floors were laid with costly marbles and decorated with carpets embroidered with gold. The walls were draped with the finest of silk curtains. The sunrays refracted through the multi-coloured crystals that layered the huge dome-shaped roof projecting a stunningly colourful and surreal visual imagery on the massive walls. There were thematic murals and paintings on display and at every corner could be seen silver lamp stands and crystal structures. At the centre of the Sabha was a lake created by crystal clear spring water gushing from the earth below. The bed of the lake was layered with stone tiles and the water was regulated to flow through a special channel that led to the garden outside. In the lake, one could spot turtles and small golden-coloured fish and also rare and beautiful swans and cygnets swimming gaily, manoeuvring between the lilies and lotuses.

I marvelled at this amazing work of Maya as I wandered around the Sabha intoxicated by the heady mix of fragrance from the flowers and the perfumed incense lit in every corner. However, as much as I was overwhelmed by the grandeur of the Sabha, I was a little let down as I was looking forward to the experience of the illusory effects that Maya was supposed to have designed for the Sabha. Just then in front of me I found a long stretch of corridor supported by tall shiny columns on either side. As I stepped forward enthusiastically, my head banged hard against a solid wall surface causing my crown to fall and break into pieces. I realised that the corridor was just an illusion. It was actually a projection of a painting on the opposite wall reflected by a mirror strategically placed to mislead. I got my first taste of Maya's illusory brilliance, and it hurt. My head reeled under the impact and I lost my balance. At that moment, I thought I heard some laughter. I looked around and saw no one. Was my mind playing tricks on me? I collected the pieces of my broken crown and continued to explore the Sabha. As I reached another area of the Sabha, it seemed to me filled with ankle deep water. I carefully lifted the bottom of my raiment to avoid wetting it as I tried to wade through the water. But as I treaded carefully, I realised that below my feet was a transparent sheet of glass that was flush mounted on the floor surface above the water, giving an impression that the floor was filled with ankle deep water. Maya did it again, and once again, I thought I could hear peals of laughter echoing across the Sabha. Was this also a part of Maya's illusion? I would soon find out.

At the centre of the Sabha was a rectangular floor area layered with intricate designs and patterns of floral sketches. I moved towards this and as I stepped on it, I fell with a loud splash into a tank of waist deep water. When I looked up, I realised that the patterns and designs were actually the reflection of the ceiling on the clear still water of the tank giving it the impression of a floor surface. As I struggled to come out of the water, I heard the laughter once again and this time there were more voices, and the resonance echoed across the Maya Sabha.

I turned towards the direction of the voices and there she was...Draupadi watching from the balcony, laughing hysterically along with her maids while brushing her long tresses. Bheema, Arjuna and the twins joined her. When they saw my plight, they too joined in the laughter. I stood there wet and humiliated as they continued to mock me. Hearing the commotion, Yudhishthira came there and when he saw my plight, he tried to control his amusement and gently admonished me. He said, "Dear Brother, I promised you a guided tour of this Sabha. You could have waited a little before setting off all by yourself." He turned around and ordered the maids to get some towels and a fresh robe for me as he offered his hand to pull me out. I refused his offer and managed to get out of the water by myself. Bheema and Draupadi continued to laugh. Yudhishthira turned to them and said sternly, "Stop this now. Remember, Duryodhana is not just our brother and a guest. He is also the Crown Prince of Hastinapur. This is no way to treat him."

And then came those words from Draupadi amidst uncontrollable laughter, "*Crown Prince of Hastinapur...of course ...blind prince born to a blind king.*"

20

The journey back to Hastinapur seemed endless. Uncle Shakuni thought it wise to leave me alone for the time being as my body burnt with the fire of silent rage. Those words and laughter echoed in my ears, stabbing me like a thousand darts... "A blind prince born to a blind king."

My father, the imperial monarch under whose banner fought the great Bheeshma and Drona who were unmatched in battle in all the worlds, referred to by such insulting terms by that woman of low virtue and that too in the presence of the Kaunteyas who did nothing to stop her...was it the intoxication from the indulgence of enjoying five husbands who took her by turns or was it her new exalted status of an empress by virtue of the Rajasuya that she forgot all etiquettes? Her arrogance was not new to me. I already had a taste of that when she insulted Radheya at her swayamvara. She had now crossed all limits of decency. I made up my mind. She needed a reminder that she became an empress only by virtue of my father's misplaced charity. As much upset as I was by all the riches and glory gained by the Kaunteyas that should have rightfully belonged to my Hastinapur, the feeling that they still revered Hastinapur was a consolation. However, whatever reverence they displayed was on the surface and I now realized that it was nothing but a figment of my imagination. I should have realised it when the Grandsire and my father were overlooked in favour of Vaasudeva for the first honour at the Rajasuya. It was clearer to me now as to why I was given the responsibility of accepting the gifts from the visiting kings on behalf of Yudhishthira. The truth was they wanted to flaunt their new-found success. Whatever their motivation may have been, they had successfully provoked a hibernating serpent to raise its striking hood and it will never lower again...not until its fangs emptied the last drop of venom into the enemy's flesh.

On reaching Hastinapur, I shut myself from the outside world for days. I could neither eat nor sleep. I confined myself to my chamber. I stopped going to the royal court for my administrative duties. Suddenly my Hastinapur seemed to have lost all its charm. In my eyes, the only way it could regain its lost sheen would be to make Khandavaprastha, now known to the world as Indraprastha, a part of it... Indraprastha, that rightfully belonged to my Hastinapur. And as for that woman of many husbands...my mind would never know rest till she was stripped of all her arrogance. It was she who suffered from blindness, the blindness caused by pride. Bhanumati, Uncle Shakuni, my mother...they all tried their best to coax me out of my depression and despondency, but my ears turned deaf to their implorations. Finally, Uncle Shakuni sent word to Radheya who was in Anga. He immediately rushed to Hastinapur.

Radheya along with Uncle Shakuni and Dushasana came to my chamber. On seeing Radheya, I lost control of myself and broke down. I narrated everything that happened at the Maya Sabha. Radheya held me reassuringly and said, "My friend, you have no right to grieve when I am with you. Just give me your orders and I'll attack and win Indraprastha for you. I will bring the Kaunteyas along with their common wife here as your slaves."

My eyes lit up and my heart was filled with joy. Those were just the kind of words I wished to hear. But Uncle Shakuni interrupted, "Brave words, Radheya, well spoken. But you forget that the Kaunteyas are no ordinary foes. You have attended the Rajasuya yourself and witnessed the various monarchs including those of Panchala and Magadha under their sway. There is too much at stake in war. You risk losing the friendship of all these kings. And don't forget, they have the entire host of the Yadavas who will do anything at the bidding of Vaasudeva, and Vaasudeva...he would do anything for Arjuna."

Radheya replied, "All those allies of Yudhishthira that you mentioned are as favourably aligned to us as they are with the Kaunteyas. Therefore, it is unlikely that they will interfere. Besides, which army would dare to oppose the army of Hastinapur, protected by the disciples of Bhargava?"

Uncle Shakuni smiled mockingly as he said, "When you speak of the disciples of Bhargava, speak for yourself. As for the other two...the great Bheeshma and mighty Drona, are you sure they will be with you on this? Acharya Drona's partiality to Arjuna and Bheeshma's fondness for Yudhishthira are no secrets."

Radheya was silent. Uncle Shakuni had a point there.

I looked at Uncle Shakuni and asked, "Then what do you suggest I do...just bear the humiliation in silence? Are you advising me to adopt the ways of the Brahmins, and abandon the natural duty of a Kshatriya? Are you advising me to allow the generations to come to mock me and refer to me as a loser? Are you advising me to bear that shame that will be worse than what I am carrying in my heart now? If I let this insult to me and my Hastinapur go unpunished, that will be a slur on the entire Kuru clan. How will I look at my Bhanumati in the eye and feel like a man worthy of her ever again? How will I ever look at my son Lakshman and feel like a worthy father to a hero? How can I even present myself in front of my father, the King, after silently bearing the insult heaped upon him by that woman of low virtue? How can I aspire for my Hastinapur without being weighed down by the guilt of allowing her humiliation? How will I face my own reflection in the mirror without repulsion? I would rather give up this life than live with a head lowered in shame. I am afraid, that is the only way ahead for me."

So saying, I drew the dagger from my scabbard and placed it against my throat ready to slit it. Quick as a flash, Radheya and Dushasana grabbed my arms and after a brief scuffle, overpowered me forcing the dagger out of my hand. We sat there on the floor. My chest heaved uncontrollably. Except my heavy breathing, silence engulfed the chamber. Uncle Shakuni shook his head in despair. He slowly walked up and sat next to me. He then put a hand on my shoulder and said in a reassuring voice, "Son, I cannot bear to see you suffer thus. You are dearer to me than my very own Uluka. I have a plan. We will discuss this over some wine tonight. Trust me when I say this, the day is not far when you will have your way with the Kaunteyas. This, I promise you."

21

Uncle Shakuni revealed his plan that night. For all the virtues credited to Yudhishthira by the sages and balladeers, it was no secret that he was a compulsive gambler addicted to the game of dice. It is a tradition amongst us Kshatriyas to never turn down a challenge for single combat or an invitation for a game of dice. Uncle Shakuni was an expert in this game, which was not only about the rolling of the dice but also the strategic movement of coins placed across a four-way board of square blocks. Elements of luck as well as skill play an equal part in the outcome of this game that is normally played for stakes and when it is played between kings, the stakes would be high. Many a time, territorial disputes between kings of equal stature and army might were settled by a game of dice to avoid needless war and bloodshed. The players always played with their own dice of which they were proud and possessive. Uncle Shakuni owned a special pair of dice, very carefully fabricated from human spinal bone with pips carefully embossed on perforations on each side to offer it differential weight in such a manner that he could manipulate the fall of the dice by sensing its dynamics in his palms while rolling it. This secret science was developed and mastered as a craft by Uncle Shakuni over years of practice and he had effectively used it to favourably settle several territorial disputes with neighbouring kingdoms of Gandhara without shedding a drop of blood. Uncle Shakuni's plan was that we invite Yudhishthira to a friendly game of dice to celebrate our newly constructed royal assembly hall. If we could get him to stake his Indraprastha, Uncle Shakuni was confident that with his superior skills at the game, he would be able to win it for me...without having to wage a war.

I found the plan distasteful. It was not the honourable way to go about. I would much rather wage war to win Indraprastha. Radheya also expressed his displeasure over the suggestion. But Uncle Shakuni convinced us with his persuasive skills that this was the best way forward. There would be no blame attached to anyone. Most importantly, we would retain our diplomatic alliances with Yudhishthira's allies. Now came the major issue. My father would have to be convinced of this proposal to invite Yudhishthira for the game of dice. I was not confident about this, especially since he never took decisions without consulting Vidura first. However, Uncle Shakuni took it upon himself to do this.

Uncle Shakuni chose an appropriate time to approach my father when he was alone. He told him about my grief and depression and also the humiliation I suffered at Indraprastha. He highlighted to my father the grave injustice he had inflicted on both me and on my Hastinapur by offering Khandavaprastha to the Kaunteyas. He warned my father that he risked losing me if something was not done about this at the earliest.

My father called for me. I entered his chamber and greeted him. He held my arms and addressed me, "Son, my brother Pandu was ever dear to me and his sons are like my own sons. I cannot bear this animosity you harbour against them. This is not good for you. Yudhishthira has earned all that he has by the virtue of his adherence to dharma. He is respected by his allies and blessed by the sages. Do not drown yourself in this despondency. It does not befit Kshatriyas to brood as such over another's good fortune."

I replied, "Father, I am unable to extinguish this fire of resentment that is burning me up. It is for Brahmins to forgive the injustice and insults heaped upon them. I am afraid that kind of magnanimity is misplaced in a Kshatriya. Firstly, they schemed and lobbied with the help of Vidura to make sure that Yudhishthira was made the Crown Prince. Then, they started propaganda amongst our people that I tried to burn them down at Varnavrat. I was deliberately assigned the responsibility of accepting the gifts and tributes for Yudhishthira from the various kings who took part in his Rajasuya. This was just a cheap tactic to flaunt their new-found opulence...and then the humiliation at Maya Sabha...the mocking laughter of Draupadi resonating in my ears has robbed me off my sleep. It was not just me that she insulted. She insulted you and my Hastinapur. I will gladly welcome death than put up with all this. My will to live hinges upon your approval to seek my vengeance. Father, allow me to attack the Kaunteyas and win back Indraprastha. With Radheya to lead our army, we have no one to fear. If that is not agreeable to you, with your permission, I will end this life. You will still have your other sons with you."

My father was alarmed. The seriousness in my tone found its mark. "No, son, please don't speak such words. You are the very reason for my living. I cannot permit you to take your life.

I need you to perform the last rites on my journey to the other world if my soul is to attain any peace. But the Kaunteyas, they are your brothers. It is not good to fight within the family. How will we ever face our forefathers? And remember, the Kaunteyas are not the same today. They have powerful allies who would come to their aid in the event of war. Right now, all of them are our allies too. We risk losing their friendship. War with the Kaunteyas is unthinkable."

This was just the little opening that Uncle Shakuni was waiting for as he moved in.

"Your Majesty, I have a solution for this that would be acceptable to all without compromising on the Kashatriya code of honour and conduct. If you may permit me, I shall explain."

My father listened as Uncle Shakuni unfolded his plan with clever use of words and logic. My father seemed satisfied at the suggestion. However, he was hesitant. He said, "Your suggestion is certainly worthy of evaluation, Shakuni, but let us also consult Vidura and the other elders tomorrow before taking a final decision."

"Father, you know how Vidura has forever been favourably aligned to the Kaunteyas. He will never allow this to happen. Alas, it is perhaps written that my destiny would be dictated by that son of a servant. What else would you expect if the Lord of Hastinapur is a mere puppet in the hands of his Chief Minister and cannot take an independent decision by himself?" My chest was heaving and lips throbbing as I spoke those words in fury.

My father was taken aback at this verbal explosion.

Uncle Shakuni then spoke to me in an admonishing tone "Son, that is no way to talk. Remember he's your King first, and then your father. He cannot afford to take decisions driven by emotion. And as for your allegation of him being a mere puppet in Vidura's hand...let me tell you, if that were true and your father had listened to the words of Vidura who wanted to put you to death the day you were born, you wouldn't be alive to speak these words today."

That was Uncle Shakuni at his best, offering a disguised and most perfectly timed reminder of that incident to my father. I apologised to my father as he stroked my face tenderly, gently wiping the tears that ran down my face. He said, "Son, what do you want from me now?"

I said, "Father, I want you to do whatever you feel is right and appeals to your judgement. Whatever your decision may be, it is acceptable to me. But I want this to be your decision and not Vidura's."

My father said, "Very well...let us discuss this in the court hall tomorrow. Now go in peace."

I looked up at Uncle Shakuni as he winked at me with a mischievous smile.

22

The following morning, in the presence of the elders and ministers of Hastinapur, my father addressed Vidura. "Vidura, it is befitting that we invite the sons of Pandu to come and visit our new assembly hall. After all, did we not enjoy their hospitality and grace when we attended the Rajasuya? I have been meaning to invite them over ever since. I would like Yudhishthira to personally inspect this magnificent hall supported by a thousand columns and designed by the best of Hastinapur's architects, and give his opinion on where it stands compared to his famed Maya Sabha. My sons have also wanted to invite them for a friendly game of dice in this hall to celebrate its completion. I would like you to personally go to Indraprastha to invite the Kaunteyas on my behalf. Choose the swiftest horses from our royal stables for your journey and proceed without delay."

Vidura was silent for a few moments. It was the first time that my father used an assertive tone while addressing him. He would normally consult him before any decision or look for his concurrence. But here he was exercising his authority without even seeking as much as an opinion on the matter. This inner strength and resolve of my father to express his will was something new to me and it made me proud of him. Vidura looked in the direction of the Grandsire, and the

Acharyas. They too were a little taken aback. They looked at each other and then slowly shifted their gaze towards Uncle Shakuni who sat there innocently stroking his beard as if he had nothing to do with what was going on.

Vidura got up and addressed my father, "Your Majesty, I do not approve of the game of dice as it is known to create disunion amongst friends and brothers. The intoxication of gambling is worse than that of wine. This game of dice is evil and could lead to nothing but ruin and destruction of peace. I plead of you, O King, to refrain from this for the sake of Hastinapur's welfare."

My father replied, "O Vidura, you have ever been thoughtful of Hastinapur as is your foremost duty and your views are noted and appreciated. Even if the game becomes the cause of disunion amongst my sons and the sons of Pandu as you fear, that would be the work of fate. Are we all not pawns in the hands of destiny? If the all-knowing Creator has something stored for us in our destiny, it cannot be prevented despite our best intentions and efforts. But you are reading a lot more into this than is necessary. This is just a friendly game and remember...I see no difference between Pandu's sons and my own. The Kaunteyas will be happy to accept my invitation. Please tell them that we can't wait to welcome them along with Kunti and Draupadi. Please proceed to Indraprastha without further delay."

My father's philosophy of conveniently shifting the responsibility on destiny amused me though I kept that to myself. But the decisiveness in his voice and the finality in his tone got the message across to Vidura. He spoke no further. The elders too remained silent. It was the first time that their

King took a decision without consulting them. They perhaps viewed this as an indication of things to come. I felt a squeeze on my arm. It was Uncle Shakuni, stroking his beard as he smiled at me. My time had finally arrived.

23

The Kaunteyas along with Aunt Kunti and Draupadi arrived to a warm welcome. After greeting my father and the other elders, they were escorted to their specially done up individual mansions. Dushasana, my cheeky brother, was curious to know with whom Draupadi would be retiring for the night and he shared his curiosity with me and Radheya, and we shared a good laugh over it. We had heard that the Kaunteyas had an arrangement that they would each take yearly turns with Draupadi, and during this period the others would not invade their privacy. Draupadi thus had five sons, one from each brother. However, we understood from the palace maids that night that Draupadi had retired to the inner chambers meant exclusively for women as she was menstruating, which explained why she did not present herself in front of my father to greet him.

The next day, after taking the Kaunteyas for a tour of our new assembly hall, we settled down towards noon for the game of dice. The hall was filled with all the male members of the royal family. We took our seats across the game board. The best of wine was served as Radheya, Dushasana and I sat around Uncle Shakuni while the Kaunteyas sat across the board with Yudhishthira at the centre and the others around him. When Bheema noticed Uncle Shakuni sitting in our centre, he looked at me questioningly. I ignored him and turned towards Yudhishthira and asked, "Dear Brother, with your permission, can Uncle Shakuni roll the dice on my behalf? You know me... I am not exactly good at indoor games. I am more of an outdoor person. However, not to worry, I shall be calling the stakes."

Yudhishthira's eyebrows lifted in suspicion as he turned and looked at his brothers for their reaction. They didn't seem too pleased. My heart was thumping in anxiety but I did my best to hide it and act calm. Uncle Shakuni then spoke, "Never mind, Yudhishthira, I see you have some constraints in playing against me. You are not to be blamed. I have a reputation of beating the best in this game. You are free to desist from playing the game. That is well within your prerogative."

Yudhishthira was silent for a few moments as he looked at the Grandsire and Vidura. They were both silent. He then said, "Dear Uncle Shakuni, up until now, I had considered this as a friendly invitation and would have had no hesitation in turning it down. But now, from your tone, it seems like a challenge. As a Kshatriya, I am bound by oath never to shy away from a challenge. I will gladly play with you."

"Well spoken, Yudhishthira," said Uncle Shakuni, "that's just what I had expected from you. Let us have some fun today."

From the corner of my eye, I could see Vidura shaking his head in despair.

"Very well," said Uncle Shakuni, "you may throw the dice first being our honoured guest."

"O Lord of Gandhara, please do not address me as a guest in my own Hastinapur. This is my home. No matter where I am, my heart belongs here in Hastinapur. Besides, the first throw rightfully belongs to Duryodhana by virtue of being my younger brother. Since you will be playing on his behalf, I invite you to roll the dice first," said Yudhishthira, indulging in his own sentiments and magnanimity...a mistake that was to cost him heavily.

The game commenced and Uncle Shakuni's genius was on display. He repeatedly won with every throw, denying Yudhishthira even a single chance to roll the dice. The game began with small stakes, starting from the precious stones and jewels we wore on our person and with every throw, the stakes doubled in value and Uncle Shakuni kept winning them for me. Soon, Yudhisthira's royal treasury was dry of all wealth. One by one, he pledged and lost his cattle, horses, elephants, slaves, army, weapons, and just about everything else that he owned. He then offered the various provinces under his jurisdiction and lost them, too. Then came the moment I had been waiting for as he nervously leaned forward and offered Indraprastha as stake.

"Are you sure about this? Don't you want to consult your brothers and get their concurrence?" asked Uncle Shakuni as he pointed towards Bheema who was now gritting his teeth and breathing heavily. His temples throbbed as he controlled his rage like a dam holding a river in spate. Arjuna too was quiet as he sat there, eyes lowered and arms crossed over his chest while his fingers dug into his own flesh.

"That would not be necessary. My brothers would not have an opinion beyond mine. So please roll the dice if you will," said Yudhishthira, sweating profusely.

"Very well, then...here we go," said Uncle Shakuni as he rolled the dice.

"Won!" he screamed in jubilation as he hugged me.

The hall erupted. My brothers congratulated me. Radheya hugged me. The Grandsire, the Acharyas and Vidura spoke nothing as they looked down in gloom. My father who was being updated on the game proceedings by his personal attender and charioteer Sanjaya kept repeating, "Who won... who won?" Sanjaya then gave him the news that he was now the Lord of Indraprastha. With a supreme effort, my father concealed his joy.

Vidura implored, "My Lord, please stop this game now. Please do not bring disrepute to Hastinapur. If this game continues, it will bring nothing but ruin and you will be blamed for generations to come. Please do as I bid you."

Uncle Shakuni became alert. He whispered to me, "Seems like your Chief Minister will spoil everything for you. If the game is stopped now, the Kaunteyas will be well within their rights to wage a fair war and claim back Indraprastha and perhaps even Hastinapur. We must continue the game till they are crippled of all freedom to wage a war. Hope your father has the wisdom to see through Vidura's intentions."

I was waiting for my father's response. My father was up to the occasion. He said, "Dear Vidura, who am I to stop the game? Yudhishthira is playing of his own free will and he is free to stop playing anytime if he so desires. There will be no objection from anybody. However, if I stop the game now, I will be denying him the chance to reclaim all that he has lost including Indraprastha. That would be unfair. So let the game continue till Yudhishthira himself feels it is time to stop. That would be the right thing to do at this time."

I was seeing a very different facet of my father. Very rarely have I seen him getting the better of Vidura, especially in the use of logic. Uncle Shakuni looked at Yudhishthira and asked him, "O Emperor Yudhishthira, would you like to continue? Do you have anything to stake to reclaim all that you have lost?"

Yudhishthira sat there motionless as if in a trance. He then looked up and said, "I have the good fortune of having these wonderful brothers mighty of arms and ever ready to serve me and wait for my bidding. Of these, I stake the youthful Nakula, handsome in looks, skilled in warfare and vibrant with energy. With him as stake, I aim to win back Indraprastha. I stake Nakula."

It shocked me that Yudhishthira looked upon his brothers as slaves or properties he owned. Even more shocking was that the brothers quietly submitted to his decisions.

The result was the same. "Won. What next?" asked Uncle Shakuni.

"Here is my brother Sahadeva, well-versed in the scriptures. His wisdom is far beyond his age and he is ever ready to provide good council even to foes. I stake him to win back all I have lost," said Yudhishthira.

Uncle Shakuni won again. He taunted, "Now that you've lost your brothers born of Queen Madri, I suggest we stop the game. You can at least retain your own brothers for yourself."

The taunt was not lost on Yudhishthira. "O wily man, know that I see through your intentions. You seek to sow seeds of disunion amongst us brothers, but you shall not succeed. My brothers are all equally bound to me as I am to them. For the sake of Indraprastha, they will lay down their lives; leave alone offer themselves as stake. Behold this mighty archer, unrivalled in marksmanship, ambidextrous, unconquered in combat, my brother Arjuna, who is ever dear to the high souled Vaasudeva. I stake him."

Uncle Shakuni won yet again.

Yudhishthira said, "Now I pledge this lion amongst men, foremost amongst wielders of the mace, having the strongest of arms, fearless in battle, terror to foes and ever ready to battle for a just cause...my dearest brother Bheema."

This was something I looked forward to. Bheema, who took delight in bullying us brothers throughout our growing years, waiting on me and carrying out my orders as my slave was something I would relish.

No sooner had Uncle Shakuni rolled the dice, than Bheema was won and now remained the last frontier...the Emperor himself. Yudhishthira pledged himself as stake in a final attempt...and he lost.

There was silence as a sudden gloom enveloped the hall. The Grandsire was sweating as he looked down at the floor. Vidura and the Acharyas were in tears. I was, however, delighted beyond words.

Yudhishthira now addressed me, "Duryodhana, we the sons of Pandu have been won by you in this game of dice with the help of Shakuni. You are our master now. I have lost everything and have nothing else to offer as stake. So do with us as you wish to do."

Saying thus, Yudhishthira removed his crown and his upper garment and laid it at my feet. His brothers followed suit. But Uncle Shakuni was not satisfied. He said, "Yudhishthira, if you so desire, we could continue the game and you could still win back everything that you lost. You still have one precious gem that you are yet to pledge as stake. Perhaps that could be your lucky stake."

That surprised me as much as it surprised the Kaunteyas. They looked up.

Uncle Shakuni said, "You still have your Queen...Draupadi."

The shock on everyone's face was to be seen as Uncle Shakuni suggested the unthinkable. Bheema charged forward to attack him only to be restrained by Arjuna. All eyes were on Yudhishthira, stripped of all his senses and devoid of all reason. He said, "Very well, I will now pledge my Queen, the pride of the Panchalas, born of the sacrificial fire, the dusky Draupadi. With her as my object of stake, I shall win back all that I have lost."

Uncle Shakuni whispered in my ear as he shook the dice and rolled it, "Did I not promise you this will be your day?"

"Won again. Alas, Yudhishthira, now the game must truly end."

This couldn't be happening. It felt like a dream. I erupted in joy and hugged Uncle Shakuni and Radheya. The elders were in a state of shock and too numb to react. "Fie, fie... shame," and such words echoed across the hall. Bheema was now hissing like a serpent in fury. He spat out words of venom at Yudhishthira. He threatened to burn Yudhishthira's hands for the misfortune that they brought upon them. Arjuna tried to pacify him as Yudhishthira sat motionless.

I ordered an attendant to go to the women's quarters and ask Draupadi to come to the hall and report to her new masters immediately. The attendant reported after a few moments all by himself. He said, "O Prince, I faithfully conveyed your message to Queen Draupadi and her reply was thus, 'Please ask Emperor Yudhishthira if he pledged me before or after he lost himself. Only on getting his response shall I present myself in the hall.' Those were her exact words."

"You fool, why do you address her as 'Queen'?" I roared, "'Queen' she is no more; she's just a slave. A slave's foremost duty is to obey her master's command. Go back and tell her to report here immediately. If she has any questions for Yudhishthira, let her come and ask him directly. If she fails to come, she will leave me no choice but to use force. Go at once!"

The attendeant left nervously only to return alone once again. He said, "O Prince, I have conveyed your message exactly the way you wanted of me. But she asked me to repeat her question to the elders of the court and insisted that she will not come till she gets her answer from them."

"Very well, then...she leaves me with no choice." My patience failed me and I never had much to begin with. I turned to Dushasana and ordered him to go bring Draupadi to the hall using force if required. It was time to settle scores with this woman whose universe revolved around her vanity. Dushasana, who was celebrating our victory with wine, was only too happy to obey as he left for the women's quarters immediately. A few moments later, he came back dragging a wailing Draupadi by her hair to the centre of the hall. She was draped in a single robe as did women in their season.

I looked at my new slave from head to toe as Radheya refilled my cup with wine. He then addressed her, "Congratulations, O Draupadi, you now have a new master and lord. Your five husbands have already enslaved themselves to him. You have been won by my dear Duryodhana in the game of dice. Come and take your place on his lap."

As he said this, I struck on my left thigh and gestured Draupadi to come over and sit on it.

The enraged Bheema roared, "Wicked wretch, I swear on all that I hold sacred that I will break those thighs in battle one day."

I retorted with a loud laugh, "Slaves don't get to battle their masters. I have better plans for you...maybe in the kitchen... or perhaps as a eunuch guarding the women's quarters."

Radheya and Uncle Shakuni joined me in laughter as suddenly Draupadi wriggled out from Dushasana's clutches and came and stood in front of Yudhishthira. His body shook nervously as he looked down avoiding her gaze. She addressed him, "O worthy scion of the Bharata race, O Emperor reputed to be the torchbearer of justice and morality, I seek your answer. Did you pledge me, your Queen, before you lost yourself or after? If it was after you lost yourself, then what right would you have over me when you have no right over yourself? If indeed it was before, even then what right do you have to use me as a stake without my permission? Please answer me. I demand to know."

Yudhishthira remained silent. She then turned towards my father and the elders as she addressed them, "O worthy heroes of the Bharata race, I come from a kingdom where women are respected and revered. When my father, the great Emperor Drupada held my swayamvara, his desire was to send me to the best of homes with the best of heroes. Here I am with five heroes, gambled away in a game of dice and not one of them to come to my aid. Is there no respect for women in the Lunar Dynasty? Even if my Lord has pledged me in the heady intoxication of gambling, I am prepared to abide by and honour his decision. But before that I demand the answer to my question...how could I be offered as stake by a man who has lost himself?" So saying, she looked at each one of them for an answer as they all looked down avoiding her eyes.

The Grandsire finally spoke up, "Dharma is very subtle in nature. There is no such thing as 'right' or 'wrong'. They are relative concepts wrapped in the foils of time and space. You must take this question back to Yudhishthira as only he can give you the answer that you seek."

Suddenly a voice spoke up, "Fie on this assembly of heroes who hide behind theories of Dharma to desist from engaging in what is right. This insult to Draupadi who has come as a daughter-in-law into the Kuru household spells doom for Hastinapur. I agree with her; what right does a man have to pledge something when he has already lost himself? I have no hesitation in stating that Draupadi has been won unfairly. Yudhishthira has no right whatsoever to pledge her."

It was one of my own brothers, Vikarna. Although I loved him the most after Dushasana, I was aware of a subtle tendency in him to play a hero in front of women. He never missed an opportunity to impress them with his well disguised nobility and chivalry, in the hope that it would extract a favourable response at the right time. This time he was aiming for Draupadi's attention, which I thought was a waste of effort since she had already become our slave. The fool thought that I could not see through him.

"Ha, Vikarna, you are still too young to delve in these matters," said Radheya. "When the great Bheeshma, the Acharyas, Vidura and others well-versed in Dharma remain silent, when even the Kaunteyas have submitted to this decision of Yudhishthira, why do you speak out of turn? It is most inappropriate. This arrogant woman needed to be shown her true place. Did she think twice before addressing your brother, the Crown Prince of Hastinapur, as the blind son of a blind king? What virtue do you find in this woman who takes five men as her husbands that you speak so much for her? She is a slave now and it is a Kshatriya's right to do with a slave as he wishes to. As a matter of fact," he turned and signalled to Dushasana, "There would be no shame even if she is stripped threadbare in this assembly."

Dushasana inebriated with wine took the cue and grabbed Draupadi's robe in an attempt to disrobe her. Intoxicated, we were completely devoid of our senses. Neither my father nor the elders did anything to stop us. There ensued a tug of war between Dushasana and Draupadi, who proved to be tougher than we thought as she fastidiously held to her robe. The Kaunteyas sat motionless with their eyes fixed to the floor. Draupadi's implorations fell on their deaf ears as Dushasana tried to disrobe her. She repeatedly taunted the Kaunteyas with her sarcasm, trying to arouse them. She said that if only Vaasudeva was there, he would not have allowed this to happen. When she realised that nothing was going to help, she stopped resisting and folded her palms breaking out into a prayer to Lord Hari, submitting herself to His will. That act of hers suddenly brought us back to our senses as Dushasana let go of the robe and dropped to the floor exhausted.

A few moments of silence filled the hall. It was broken by the thundering voice of Bheema, "Let all the Gods and the Kshatriyas who lived in this world, are living and are yet to be born bear witness to my oath. If I do not tear open the breast of this wretch Dushasana in the battlefield with my bare hands and feast upon his blood, let me be denied the auspicious regions attained by my forefathers."

24

The terrible words from Bheema who was seething in fury sent a panic alarm across the hall, especially among the elders and my father. Dushasana looked at me, awaiting my advice.

I got up from my seat and addressed the Kaunteyas and, in particular, Bheema, "You brothers now listen to me carefully. I empathise with you about your situation and the indignation at whatever you are undergoing, but your rage is misdirected. You seem to forget the fact that you have all been won by me in a fair game. However, I will still respect your individual rights and offer you freedom if you proclaim that this man, Yudhishthira, is not your master and had no right whatsoever in offering you as stake. If you do this, I shall return everything that I have won in this game from Yudhishthira and that includes Draupadi. This is my promise to you in the presence of the King of Hastinapur with the elders here as witness."

My words were greeted with appreciation across the hall. I considered this as my master stroke. I had the Kaunteyas tongue-tied. This was the moment of truth for them. It was a test of their unity. They looked at each other while Yudhishthira remained silent with his eyes fixed to the floor. Bheema was about to respond when Arjuna interrupted him and addressed me. "This man you refer to is not just our brother. We revere him as we would our father. He is the embodiment of truth and righteousness and has forever been our guide in the path of dharma. Know you must that what he has withstood on this black day in the history of our dynasty is not a reflection of his weakness. He has done it out of higher considerations as he is blessed with the gift of foresight. He has performed many a sacrifice and has the grace of the Gods shining on him. We take pride in the fact that he holds complete sway over us as our master. If he has staked us brothers, we will submit to his decision. Do with us as you please."

"Does your wife Draupadi also take your stand?" asked Radheya mockingly.

All eyes turned to Draupadi. I repeated my offer to Draupadi, "Freedom shall be yours, O Draupadi, this I promise. All you need to do is challenge Yudhishthira's right as your lord to pledge you and I shall release you from your bondage."

Draupadi now looked at the elders and once again implored, "O Great Lords of the earth, I will consider it my honour if I was staked by my lord to win back Indraprastha. However, I will still ask my question, which remains unanswered. If he pledged me after he pledged himself, is that acceptable?"

The Grandsire looked at her with helpless pity as he said, "O Daughter, I said this before and I say it now again...your question can be answered by none but Yudhishthira. As long as he remains silent, the question will remain unanswered."

Radheya, who was running out of patience said, "Let me answer this to the best of my knowledge of dharma. The moment Yudhishthira pledged himself, it was understood that it was inclusive of everything that belongs to him, including his queen. Now he belongs with all his possessions to Duryodhana, and that includes Draupadi. Dushasana, waste time no more discussing this slave woman. Take her away to the slave chambers where she may be assigned her chores."

Dushasana grabbed Draupadi's arm and began pulling her, when she once again wriggled out of his grip and came and stood in front of my father and the elders. She folded her palms and addressed them, "O glorious King, O illustrious elders of the Kuru court, know you all that I was dragged by my hair and brought to this assembly while I am in my season and draped in a single cloth. In my agitation on hearing that I was staked in this game of dice, I failed to offer my proper respects to you all. I seek your pardon for the same. I, Daughter of the Emperor Drupada of Panchala, born of the sacrificial fire, sister of mighty armed Shikhandi and Drishtadyumna, queen of five mighty heroes whose sway extended across the earth until this morning, and an honoured daughter-in-law in the Kuru clan, offer my respects to Your Majesty and the elders in this assembly."

I wondered where all this respect was on that day in the Maya Sabha when she addressed me as the 'blind son of a blind king'? However, her sarcasm was not lost on the elders as they looked down in shame. Beads of perspiration appeared on my father's forehead. He then spoke in a gentle tone, "O sinless one, whatever happened today is the work of fate. Let none be blamed for this...or let everyone take their share of responsibility. However, as the King of Hastinapur, I shall take the major share of the blame, but I shall also make amends. Please ask of me any wish you may want me to grant you in my capacity as the King. It shall be honoured."

"What is he doing? The old man is going to ruin all our efforts," whispered Uncle Shakuni. I could do nothing but watch as Vidura heaved a sigh of relief.

Draupadi replied, "O Great King, if you must grant me a wish, please give my lord Yudhishthira his freedom from this bondage."

"Consider it granted. Please ask me for one more wish and I will grant you whatever it may be that you seek," said my father.

"O King, if I may ask for one more wish, let it be that the other Kaunteyas also be released from bondage and their weapons, chariots and insignias returned to them."

"Of course, Daughter, but I am still not satiated. Please ask me for one more wish and I shall be happy to honour it."

"Your Majesty has granted me everything that I need and asking for more would be misusing your magnanimity. Please grant us permission to take leave."

Uncle Shakuni was silent and so was I. All our efforts were brought to nothing.

"Truly this woman is commendable," said Radheya. "Single-handedly, she has rescued the Kaunteyas like a raft rescuing drowning men and ferrying them across turbulent waters."

The Kaunteyas remained in a silent state of shock as the assembly quietly dispersed, equally shocked by the turn of events. Later, I met my father in his chamber along with Uncle Shakuni. Uncle Shakuni spoke to him, "Your Majesty, as much as your magnanimous gesture will be spoken of generously, I fear that it might turn out to be a bad decision as far as Hastinapur is concerned. We virtually won everything without shedding a drop of blood and now you have given it all back leaving us much worse than we were when we started."

My father said, "Why do you say that, Shakuni? I have only given the Kaunteyas their freedom from our bondage. But we now have Indraprastha and all its wealth at our disposal. Isn't that what my dear Duryodhana wanted in the first place?"

"My Lord, you are too noble to see through the intentions of that devious woman Draupadi. When you were ready to grant her a third wish, why do you think she refused? She was satisfied with the release of the Kaunteyas along with their weapons and chariots. She could have asked for Indraprastha to be returned, but she didn't. That is because she prefers Indraprastha to be won back by war, which the Kaunteyas now have the freedom to wage with us, and not to forget, they will have the Panchalas and their allies to support them. All you have done now is perhaps empowered Bheema to fulfil his oath."

My father was now worried. He hadn't thought about this. He sat deep in thought. Perhaps Bheema's words were still echoing in his ears. He finally spoke, "What you say is possible, Shakuni. Even Vidura warned me earlier that the Kaunteyas are not going to bear all the humiliation they suffered today in silence. So what do you suggest we should do?"

I spoke, "Father, since things have reached this far, peace with the Kaunteyas is now unthinkable. Let us call the Kaunteyas for another game of dice before they leave Hastinapur and this time let the conditions be different. Let the losers go into exile for thirteen years, twelve in the forest and the thirteenth incognito. If they happened to be traced and found out in the thirteenth year, they then will have to repeat the same for another thirteen years."

My father seemed pleased and convinced of the idea though he was sceptical about Yudhishthira accepting the invitation a second time. He, however, took the chance and sent a messenger to invite Yudhishthira once again, and as expected, Yudhishthira once again did not disappoint us. The Kshatriya's code of honour did not permit him to turn down the invitation and Uncle Shakuni delivered the goods once again.

It never ceased to amaze me how these man-made codes of honour and pride often misguided the most sensible of men to their fall.

25

The Kaunteyas took leave for the forest after offering their respect to the elders. They were led by their priest Dhaumya, who chanted certain hymns from the Sama Veda meant for Yama, the deity of death. They were attired in nothing but deerskin. Draupadi accompanied them, in a single cloth with her tresses let loose. I was informed to my amusement that she vowed to let her hair remain that way till it was washed with the blood of my brother Dushasana. She wanted Bheema to be reminded of his oath every time his eyes fell on her dishevelled hair. The citizens thronged the streets to give them a farewell and accompanied them as far as they could. I did not stop them. It was heartening for me to see the Kaunteyas sent back to where they came from in the first place one fine morning years ago...the forests.

Aunt Kunti stayed back in Hastinapur. She stayed in Vidura's palace, much against my father's wishes. He wanted her to stay in the royal palace with my mother. I occasionally paid her a visit as per my father's wish. He felt it important that she held no resentment against me. I did attempt to explain to her my side of the story of the events that occurred including the insult at the Maya Sabha and why destiny was to be blamed and not me, a line that I borrowed conveniently from my father. She listened to me patiently as she looked at me with what seemed like empathy. It is only now I realise that it was in fact sympathy.

She said to me, "Son, I harbour no ill will towards you or anyone for that matter. Yes, whatever happened was destined to happen, and whatever will happen is also perhaps destined. None can change the work of fate. You have won lordship over Indraprastha. But to fit into Yudhishthira's shoes, you must let only truth be your guide. Now reign over Indraprastha wisely, this Indraprastha that your brother Yudhishthira built from scratch. Let the welfare of its subjects be on the top of your priorities. Make your victory valuable and meaningful to them."

Although her words seemed straight enough from the heart, the emotion behind it was something that confused me. Was there some kind of a warning veiled behind those words? Anyway, I lay to rest those thoughts. I focused on the road ahead as I had no intention of fitting into Yudhishthira's shoes. I always followed my own ways. Indraprastha was a vast kingdom with many allies. With the Kaunteyas gone, it was important that we kept Indraprastha safe from any insurgency by Yudhishthira's loyalists. We discussed this amongst ourselves and Uncle Shakuni came up with the solution. We needed to entrust the governance of Indraprastha with someone loyal, someone who was not only feared but also respected by the Kaunteyas and their allies. That way, we would ensure that Indraprastha remained in safe hands. We decided that Acharya Drona would be the best person to fulfil this role. That would not only be acceptable to the people of Indraprastha but would also keep potential enemies and rebels at bay as his prowess was known to the world. He was highly respected by all the kings in the land of Bharata. Acharya agreed to take up the responsibility but chose to govern as a supervisor from Hastinapur. He delegated the daily administration to a carefully chosen group of loyal ministers whom he stationed at Indraprastha to report to him.

Uncle Shakuni organised for a network of trusted spies and informants to update us on the Kaunteyas and their whereabouts in the forests. The last we had heard was that they were camping in a clearance in the Kamyaka Forest by the River Saraswati, in the company of sages. We received information that the Yadavas headed by Vaasudeva and the Panchalas led by Drishtadyumna paid them a visit. That was not surprising, considering they were tied to the Kaunteyas through matrimonial alliances. We were also informed that they had other regular visitors, most of them sages and notable among them was Markandeya, famed for his rigid vows and knowledge. Many of these sages came to visit Hastinapur, too...with their ears filled with the lamentations from the Kaunteyas and Draupadi about the alleged injustice heaped upon them by me. The main objective of their visits was to admonish my father, the King, for whatever happened and give unsolicited advice to call the Kaunteyas back and return whatever we rightfully won from them or face our doom at the end of thirteen years. They came to us with a prejudiced mindset after hearing just one side of the story. I did not care much for them. I was not one to give in to threats. So was my father. But he had the wisdom to extend the customary courtesies to these sages and hear them out fully before giving them his tested and approved theory that whatever was happening was the work of fate and that neither he nor anyone could disentangle themselves from the web of destiny.

I felt that as the king he was accommodating more than he should be. I certainly lacked that kind of patience and tolerance.

I told my father to call for me the next time he had to listen to these sages and their sermons on this issue. I told him to ask them to speak to me directly and that I would handle them. Uncle Shakuni had alerted me that many of these sages who came visiting could actually be Yudhishthira's spies or informants and that we should be careful while talking to them. These sages had an unwritten license to wander around from kingdom to kingdom and were not subject to the regulatory checking or entry restrictions at the borders that normal citizens were subjected to. They were received with honour and treated as royal state guests wherever they went as their visits were supposed to be auspicious. I gave orders to the guards at our borders to bar entry for these wandering sages unless they came on invitation or prior approval from the King. However, Vidura convinced my father to revoke the orders. He convinced my father that the sages' blessings played a big part in the prosperity of Hastinapur. They bring auspiciousness with their presence in the kingdom. They were men with special powers earned from their rigid austerities and antagonising them would be at our own peril. The last thing that the people of Hastinapur wanted was their curse on our heads. My father became a soft target for yet another one of his wily minister's schemes, this time to offer Yudhishthira's informants free access to Hastinapur.

One day, I was summoned to the assembly hall by my father. It was to welcome the renowned sage Maitreya. He had come on the specific request of sage Vyasa to counsel us to call back the Kaunteyas. My father received him with the customary traditional honours. The sage began his counsel, which was not any different from what we had heard before. He sang flowery praises of the Kaunteyas and their prowess. He accused me of cheating in the game of dice and winning over everything I had by deceit. I could do nothing to this man while he insulted me, as he was a guest of my father and a Brahmin. Anyone else in his place would have had his head severed in that very hall. I remained silent and turned a deaf ear to him. I kept slapping my thighs in impatience as I sat there wondering how long he would take to leave. This was not lost on him and he felt slighted. Eyes red with wrath, he got up from his seat and roared, "O haughty Prince, you have invited your own destruction with your insolence. Those thighs that you slap in arrogance and pride will one day be broken in the battlefield by that foremost of wielders of the mace, Bheema. This is my curse. I have been a man of truth. The words I utter will never be falsified and may this help Bheema in fulfilling his oath." Uttering his curse thus, he took a handful of water from the small earthen container he carried with him, sprinkled it in my direction and left the hall in a rage.

My father was anguished over the sage's curse. He and the other elders implored me to call back Maitreya and beg for his forgiveness. I had a good mind to call back the sage, not to ask for forgiveness but to chain him and throw him in the dungeons. However, I could not do that, as my father would not approve of it. I got up and walked away from the hall to my chamber. I needed some respite from all this endless drama.

As I walked into my chamber, I saw Bhanumati standing alone in the balcony, waiting for me. Her silhouette against the evening rays of the setting sun made her look more desirable than ever. She seemed to be in a melancholic trance. I hadn't spent much time with her in the last few months, especially after the game of dice. I had neither sought her opinion nor shared my thoughts with her on the matter.

As I came near her, I observed tears in her eyes. I got concerned. I asked her the cause for her grief. She said, "My Lord, I have been silent all along and have never interfered in your state affairs. You are the best judge to decide if your actions fall within the sphere of dharma. I have no fear of the words of the sages coming true. I know that you are stronger than that."

I held her in my arms, looked her in the eye and said, "Never have I been more proud of you. You please me with your faith in me. Then pray tell me, why this despondency? Why do I see your eyes wet? If it is anxiety, tell me the cause. Are you unwell? You look tired. Haven't you had enough rest?"

She replied, "My Lord, I have known no sleep for the last many days as I am haunted by a recurring dream every time I close my eyes and that gives me no peace of mind."

I laughed aloud. "A dream? Is that what this is all about?"

"My Lord, I feel this is more than just a dream. It appears to me as a presage for some great calamity that is to befall us. I keep getting this dream of a hundred serpents with their hoods raised and swaying majestically in a grassland. Out of nowhere emerges a mongoose, which single-handedly kills each and every serpent and relishes them for a meal. At this point, I wake up perspiring. I see no relief from this dream that spoils my peace of mind. I feel that it is a warning that the path you have chosen will lead to our destruction. Perhaps it is an indication of what destiny has in store. Is this the way of our Gods to tell me that the hundred sons of Gandhari would meet their end in the mighty arms of Bheema?"

I laughed as I held her close to me. "Dear, this kind of fear does not befit a Kshatriya woman. Your Lord is the Crown Prince of Hastinapur under whose banner fights the mighty Bheeshma, Drona, Radheya, Jayadratha, Ashwatthama and a host of the foremost warriors in this land of Bharata. I know that you do not approve of what happened to Draupadi. But it was done to teach her a lesson in humility. She insulted Radheya at her swayamvara. She insulted me, and more importantly, the King of Hastinapur at the Maya Sabha. Not for a moment do I regret my actions. I do not care if the whole world goes against me as long as you and Radheya understand me and stand by me. Now forget about your silly dream. Dreams are nothing but a reflection of our thoughts. Let's live in the present and indulge in every moment of it."

I poured some wine in a cup and offered her to join as we both settled down for an evening of entertainment by a troop of visiting musicians who gave us a private performance in our chamber. The music seemed even more delightful when it was coupled with the thoughts of the Kaunteyas languishing in the deep woods.

26

Seasons came and went, rolling undisturbed and it was now time to take account of our livestock as well as wildlife. This was a very important exercise we conducted every three years. Dairy and venison played a big role in shaping the kingdom's food economy. Game hunting in the forest was permitted with restrictions as it was important to retain the ecological balance. Hunting of deer, bison, wild boar, wild rabbits and other animals as such with edible meat was permitted strictly for food. Wild elephants and horses were mostly captured young and trained in the royal stables. Hunting of big game, especially wild cats was permitted only if their population was threatening to be a menace and they were leaving their habitat in the deep woods and meandering into the villages.

We had reports from our stations in the woods that there was a significant drop in the deer and bison population in the surrounding areas of the Kamyaka Forest. This had resulted in the big cats leaving the deep jungles and wandering into the villages in search of food causing panic amongst the villagers. I had information that the Kaunteyas were residing in the Kamyaka Forest towards the north near Lake Dwaita, along with a host of Brahmins and sages. Various other sages and their entourage of disciples regularly visited them and camped with them for days. The Kaunteyas had literally converted the rich Kamyaka Forest into a settlement. I also had information that they played host to these sages and visitors, and served them regular feasts of venison, which they gathered from hunting. This explained the sudden drop in the deer population. However, I decided to go to the forest and examine things for myself. My brothers along with their families, Radheya and Uncle Shakuni decided to join me as they wanted to enjoy an outing in the woods.

After taking my father's permission, our retinue set out to the forests. We made sure that our slaves carried enough meat and wine to last the trip. My father gave us strict instructions to stay away from the vicinity of the Kaunteyas to avoid any unnecessary friction and trouble. Nothing suited me better. We came upon a clearing in the deep forest where we decided to set camp. It was a beautiful setting filled with wild flowers and tall trees with their branches forming a lush canopy. The slaves lost no time in setting up the camp and putting up our tents near a little stream. I called the various team leaders of the census team and divided the work to be done amongst them. I had the forest divided into areas and assigned a team for each area. I always believed that effective delegation was the key to get work done. The teams were equipped with the assembled machinations and traps. The quadrupeds captured were to be checked for their identity code stamped along with the royal emblem of Hastinapur and if they did not carry them, they were to be stamped with a new code that fell in serial and let back free to the forest. After assigning the teams their tasks and setting them forth in different directions, I decided to relax and indulge in some wine and sport in privacy with my brothers and Radheya. I retained just a handful of our eunuch bodyguards to guard our womenfolk who were having a nice time sporting in the stream of clear water that ran down from the distant Himalayas.

Towards evening, as we lay in our camps intoxicated with the heady wine, we heard sudden shrieks of the women from the stream. I rushed to find the bodyguards dead with their heads severed from their bodies. The womenfolk, my Bhanumati included, stood there half-naked and in horror. We were being attacked by a group of Gandharvas. The Gandharvas, like Danavas, were a group of sub-celestial beings with special gifts and powers. They dwelled in the base region of the Himalayas. They were specialised in the art of fighting from the air and their feet never touched the earth. Their strength grew with the onset of darkness.

My bodyguards rushed to the rescue of the women but were overpowered and butchered before my very eyes. It was all too sudden and I was at a loss for reaction. Hearing the commotion, my brothers along with Uncle Shakuni and Radheya came out. Soon there ensued a terrible fight between the Gandharvas and us. The Gandharvas greatly outnumbered us. We were still inebriated from wine. One of the Gandharvas, who appeared to be their chief sought out Radheya for single combat and hurled all kinds of shafts at him. Radheya managed to counter the onslaught but began to fatigue against the relentless attack. He was struck by a powerful shaft that made him swoon. His charioteer appeared in the nick of time and rescued him. The chief of the Gandharvas then turned his attention towards me. The fight went on too long. I withstood the attack along with my brothers and slowly gained ground. I methodically disarmed the Gandharva chief and took up my prized possession, my mace that I treasured.

I whirled it in the air a couple of times as I took aim at his skull when I heard a loud wail. I turned around to see that the Gandharvas had taken the women hostage. One of them held a sword against Bhanumati's throat threatening to slit it. I held back. The Gandharva Chief, then spoke, "Put down your arms, you fools, if you value the lives of your women."

I dropped my mace and my brothers also dropped their weapons. The Chief then ordered for us to be taken captive and tied up against a tree.

I stood there humiliated as he came up to me. "O foolish man, tell me who you are and where you come from? What gave you the courage to set camp here in this forest? Don't you know this region is meant for us Gandharvas once the sun has set? I am Chitrasena, the Chief. We have been allocated this region by our Lord Kubera. If you have treaded into this region out of ignorance, then you may seek my pardon and take leave with your womenfolk at the break of dawn."

"Shame on you, shame on you that you should seek refuge behind these women whom you have taken hostage. Know you that I am Duryodhana, the Crown Prince of Hastinapur and this region that you claim to have been allocated by your lord falls in my domain. You have no claim to it whatsoever. This victory that you have won is only temporary. My friend Radheya will soon be back. He is the master of all missiles. Don't be misled into thinking that he has retreated out of fear. He was unprepared for this and heady with wine. But he will soon return and once he is back, you and your entire host will be sent to the abode of Yama."

Chitrasena let out a loud laughter. "Very well, then, we shall wait and see."

Just then, at a distance, we saw a couple of men approach us. They were tall, well-built with broad shoulders and dressed in deerskin. They carried a torch flame with them. They looked familiar although I could recognise them only when they came near. It was Bheema and Arjuna. What were they doing here? Then I saw Chitrasena welcoming them and exchanging pleasantries. So did they plan this whole thing? Was Chitrasena and his horde of Gandharvas acting on the Kaunteyas' behalf? They had a long animated conversation, occasionally turning and looking towards me. I could not hear them as they were at a distance. After some time, Bheema and Arjuna took leave of Chitrasena but not before they cast a mocking glance at me. My blood boiled with fury. The intoxication of the wine had long gone and all I could feel was a throbbing headache added to the niggling pain of the bruises from the fight.

Chitrasena now came to me and spoke, "You are indeed fortunate that you belong to the same family as that gem amongst men, Yudhishthira. It seems obvious that you have ventured this far into the woods just to derive mocking pleasure from watching the living conditions of the Emperor and his brothers in the forest. Yet, he has sent word through his brothers seeking your freedom and it will be my privilege to honour his wish out of my respect and allegiance to him. I spare the lives of you and your brothers and you should all be grateful for this to Yudhishthira's magnanimity. I order you to leave this forest at once with your retinue and never make the mistake of coming back. If you do, it will be at your peril."

He ordered our release. The humiliation was too much for me to bear, that too in front of the women. Where was Radheya? Where was he when I needed him the most? What took him so long? We retraced our path back to the city. Bhanumati was quiet as she stayed by my side. Uncle Shakuni, Dushasana, Vikarna, Uluka...none spoke a word. The smug look on the faces of Bheema and Arjuna at seeing my plight kept playing in my mind. Added to this was the convenient allegation that we were there just to derive pleasure from watching them suffer in the woods...a thought that I had not entertained in my mind even for a moment. How did the Kaunteyas know that we were camping there? Were they informed by one of my slaves? That cannot be. My slaves knew better than that. They knew that I preferred death to such humiliation. Perhaps their spies informed the Kaunteyas about our coming. Perhaps they were the ones who alerted Chitrasena and asked him to attack us when we least expected it. After that, they carried out this drama of securing our release just to humiliate us. If only Radheya had held his ground, things would have been different.

The news would have reached Hastinapur by now. How was I going to face my father, the King, or my son Lakshman for that matter? How was I to face the Grandsire and the Acharyas? How was I going to handle the smirk on Vidura's face when I meet him? The thoughts kept gnawing into my soul. Shame enveloped my entire being and suddenly my very existence lost its meaning and my life lost all essence. Towards dawn, as we reached the edge of the forest closer to the city outskirts from where the women could be safely escorted back to the city, I stopped my chariot and got down. I addressed Bhanumati and my brothers, "Dear loved ones, I always held my self-esteem dearer to me than my life. It is said that a Kshatriya devoid of his pride is a living corpse. This life as a beneficiary of the Kaunteyas' magnanimity is worse than the burning fires of the worst hell. Please tell the King that I have lost the right to call myself a worthy son, leave alone a worthy Crown Prince to Hastinapur. Please return to Hastinapur, all of you, and choose a worthy one amongst you to be the new Crown Prince. As for me, I shall stay back here. I shall forego food and water till death embraces me. This is the only way that I see to redeem myself."

My brothers were devastated by my words. They implored me to change my mind. Dushasana wept as he fell to his knees begging me to come back to Hastinapur. Uncle Shakuni also used the best of his persuasive skills trying to convince me to leave the episode behind. But I was firm in my decision. Bhanumati who was quiet all along approached me with folded palms and said, "My Lord, I am aware that once you resolve to do something, there is no turning back. However, if redemption is what you seek, then pray listen to this better solution that I have before you. Giving up your life will not only be a slur on your name but on the family as well. Suicide is not the path to glory for Kshatriyas. Instead, this is your chance for repaying magnanimity with magnanimity. Call the Kaunteyas and return Indraprastha to them as a token of your appreciation for securing you your release. This will not only neutralise their gesture towards you, but it will enhance your stature across the world."

The suggestion appealed to everyone present. I also found this palatable. Bhanumati had a gift for saying the right things at the right time and here she was once again offering her wise advice when I needed it most. Just then we heard a chariot approaching. It was Radheya. He rushed towards me and embraced me. "Dear friend, I am so heartened to see you safe. I was so concerned about you. I had swooned in my chariot after being struck by a powerful shaft and my charioteer had taken me far away to a safe place. When I regained consciousness, I realised that I had come too far. I rushed back to our camp to see it empty. There was no sign of the Gandharvas as well. I was worried no end on account of your safety. I was planning to get back to the city and bring back an army to search for you and to rout those Gandharvas. But I see you are safe. You have defeated them, which is remarkable considering that even I had to temporarily retreat from their relentless attack. I am so proud of you."

All my anger at Radheya for deserting me vanished as he spoke to me. I broke down in tears as I narrated everything to him. I also told him about my decision to return Indraprastha to the Kaunteyas as advised by Bhanumati to redeem my honour and pride.

Radheya laughed lightly and said, "O dear friend, your self-esteem is matched only by your guilelessness. It is evident that this whole drama was plotted by the Kaunteyas. Assuming that it was not the case, even then, what have they done so extraordinary or meritorious to claim magnanimity? You are the Crown Prince of Hastinapur and the Kamyaka Forest where they dwell falls within your domain. They owe their existence in that forest to you. They are in effect your subjects even if in exile. It is the highest duty of the subjects to do what is within their power to protect their Crown Prince from danger, and that is exactly what they have done. It is not an act that deserves any reward or gratitude. You have no reason to be ashamed or feel crushed under the weight of debt towards them. If, however, you return Indraprastha to them on this account, that will be perceived as an undoing of a wrong that you have committed towards them, out of a sense of guilt. Please clear your mind from these clouds of fallacy. You have great things to achieve as Hastinapur awaits you. Cheer up now, your brothers look up to you for leadership. It is not right that you give in to such needless despondency."

Radheya's words inspired me out of my gloom. Yes...what he said made sense. I had no reason to feel shame for I was the Crown Prince of Hastinapur and as long as the Kaunteyas lived in my domain, they had an obligation to me. Once again, Radheya lifted my spirits. My brothers were relieved too. Uncle Shakuni said, "Radheya is right, Son. Forget whatever happened as a bad dream. Now let us get back to Hastinapur."

He was right. I had to forget this episode and move forward. We resumed our journey back to Hastinapur. If Bhanumati was upset about my not following her advice, she never showed it. I, on the other hand, had more important things to worry about...the reaction of my father and the Grandsire. Whatever happened was a big slur on the Bharata race. This would be discussed amongst the citizens and sung by balladeers for a long time and, of course, the wily Vidura was also there to add fuel to the gossip with his ever active propaganda machinery that always worked in favour of the Kaunteyas.

27

We reached Hastinapur to a cold reception. Nobody spoke anything the day we returned, but I could sense it was the calm before the storm. My guess was right. The following day, we brothers along with Radheya and Uncle Shakuni were asked to be present at the assembly hall for an enquiry about the incident in the forest. What followed was not an enquiry but an admonishing session. Firstly, I was reprimanded by the King for venturing close to where the Kaunteyas were dwelling despite repeated instructions not to. This was followed by a volley of accusations and insults by the elders led by the Grandsire and Vidura against Radheya. He was harshly criticised for deserting me and fleeing from the battle when it mattered. He was accused of irresponsibility and told that his proficiency in rhetoric far outmatched his proficiency in warfare and that he wouldn't stand up to Arjuna in real battle. He was accused of misleading me into a false sense of security with the endless bragging of his prowess. Arjuna, he was told, had now in his possession the incantations to invoke the divine missile called 'Pashupata' that he received by propitiating the great three-eyed Lord Shankara through rigorous austerities. This missile was capable of rendering the whole world lifeless. He also had in his possession fourteen other divine missiles that he received from Lord Indra, the Chief of Gods. According to the Grandsire and the Acharyas, these missiles made him invincible in battle. They insulted Radheya saying he wouldn't measure up to even a fourth of Arjuna in single combat. Poor Radheya took it all with his chin up but I knew he was hurting and burning deep inside. His hands were itching to grab the sword from his scabbard but he exercised maximum restraint.

As expected, all the admonishing led to the oft repeated counselling of recalling the Kaunteyas and establishing peace with them. I could stand this no longer and I stormed out from the assembly hall followed by my brothers. Later that afternoon, when I found Radheya alone, I apologised to him on behalf of the Grandsire and the others for the insults heaped on him.

He said, "Dear friend, I hold no ill will against the Grandsire. Whatever he spoke was in your best interest. The Grandsire has always disliked me and he has openly displayed his hatred for me on several occasions. I am aware that Vidura and the Acharyas also do not think highly of me. They are blinded by their fondness for Arjuna and hence behave that way. I am not disturbed over that in the least as their opinion about me has little bearing on me. However, there is one thing that I fear of losing because of all this and that is the trust of His Majesty. These old men have the privilege of proximity to His Majesty and the more they speak ill about me in his presence, the more likely that his trust in me gets eroded over a period of time and I fall out of favour. That is something I cannot live with."

I said, "My friend, you forget that I will not let that happen. You are the firm ground on which I have built my dreams for my Hastinapur."

He said, "I am aware of that, my friend, but it is important to let the world know that your trust and confidence in me is not misplaced. There is only one way to achieve that. I will set out in all the four directions in conquest and bring every kingdom in this land of Bharata under your sway, just as the Kaunteyas did in the past. I shall conquer the earth for you and bring it under your subjugation. When I return, I promise you that there would be no room in your coffers to store the tributes that I shall bring from all the conquered monarchs. I shall not rest till I see you as the Lord of the Earth. History will bear witness to my feat and these old men will eat their words. Even as Yudhishthira conducted the Rajyasuya sacrifice, so will you. All I seek is your approval."

'The undisputed Lord of the Earth'...this was a title that every Kshatriya king dreamt of. Radheya's words thrilled me as I embraced him in joy. After seeking my father's blessings and approval for the venture, the royal priests and astrologers were consulted. My father was advised that as long as Yudhishthira was alive, it would be against the scriptural injunctions to conduct the Rajyasuya as there cannot be a second member from the same family conducting the sacrifice when the first one was alive. They came up with the suggestion to perform another sacrifice that was as meritorious as the Rajyasuya and it was called 'Vaishnava'. This was also a sacrifice performed by someone who had undisputed claim to the title of 'Emperor'.

On an auspicious day, after making the customary offerings to Lord Hari, Goddess Durga and the Sun God, Radheya set forth on his conquest with his carefully chosen army. My father, however, advised him to ensure that our diplomatic relations with the kingdoms where we had familial ties were not disrupted on account of the conquest. The Grandsire and the Acharyas appeared sceptical about the success of this venture. This is what Radheya too preferred, as nothing would please him better than proving them wrong. He did not bother to seek their blessings. I ordered for a lamp to be lit in the royal temple in front of the idol of Lord Hari. Special instructions were given to ensure that the lamp remained filled with oil to the brim and the flame never doused till Radheya made his triumphant return.

Radheya began his campaign by first laying siege on Panchala. After its subjugation, he proceeded, bringing all the kingdoms and tribes on his way under his sway and collecting tribute from them. True to his word, he covered all the four quarters meeting little resistance on the way. He not only amassed huge wealth as tribute from all these kingdoms but also struck strategic diplomatic alliances with them. When he returned several months later to a hero's welcome, Hastinapur erupted in celebration. I personally went to receive him as he rode into the city in his chariot, proudly waving the flag of my Hastinapur. I embraced him and led him into the royal assembly with all the honours. He strode majestically like a lion towards my father. After offering his respects, he gave him the report of his successful campaign. My father was delighted as he said, "Dear Radheya, you have made Hastinapur proud today. It was at a blessed moment that Duryodhana chose your friendship. With you by his side, I have no need to fear on his account. The Kaunteyas, even if they come with the entire host of Panchalas and the Yadavas, will not be able to measure up to you. Of this, I am now convinced. You are as dear to me as my son Duryodhana. It is my wish that you never leave his side. May you be his ever-dependable refuge. Consider him as your own brother. May God be with you and may your fame last forever."

Radheya addressed the King, "Your Majesty, Duryodhana is but a part of me as I am a part of him. I am bound to him as a soul to the body. As long as I live in flesh and blood, Duryodhana shall remain the Lord of the Earth. Today, you have the crowns of all the monarchs of the land of Bharata at your feet. The moment is right to conduct the Vaishnava sacrifice as advised by the sages."

No time was wasted in preparing for the great Vaishnava sacrifice. Invitations were sent through messengers to all our friends, allies and vassals. The city of Hastinapur was done up for the occasion. Fountains and floral decorations filled the streets. Statues and numerous works of art and architecture were displayed all over the city. Various rest houses and pavilions were constructed on all the highways of the city outskirts with provisions for rest and recreation for visitors. Responsibilities were delegated to ensure that no detail was neglected. Special mansions were constructed to accommodate the various royal dignitaries. The best of knowledgeable Brahmin priests, well-versed in the Vedas, were invited to perform the rituals and recite the sacred incantations. They were all honoured according to their stature and so were the various monarchs and princes who arrived from all over Bharata. A golden plough sanctified through sacred incantations was used to dig the sacrificial pit at an auspicious area of the earth around which the sages were to perform the holy sacrifice.

Meanwhile, unknown to me, Dushasana had sent a messenger to the Kaunteyas in the forests, inviting them, too, to attend the sacrifice. When I came to know of this, I did not approve of it. It would have appeared as an attempt to gloat about our success in front of them the way they did to us during the Rajyasuya. I thought myself to be above such pettiness. However, to my relief, the messenger returned with the message that they would not be attending the sacrifice. He also brought a personal message from Bheema to Dushasana that they would come at the end of the thirteenth year to take part in a greater sacrifice where the sacrificial offering would be my brother's blood. The message was met with silence. Dushasana looked at me for a reaction. I shrugged, nodding my head in disapproval of his decision to send the invitation in the first place. Then Radheya laughed breaking the silence and making light of the matter. He said, "Poor Bheema, all these years of hardship in the forests must have taken its toll on his senses and right thinking. Let us not dignify his threat with a response. Come, we have more important things to take care of."

The matter was soon forgotten as we busied ourselves with the ceremony. The Vaishnava sacrifice was a grand success. Gifts and tributes poured in from the various kingdoms. Excellent feasts with variety of meat and delicacies were served and gifts were presented to the various guests and the Brahmins who came to take part in the sacrifice in thousands. They went away happy, singing our praise and offering the choicest of blessings to me and my Hastinapur. Of course, comparisons were made to the Rajyasuya of Yudhishthira, and that was inevitable. I had my informants mingling with the public and the feedback from them was that my Vaishnava sacrifice surpassed the Rajyasuya by far in grandeur. It was all thanks to my dear Radheya who simply stood by my side allowing me to bask in all the glory, which rightfully belonged to him.

However, there was one small niggling factor that dampened the success of the sacrifice. It was the absence of someone whom I eagerly looked forward to meet and honour at the sacrifice. He was one of the firsts to have been invited for the sacrifice and much to my embarrassment, everyone including the sages noticed his absence...especially considering that he was the father-in-law of my only daughter Lakshmanaa. Yes, for reasons best known to him, Vaasudeva of Dwaraka chose not to attend the ceremony.

28

It was the thirteenth year of the Kaunteyas' exile; the one that they had to spend incognito. Uncle Shakuni had spies sent in all directions with instructions to comb the forests and the neighbouring kingdoms and report immediately if they had even the faintest knowledge or suspicion of their whereabouts. However, we received no such feedback from them. This made my father very nervous and worried. He was certain that if the Kaunteyas successfully completed their final year of exile without being discovered, they would definitely return to wage war with Hastinapur to claim all that they had lost. I, however, lost no sleep over this and neither did Radheya for that was exactly what we preferred in the first place, war with the Kaunteyas and their annihilation.

Then one day, King Susharma of Trigarta paid us a visit. Trigarta was a neighbouring kingdom to the north with Prasthala as the capital. Susharma was a very brave and committed ally of ours. He was prompt in his annual tribute and in return, we had promised him our protection from the neighbouring Kingdom of Matsya. Matsya was a sovereign kingdom ruled by the aged King Virata. Matsya was a kingdom with which we had a neutral relationship. We did not attempt to bring it under our dominion out of respect for my great grandmother Satyavati. King Virata was her twin brother who was separated from her at birth. They were found abandoned on a riverside by a fisherman chieftain who took them to King Uparichara. The king decided to adopt the boy and the fisherman adopted the girl child. The boy grew up to be a great warrior and founded the Kingdom of Matsya. He was Virata. The girl was Satyavati, my great grandmother and the mother of Sage Vyasa. Vyasa himself told us about this during one of his visits.

King Virata had a queen much younger to him named Sudheshana whom he was exceedingly fond of. She was younger to him at least by a couple of generations. On her request, he had appointed her brother Keechaka as the commander of his army. Keechaka was a strong-armed man famed for his valour and skill in warfare. He had a mighty army and was ably supported by his brothers. Under his leadership, Matsya had expanded its territorial domain, significantly. Keechaka, with his ferocious army, had annexed vast territories of Trigarta that were under territorial dispute for a long time. He met very little resistance from Susharma whose army was no match. He would have made further inroads into Trigarta if Susharma had not strategically signed a treaty of alliance with us. Post the treaty, Radheya had an infantry of soldiers stationed at the Trigarta-Matsya border and ensured that there was no further advancement from Keechaka.

Susharma came to us with the shocking news of the death of Keechaka and his brothers. They were believed to have been killed in a skirmish with some Gandharvas. The Gandharvas attacked him and his brothers in the night when the Gandharvas become naturally stronger and more powerful than humans. Now with Keechaka gone, the Matsya army was like a rudderless raft. It was the perfect time and opportunity for Susharma to reclaim all the land that he had lost to Matsya. For this, he needed our help and as an ally, we could not refuse.

I asked Dushasana to arrange for a quick meeting with Grandsire Bheeshma, the Acharyas, Ashwatthama, Radheya, Susharma and some of the important cavalry chiefs of our army to discuss our strategy. I could have done this with Radheya alone but my father wanted me to do it in consultation with Grandsire Bheeshma and the others. It was decided that Susharma along with his army would lay siege on Matsya from the north-west front and engage the army. When the entire Matsya army was occupied thus, we would attack them from the south and make inroads. King Virata maintained his cattle farms in the south. It was decided that we would attack him from there and capture his cattle. This would psychologically cripple Matsya, for a kingdom's health is determined vastly by its cattle wealth, even more than its gold. Dairy played a huge part in the economic prosperity of a kingdom. Virata would find it difficult to manage this two-pronged attack and would be forced to concede defeat. The strategy was explained to us by the Grandsire who seemed enthusiastic like a child. It was the first time in the last thirteen years that I saw him so excited. For all his affectionate nature, he was a warrior at heart and nothing thrilled him more than the call of the battlefield.

We moved as planned. Susharma laid siege on Matsya and King Virata personally led his army to counter him. It was the Grandsire's instruction that we would make our move only if Susharma's position was weakened and he needed our intervention. The battle went on for twenty-eight days. We received information that Susharma was losing ground.

We decided to make our move. We gathered an infantry and attacked Matsya from the south, which was left unguarded. We attacked the farms and took possession of the cattle in huge numbers. We captured the caretakers of the farms and ordered them to go forth and deliver our message to Virata's camp announcing our intention to capture his cattle and challenge him to stop us if he could.

While we waited, one of our informants approached us from Susharma's camp. The news he brought was disturbing. Susharma's army was completely routed by Virata and he was taken captive. To make the humiliation of defeat even bitter, he was released with a royal pardon for his indiscretion.

"How could this happen?" I asked in disbelief. "Virata is just a toothless lion without Keechaka."

"My Lord, King Virata's army was led by some new recruits extremely accomplished in warfare. In fact, these men are not even regular soldiers. They are just servants of the King. One is a counsellor named Kanaka whom the King consults in matters of statecraft. He is extremely competent in wielding the spear. Another is a caretaker of the stables and well-versed in handling the steeds. There is another who in fact takes care of the cattle, and of course the fourth and the most important one, a giant of a man with a slender waist like a wolf, broad shoulders and strong arms, who roars like a lion and moves like the wind, destroying everything in his path. He is a cook in King Virata's royal kitchen. He was the one who took King Susharma as captive and produced him before King Virata, grabbing him by his hair and repeatedly smashing his head against the earth. King Virata, however, granted him a royal pardon and set him free on the advice of Kanaka."

We stood there in silence after listening to this information. My heart was thrilled. I looked at Radheya and Ashwatthama and they too seemed excited at the news. I turned around to Grandsire Bheeshma and the Acharyas and looked at them questioningly.

Acharya Kripa spoke first. He said, "Yes, son, we know what is on your mind. You need not entertain any doubt. From the description, it seems like it was the Kaunteyas who fought for Virata. The counsellor Kanaka seems to be none other than Yudhishthira and the cook's description fits that of Bheema. The other two may be the twins. As for Arjuna, I am certain that he is not far away."

I removed the pearl necklace that I wore around my neck and gifted it to the informant. "You have brought me great news." I exulted, "The Kaunteyas will now have to go back to the forest for another twelve years."

"Son, you speak too soon," said the Grandsire. "Even if you ascertain that all the Kaunteyas are in Matsya, the thirteenth year of exile has long been completed. Ever since their exile, I have been in regular consultation with scholars well-versed in the science of celestial movements and it is their opinion that the scale of time based on the different units of measure as well as relative movement of constellations undergo a deviation every year gaining two months for every year. By that measure, the Kaunteyas have completed their thirteenth year months ago. Therefore, if you have indeed discovered them, it behooves you to return their kingdom back to them. This will be the best course of action for everybody."

I said, "O Grandsire, with all due respect, I find it difficult to favourably dispose myself to your proposition. It is now clear that you speak out of partiality for the Kaunteyas. You have always been favourable to Yudhishthira. Even if what you say is true and the period of exile was over months ago, why has no one spoken about it till now? Even the Kaunteyas themselves have not come forward with any claims. Therefore, I do not buy your story."

"The son of Ganga speaks the truth," Acharya Kripa said, "The period of exile is well past us. It will be in the best interest of Hastinapur to return Indraprastha to the Kaunteyas for the sake of peace. Harbouring animosity for them will only lead to the destruction of the entire Kuru race. Who can match Bheema's strength and energy, especially when it is fuelled by his terrible oath? Does anyone have it in us to face the endless stream of arrows from the Gandiva–Arjuna's mighty bow? He is now more powerful than ever before after gaining the knowledge of the divine missiles from the Chief of the Gods, Lord Indra himself. I've also heard that his son Abhimanyu, born of Subhadra, is no less an archer than his father and has been trained by none other than the great Vaasudeva, and not to forget, Vaasudeva who considers Arjuna to be his very life, will himself be on their side."

Radheya spoke out, his voice filled with sarcasm, "Blessed indeed is my friend Duryodhana. With such well-wishers in his flank, what need is there for enemies? O Acharya, you don't surprise me with your advice to my friend. Meekness is an inherent quality in Brahmins. But you must know that between the Kaunteyas and Duryodhana stands this Radheya with his mighty bow famed world over by the name 'Vijaya'. I have the answers to all the divine missiles that Arjuna may bring to battle. My shafts will break into the enemy ranks like furious serpents filled with virulent venom. You Brahmins can stay by the side and watch, and once victory is achieved, you shall be invited to partake your free share of the spoils. After all, isn't that what you are all about?"

Unable to bear the insult to his uncle, Ashwatthama, who was silent all along sprang up. "Ha, Radheya, on what pedestal do you see yourself to judge? You are just a crow pretending to be a swan. You are neither from a royal household nor are you a warrior of stature. Need I remind you of the humiliation that you suffered at Arjuna's hands at Draupadi's swayamvara? You are just a low born braggart whose words far outmatch his valour and prowess."

"Well, we shall settle that matter right here and right now!" said Radheya as he took his sword and jumped out of his chariot heading towards Ashwatthama. Ashwatthama too jumped out of his chariot ready for the duel. I rushed and stood in between the heroes before things got out of hand. I implored, "This is no time for you heroes to behave thus. You are both important to Hastinapur and me. Please withdraw, restrain your anger and save it for the enemy. You both are mighty warriors and when your energies combine there will be no force on earth capable of stopping you. So please desist from this fight which is not doing us any good."

Acharya Drona addressed Ashwatthama, "Yes, Son, Duryodhana is right. Our allegiance is to the King of Hastinapur. We must not let our likes and dislikes dictate our actions. Please make peace with Radheya for he has the best interest of the Crown Prince at heart, though his judgement may be clouded by his hatred for the Kaunteyas."

Amidst this chaos, we heard the shrill blow of a conch. The sound was familiar. Grandsire Bheeshma at once recognised it as the sound of 'Devadutta', the famed conch of Arjuna. This was followed by a loud thunder-like twang of a bow. From the distant horizon, we saw two shafts swiftly speeding in the air towards us. One of them came and fell at the ground next to where stood the Grandsire's chariot and the other knocked out his flag mast carrying his famed palmyra banner.

"That was the twang of the Gandiva, the mighty bow of Arjuna...the echo of which strikes terror in the heart of foes," said Acharya Drona. He turned to the Grandsire and said, "With that shaft aimed at your feet, O Son of Ganga, he has offered his salutations to you and with the other, he has challenged your army to duel."

As we looked up, in the distant horizon we could see the smoke of dust as a silver chariot steered by four excellent white steeds sped towards our direction. It was driven by a young man and mounting it, holding a massive bow in hand, was a tall, figure with broad shoulders and familiar features, except that he had long waist-length hair pleated together. As the chariot approached us, the emblem of the monkey god on its flag banner became clear. Yes, no doubt, this was Arjuna... but why was he in the guise of a eunuch?

Grandsire Bheeshma turned to me and said, "Duryodhana, you must take the cattle with you and also a quarter of the army and set forth in Hastinapur's direction immediately. I, along with the Acharyas and Ashwatthama, will hold back Arjuna. As for Radheya, he can do as he pleases. He can either accompany you or stay here. His presence or absence will not make a difference. But you must do what I say without delay, before Arjuna's chariot reaches here."

It was a needless insult to Radheya and at the wrong time. He said, "O Grandsire, time and again you insult me for no fault of mine. I will not turn my back to the enemy and I am certain that neither will the Crown Prince. Let Arjuna or even Indra come. I will vanquish them in your very presence."

Acharya Drona said, "This is no time for idle bragging. Duryodhana, you should take the cattle to a safe place. Please take the necessary forces with you to ensure that."

I ordered a unit of forces to move the cattle to a safe distance under my supervision. Before we knew, Arjuna's chariot was right in front of us. There ensued a tremendous duel between him and the various commanders. The shafts left his bow at tremendous speed as he individually challenged and defeated all the warriors including the Grandsire, both the Acharyas and Ashwatthama. It was quite obvious that they were engaging Arjuna, half-heartedly. Radheya stood as a mute spectator. He knew that if he intervened to help, these great warriors would take that as a personal insult.

Arjuna then turned his attention to me. He used special shafts called 'Shatagni' charged with special incantations. They had the power to multiply exponentially as they sped through the air. They fell upon my army killing them by hundreds. Using the 'Shatagni', he created a barricade blocking my army unit and the cattle.

He then turned his attack on me but I held my ground against his onslaught. He was fighting like someone possessed when, suddenly, Radheya's chariot came and stood between us. There ensued a wonderful battle between the two, with Radheya matching Arjuna shaft for shaft. The battle raged on as the world seemed to stand still. Both were wounded several times and they were bleeding.

Then all of a sudden, a fog of smoke appeared out of nowhere. It spread across the army and caused everyone to swoon. Before I knew what was happening, I passed out. Much later when I woke up in my chariot and looked around, I found Radheya, Acharya Drona, Ashwatthama and all the others in the same condition...just waking up from a deep sleep in their chariots. We noticed that the piece of raiment that we wore on our shoulders as a cape was missing. As we looked around, we realised that the cattle too were missing. The only one who seemed unaffected by all this was Grandsire Bheeshma as he stood tall in his chariot watching us with a smile.

"There is no need to look for the cattle. Arjuna has rescued the cattle. His charioteer was Prince Uttara, the son of Virata. They have returned to Matsya with the cattle. Your capes were removed by Uttara and taken as a souvenir for his sister Princess Uttaraa. We have been truly defeated. But there is no shame in this for we lost to the greatest warrior on the face of the earth."

"How did this happen, O Grandsire?" asked Dushasana. "How did they win over us and rescue the cattle? What was that fog? How did we fall into this slumber?"

"Arjuna had dispatched a special divine missile called 'Samohan Astra'. He must have received the knowledge of its incantations from Lord Indra himself. This missile causes the enemy to fall into deep slumber. There is no one on earth who knows the incantations to counter this missile save me. Arjuna could have attacked and killed you all in your sleep, but he was too chivalrous to do that. Instead, he had Prince

Uttara remove your capes and take them back with him to Matsya as souvenirs for their womenfolk."

I was livid. I asked the Grandsire, "If you knew the counter incantations, why did you not stop them, O Grandsire? What was your constraint?"

The Grandsire said, "Son, I was helpless in this regard as they had sought my blessings and permission first before taking away the cattle. Besides, what need is there of Virata's cattle for us? We came here to help Susharma reclaim his lost territory. But Susharma having retreated to Trigarta after being defeated, what need is left for us in this war? What benefit is there in us continuing to fight? After all, we have no direct conflict with Matsya. So let us head back to Hastinapur and put this behind us. This is an occasion to celebrate as we finally know that Kaunteyas are safe."

I knew it was meaningless to argue further with the Grandsire on the matter. We gathered our forces and headed back to Hastinapur. My mind was filled with mixed emotions. The exhilaration of having discovered the whereabouts of the Kaunteyas before the completion of the exile period was dampened to some extent by Grandsire Bheeshma's view on the same. But what really hurt was the sting of defeat at Arjuna's hands. Radheya, for all his bravado, did not expect Arjuna to use the divine missiles in the fight without alerting first. This was against the code of war ethics and Radheya was least prepared for this.

29

The following days in Hastinapur were spent over extensive discussions and debates on what should be our course of action. Grandsire Bheeshma, Vidura and Kripacharya insisted that Indraprastha be returned to the Kaunteyas as they maintained the view that the thirteenth year of exile had been completed a few months earlier. There were also many who felt that that was not the case. But this was not just about technicality. It was also about morality. In my view, Yudhishthira had lost the moral right to rule the moment he staked his kingdom...a kingdom that should have belonged to Hastinapur in the first place. There was no question even for a moment in my mind of willingly returning Indraprastha to the Kaunteyas. Radheya stood firm by my side on this stance like a rock. Uncle Shakuni advised me to make preparations in the eventuality of an all-out war with the Kaunteyas. He advised me to embark on diplomatic missions and gather allies.

Meanwhile, advice poured in for my father from all sides. The sages who visited him had no advice to offer except the return of Indraprastha to the Kaunteyas. Discussions went on every day in the royal court and my father's mind was muddled with opinions. Amidst this, one day, we received a messenger from Virata. We expected a strongly worded message from Virata regarding our attempt to take his cattle but we were surprised. Virata had sent an invitation to my father to attend the wedding of his daughter Uttaraa to Abhimanyu, the son of Arjuna and Subhadra. Although this was unexpected, it left no doubt in our minds that the Kaunteyas had indeed sought refuge in the Kingdom of Matsya during the thirteenth year. The information that I gathered from my spies was that Arjuna had disguised himself as a eunuch by the name Brihannala and taken up the job of a music and dance teacher in the royal household of Virata. From where he actually picked those skills, I will never know. I've heard the balladeers say that he acquired those skills from Chitrasena, the Gandharva Chief. As a gesture of gratitude for rescuing his cattle from us, Virata had offered the hand of his daughter Uttaraa to Arjuna who instead, accepted her as a bride for his son Abhimanyu.

My father was understandably upset that the invitation was not sent personally by Yudhishthira or Arjuna, and instead came from Virata. He felt that by this the Kaunteyas were showing disrespect for familial honour and courtesies. He was justified in feeling that way. It was jointly decided that none would go from Hastinapur to attend the wedding. Vidura did not seem too happy about the decision, though he was now but a mere shadow in the background. He did not matter anymore in the decision-making processes of Hastinapur.

30

Uttaraa and Abhimanyu's wedding ceremony was followed by a meeting at Upaplavya hosted by Virata and attended by the chiefs of Panchala and Dwaraka. The meeting was presided over by King Drupada. Our spies informed us that this meeting was convened primarily to decide the course of action to be taken by the Kaunteyas, now that their exile period was over. Passions ran high at the meeting and the majority was of the opinion that the Kaunteyas should wage war with us to reclaim Indraprastha. The most vociferous in his support for the Kaunteyas, I was told, was Satyaki, a powerful chief of the Vrishni tribe who had a whole 'Akshauhini' under his command. An 'Akshauhini' is a unit comprising 21,870 elephants, 21,870 chariots, 65,610 horses, and 109,350 foot soldiers. Satyaki went on a tirade against my brothers, Radheya and me, accusing us of falsehood and deceit. He did not even spare his kin Balarama who was at the meeting and was the only one who had a few kind words for me, his favourite student as I was. I must admit that I was surprised on hearing about this. I had enjoyed a very good and friendly relationship with Satyaki during my days in Dwaraka. We used to sport together. His judgement was perhaps clouded by his gratitude for Arjuna whom he looked upon as his teacher for imparting certain esoteric knowledge of missiles to him.

Although Yudhishthira was silent, Drupada, Dhrishtadyumna, Shikhandi, Virata and his sons; Arjuna, Bheema, the twins, and just about everyone else present echoed Satyaki's sentiments. In the midst of all this, however, there were two people who spoke in favour of peace–Balarama and the wise Vaasudeva. I was told that finally, Vaasudeva's wisdom prevailed as always, and it was decided that an emissary would be sent by Drupada on a diplomatic mission to Hastinapur to demand the return of Indraprastha to the Kaunteyas. Drupada also advised the Kaunteyas to gather the support of as many allies on their side as possible in the meanwhile, and to be prepared in the eventuality of war with us. On this note, the various heroes returned to their respective cities while the Kaunteyas remained in Upaplavya as Virata's guests.

On receiving this information, we decided to expedite our mission of fortification and garnering support from our allies to prepare for the impending war with the Kaunteyas. Uncle Shakuni advised me to head for Dwaraka at the earliest. He wanted me to seek the support of Vaasudeva and Balarama in the war first. I was a little sceptical about getting Vaasudeva's support, knowing his fondness for Arjuna, but he was also the father-in-law of my daughter Lakshmanaa. As for Balarama, I knew for sure that I had his moral support. But would that translate to military support? I was not sure. I made haste towards Dwaraka. I was well-received by Sambha and Lakshmanaa, and spent a pleasant evening in their company and hospitality. I was pleased to know that Lakshmanaa was happy in the Vrishni household. The next afternoon, I headed to Vaasudeva's palace. The guards ushered me into his inner chamber. Vaasudeva was alone and in restful sleep. I quietly took a seat at the head of his bed so as to not awaken him. Even in his sleep, he seemed to have that bewitching half-smile on his lips. He seemed so restful in his sleep and yet one got an impression that behind that relaxed appearance was a mind that worked all the time, even in sleep. It was hard to describe Vaasudeva. At best, he could be compared to the waters of the deep ocean. Calm and peaceful on the surface and yet running deep and mysterious. As I sat there watching him, I heard someone enter the chamber. It was Arjuna. What was he doing there? We were both surprised to see each other and there was an embarrassing moment of silence. All those years in the forest did not seem to have any effect on him. He seemed to have got younger with age. Hearing the noise of him entering, Vaasudeva woke up. His eyes first fell on Arjuna and they greeted each other. He then turned around as I greeted him and he was surprised to find me there.

After exchanging pleasantries, I broached the subject of the impending war with the Kaunteyas. Vaasudeva turned and looked at Arjuna for his reaction. Arjuna was silent. Vaasudeva said, "Dear Duryodhana, this is entirely a family matter that must be settled amicably between you cousins. Your father is a just king known for his sense of fairness, and surely, with the help of the learned men in his court, he will do what will be pleasing and acceptable to everybody without going to war. So why involve me in your family feud?"

I ignored the tone of sarcasm in Vaasudeva's voice. I said, "Vaasudeva, you are very much a part of our family. Nothing gives Bhanumati and me more joy than the knowledge that our daughter is happy in your household under your care and protection. You are equally dear to us as you are to the

Kaunteyas. You are famed for your wisdom across the world. No one needs to tell you the right from the wrong. You already know the sequence of events as they unfolded over the years and also the truth behind them. It is important to know that we have your support in the event of a war with the Kaunteyas."

Vaasudeva said, "What you say is true. You are dear to me as are Yudhishthira and his brothers. Therefore, it is difficult for me to choose a side based on relationships. Hence, I have a solution to offer in the event of a war. I have an army of fierce warriors known as 'Narayanas', comprising one Akshauhini. They are well-trained in combat and highly skilled in the use of all weapons. I shall offer this army of mine to one of you. On the other side, I will offer myself, alone and unarmed. I will not directly fight in the war and will offer my services only at an advisory level."

This was a very strange diplomatic strategy that got me thinking whether there was a hidden motive somewhere. Vaasudeva was not the kind to indulge in self-importance, equating himself with an Akshauhini. Also, there was a lack of clarity on the moral stand that he was taking here. He appeared to be trying to row with his feet in two boats. I was confused as to what should be my choice. However, he saved me the trouble by offering the first choice to Arjuna by virtue of him being younger in age to me.

Arjuna folded his palms and said, "O Vaasudeva, you are well aware that any day I would choose you to all the armies in the world. Of this, there is no doubt. With you on our side, the world will know that Dharma was on our side. History will record our war as just."

Nothing suited me better. I was happy with the arrangement. I thanked Vaasudeva and took leave of him. I went next to meet Balarama. We discussed the war over some wine. Balarama was not happy at the turn of events. He said, "Dear Duryodhana, I wish to see peace prevail among you brothers. You must know that I spoke for you in the council we had at Upaplavya. I truly believe that whatever happened was a result of Yudhishthira's addiction to gambling. I was of the opinion that Yudhishthira should make peace with you and be grateful for whatever you may decide to offer him out of your magnanimity instead of demanding the return of Indraprastha as his legal right. However, my words were met with furious resentment and resistance. If there should be war, I will not fight for the Kaunteyas as I see no moral ground in their cause. At the same time, I cannot fight for you as long as my brother Vaasudeva who is my very life sits on the other side. Therefore, all I can offer you is my blessings. Fight in the true spirit of a Kshatriya and attain fame and glory."

After getting the blessings of Balarama, I met Kritavarma, another Yadava hero of the Andhaka tribe whom I knew was favourably disposed towards me. He too promised to bring an army of one Akshauhini to fight on my side.

I left Dwaraka feeling content that my trip was a fruitful one. On reaching Hastinapur, I narrated everything to Uncle Shakuni expecting him to congratulate me on the success of my mission. Instead, he berated me for my judgement.

He said, "Son, I do not know how to react. You may have just ensured your defeat. How are we to be certain that Vaasudeva's army would be sincere when they fight on our side? How can we know if mingling amongst us, they would not serve the Kaunteyas as their informers and spies? How could they put their hearts into their fight for us when their master sits on the opposite side? You should have refused Vaasudeva's army."

I said in defence, "But refusing Vaasudeva's army would be deemed as a personal insult to him which I want to avoid, considering that my daughter is married to his son."

"Well..." said Uncle Shakuni, "I hope you realise that this was a master trick by Vaasudeva, and he played it well by giving the first choice to Arjuna. He sees things well ahead and plays his game accordingly. Let me tell you something, Son, the way I see it, the Kaunteyas will not be your problem. The real problem you should be worried about is–Vaasudeva."

31

Preparations were in full swing on both sides for the war. We were informed that Vaasudeva would be playing the role of Arjuna's charioteer if there were to be a war. The charioteer had a pivotal role to play in the success of a chariot warrior. The best of warriors made sure that they also had the best of charioteers steering their steeds. The charioteer was responsible for the protection of his master. He not only played a critical role in protecting his master through skilful manoeuvring of the chariot and taking timely decisions in the best interests of his master's safety but also played a pivotal role in keeping the spirit and morale of his master high by counselling him with words of wisdom and encouragement. He had to be a strategic thinker and ever alert to the happenings on the battlefield. He had a full-fledged support team at his disposal under him. Its function was to protect the wheels on either side and provide replenishments of food, water, weapons and other necessities. The charioteer was as important as his master and the master was also duty-bound to protect his charioteer from harm.

When Radheya heard that Vaasudeva was to steer Arjuna's chariot, he became despondent. He knew that there was none to match Vaasudeva's charioteering skills. He also knew that Vaasudeva was a storehouse of knowledge and wisdom and with him holding the reins; Arjuna could focus entirely on the fighting and would have nothing else to worry about. It was a huge advantage that could make all the difference between victory and defeat for Radheya. We held a lengthy discussion on this with Uncle Shakuni. It was then that Radheya came forward with a suggestion. He felt that there was only one person who could match Vaasudeva's skill as a charioteer and that was King Shalya of Madra. If there were some way that we could get him to fight on our side and convince him to take up the reins of Radheya's chariot, victory would be assured. However, the question was how to go about this. Shalya was the maternal uncle of the twins Nakula and Sahadeva by virtue of being the brother of Aunt Madri.

Madra was situated to our west. We got information that King Shalya was setting out with his retinue to meet Yudhishthira at Kampilya. He had to pass through the outer ring of the road on the outskirts of our domain to reach Kampilya. Uncle Shakuni and Radheya advised me to leverage this excellent opportunity to sway Shalya to our side. As instructed by them, I had a special resting camp put up in his travelling path that was part of my domain. I had the best of my hospitality staff appointed in these camps to represent me with instructions to welcome Shalya along with his retinue and not just to please him but delight him too. They were supported by the best of cooks offering the choicest delicacies and also musicians and dancers offering the best entertainment. My efficient staff did not let me down. Shalya stayed put in the camp for a few days indulging in my hospitality. When I gathered that Shalya was preparing to leave the camp, I decided it was time to go and meet him personally, along with Radheya.

Shalya was very happy to see me. I greeted him and offered him all the due respects. He hugged me and said, "O Duryodhana, you have pleased me no end. I wanted to pass by Hastinapur unannounced, but you have outsmarted me. I wish to return this favour and hospitality that you have bestowed on me. Please ask of me something that your heart desires. I shall honour your wish."

I said, "O Lord of Madra, you are as dear and revered to me as you are to the Kaunteyas. Please don't insult me by such undeserving gratitude. I was only doing my duty and I consider that in itself as my greatest blessing."

Shalya smiled and said, "Your reputation is certainly very misleading. I find it hard to believe all those things I have heard about you. You must ask of me something. This, I insist. Otherwise, I will consider myself indebted to you."

I folded my palms and said, "Mighty one, please refrain from using such strong words like 'debt'. If you must grant me a wish, I would like to have your blessings and support in the event of a war with the Kaunteyas, which seems imminent. As you may be aware, Vaasudeva has decided to take up the reins of Arjuna's chariot and this puts Arjuna at an advantage over my friend Radheya here. There is no one in the world who can match Vaasudeva's skills save you. Therefore, it is Radheya's most cherished wish that he be honoured by you taking up the reins of his chariot in battle."

Shalya was silent for a few moments. It wasn't what he had expected. This was a moment of truth for him. Would he succumb to the demands of his pride and honour his word? Radheya and I glanced at each other. I then broke the silence.

I said, "Lord, if what I seek from you causes you even the slightest distress, then I take back my request. You can forget that I even asked."

Radheya and I both knew that I was perhaps pushing it. We waited for Shalya's response. He then rose from his seat and smiled at me. He came and put his arm on my shoulder and said, "Duryodhana, know you must that in this conflict, I am morally with Yudhishthira and I had set out from Madra with the intention of meeting him and offering him my support. But now that I have given you my word, as a Kshatriya, I am duty-bound to honour it. You will have my support in the event of a war with Yudhishthira and his brothers. My army comprising one whole Akshauhini will be at your disposal in the war and I will fight on your side in whatever capacity that you may demand of me. But before that, I must meet Yudhishthira and explain everything to him. So please allow me to proceed."

Radheya and I bowed down in gratitude to Shalya as he took our leave. We returned to the palace. I couldn't wait to give the good news to Uncle Shakuni. He would have been proud of my performance if he were with us that day.

32

After roping in Shalya, I lost no time in reaching out to all our allies to garner support for the war. It was not about who had the bigger army. It was about showing who had greater moral support and, therefore, reflecting the general perception as to the side on which lies truth and justice. The forces that came forward to fight on our side included the army of King Bhagadatta, the son of Naraka of Pragjyotisha who was killed in battle by Vaasudeva and also of Bhurishravas of the Kingdom of Bahlika, founded by his grandfather of the same name. His grandfather was the elder brother of my great grandfather King Shantanu. My brother-in-law Jayadratha of Sindhu also came forward offering an Akshauhini of troops. The chiefs of Magadha, Kalinga, Avanti, Mahishmati, Trigarta, Kekeya, Khamboja and a host of other domains, all came forward with their armies, not to mention the army of 'Narayanas' offered by Vaasudeva and also the host of fierce Bhoja and Andhaka tribe warriors brought by Kritavarma. The Kaunteyas were chiefly supported by the armies of Drupada and Virata. They also had Satyaki commanding an Akshauhini. Their other main supporters were Dhrishtaketu, the son of Shishupala of Chedi, and Pandya from the south of the Vindhyas. In all, there were eighteen Akshauhinis ready to battle. I had the support of eleven, which was four more than what the Kaunteyas could manage as per the information I received.

I had special areas designated on the outskirts, at the banks of the rivers Ganga and Yamuna, for my huge army of eleven Akshauhinis. They were accommodated and it was ensured that there was no shortage of food, water, medicinal herbs and other amenities like facilities for training and drill, not to mention the support staff like cooks, physicians, message carriers, and musicians and so on. In the middle of overseeing the provisions for all the logistical support required for the army, we received the news of the arrival of a Brahmin priest assigned by Drupada to carry a message from Yudhishthira for my father. I had expected him to arrive sooner. Yudhishthira was perhaps buying time to prepare for the battle.

The Brahmin priest was received with due honours in the royal assembly by my father. After enquiring about the welfare of the Kaunteyas, my father asked him to deliver his message.

The priest said, "O King, I bring you and the elders of the Kuru household the highest respects of Emperor Yudhishthira. The Emperor wants me to convey that he and his brothers have dutifully fulfilled the conditions stipulated at the game of dice thirteen years ago where they were defeated through deceit and cunning. They have endured the hardships of the forest life for twelve years without complaints and followed it up with one year of servitude incognito, in the refuge of King Virata of Matsya. For the sake of Dharma, Emperor Yudhishthira, the performer of the exalted Rajyasuya sacrifice; Bheema, who boasts of the strength of ten-thousand elephants; Arjuna, unmatched in valour and now the master of divine missiles; the twins who have never known the taste of defeat and the pious Draupadi, born of the sacrificial fire...they spent an entire year as servants of King Virata enduring hardship and humiliation. Now that the stipulated period is over, the Kaunteyas seek to have their Indraprastha returned to them. Yudhishthira is aware of Duryodhana's efforts in mobilising his allies for war. But war is the last thing that Yudhishthira has in mind. He is ever for peace. However, the Kaunteyas will not hold back if pressed in to battle. They have seven Akshauhinis at their disposal, led by that tiger amongst men, Dhrishtadyumna. They have the mighty, well-trained forces of Panchala and Matsya to fight for them under Yudhishthira's banner. They have the best of chariot warriors to command their forces including Shikhandi, Satyaki and Abhimanyu, not to mention the Kaunteyas themselves who are individually more than a match for any army. Above all, they have the son of Devaki as their counsellor. It would take a man deprived of his right thinking to challenge them and invite them to war. Therefore, it behooves you, O King, to respond to the call for peace and propriety and return to the Kaunteyas what is rightfully theirs."

There was silence in the hall.

Then the Grandsire spoke up, "The Brahmin has given us excellent counsel, O King. There is no merit in war amongst brothers. Besides, what chances do we have in war when pitted against the skill and valour of Arjuna combined with the wisdom and alertness of Vaasudeva, who has offered the Kaunteyas his protection? Therefore, I appeal to the best of your wisdom and judgement to return whatever Emperor Yudhishthira seeks rightfully and let peace prevail."

"Emperor?" asked Radheya mockingly. "What claim does Yudhishthira have to that title when he lost it all over a game of dice? O Brahmin, you claim that Duryodhana won their kingdom through deceit and cunning. Tell me, how is it possible to cheat in a game of dice? It was only after Yudhishthira's approval that the Lord of Gandhara rolled the dice for Duryodhana. So where is the deceit? Besides, we had discovered Arjuna before the completion of thirteenth year, no matter what the elite scholarly advisors of Grandsire Bheeshma may opine. Even if that were not the case, when His Majesty out of his benevolence gave the Kaunteyas their release from bondage on Draupadi's request, he never proclaimed he was returning Indraprastha. He only gave them their personal freedom. When Yudhishthira played the second game of dice, he was no longer the Lord of Indraprastha. So on what ground is he staking his claim to Indraprastha? Besides, you must know that my friend and the Crown Prince Duryodhana is someone who will give in to neither direct nor subtle threats. If it is the might of Yudhishthira's army that we are talking about, then we have eleven Akshauhinis at our disposal. If it is the might of his commanders and chariot warriors, we have a galaxy of them, each well versed in the knowledge of the best of missiles to fight for Duryodhana's cause. Therefore, the tone of threat is most inappropriate to use in this matter. However, if the Kaunteyas are willing to go back for another period of thirteen years of exile and then return seeking refuge in Hastinapur, I am certain that my friend Duryodhana would be magnanimous to consider that."

"Ha, Radheya! Brilliant as always with words...but just that," said Grandsire Bheeshma. "Need I refresh your memory as to what happened not so long ago at Matsya, when Arjuna single-handedly defeated all of us and took back Virata's cattle? Why was all this bravado not on display then?"

Yet again, a lengthy argument broke out with Radheya, Uncle Shakuni and me on one side and the Grandsire, the Acharyas and Vidura on the other. Accusations and counter accusations flew across the hall. Drupada's priest looked at my father and said, "Why is the King silent? Is it in the tradition of Hastinapur that when the King is addressed, everybody responds except the King?"

The verbal missile found its mark and everybody fell silent. They say that a Brahmin's tongue is sharper than a Kshatriya's sword. My father lifted his hand gesturing everybody to settle down. He then addressed the Brahmin, "O venerable Brahmin, thank you for your message and counsel. My response would have been different and more welcoming if Yudhishthira had personally come to me and made his request. After all, this is a family matter and though I may be the King, he is still my nephew, my beloved Pandu's son. However, he chose to give it the official garb by sending an emissary from another sovereign kingdom on his behalf. Since he wants to deal with it that way, it is only appropriate that we do the same. Please convey our regards to him and tell him that he will be receiving an official response from Hastinapur at the earliest. Do convey our regards to King Drupada too. You may proceed without delay."

The Brahmin paid his respects and took leave.

33

The days that followed saw my father immersed in consultations with Vidura, the various other ministers, army commanders, Grandsire Bheeshma and the Acharyas. They were all of the opinion that the best way forward would be to avoid a war. The justifications for their stand on the matter were based less on moral ground and more on fear. They almost succeeded in brainwashing my father into submitting to their opinion by repeatedly exaggerating the prowess of the Kaunteyas and their allies, especially Vaasudeva. My father's mind began to waver. On the one hand, he knew that I was the one who was denied justice in the first place and had every right to feel so, but on the other, he wasn't willing to be answerable for the aftermath that the war may cause. I, however, held my ground. There was no question of returning anything to the Kaunteyas. Radheya stood firm with me in support.

After a lot of deliberation, my father decided to send Sanjaya as his personal messenger to Yudhishthira with a lengthy message. I was not given access to the contents of the message but I gathered that the gist of it was that we would not be returning Indraprastha to the Kaunteyas. This made me happy and proud of my father for showing spine. However, that was short-lived. When my informants from Kampilya brought me the news of Sanjaya's visit and the contents of the message delivered on behalf of my father to Yudhishthira, I felt deeply anguished and let down. In his message, my father absolved himself of all the responsibility for whatever was happening. He blamed me for everything and accused me of being obstinate and unheeding to good counsel. He tried to evoke Yudhishthira's empathy at his helplessness and failure in making me see reason. At the same time, he praised Yudhishthira sky high for his adherence to virtue. He appealed to his sense of commitment to peace, pleading him thereby, to seek satisfaction in the current status and let go of his 'rightful' claim to Indraprastha for the higher purpose of harmony, as there should be no fight within the family.

This did not sound like a firm stand. There was no resolve, just a spineless placation for peace. I was extremely upset at the way my father went about this, not only demeaning himself as the King but also making me appear to be the villain behind the whole situation. This was not the way of Kshatriyas and I spoke my mind to him about this. It was the fear of war with the Kaunteyas induced by all the needless counselling from the elders that made him send such a message. What he did not realise was that, with this message, he offered the moral ground, which was so critical in this war, on a platter, to the Kaunteyas. This was poor judgement on his part.

Sanjaya delivered my father's message to the Kaunteyas and their allies in their camp. As expected, the Kaunteyas did not take kindly to the message. Yudhishthira rejected my father's appeal and made it amply clear that they would very much like to go to war with us if that was the choice we offered them and they were fully prepared and equipped to do so. His brothers and all the allied chiefs in his camp echoed his feelings. Arjuna even had the audacity to warn Sanjaya that he would burn up Hastinapur with his special shafts if Indraprastha was not returned to them. However, Vaasudeva intervened and said he would personally visit Hastinapur and counsel my father as a last attempt for peace.

34

The news of Vaasudeva's proposed visit spread excitement all over Hastinapur. My father called for a meeting with all his counsellors to discuss the arrangements to be made to receive Vaasudeva. Orders were given to have the roads cleaned and specially decorated. Provisions were made for the citizens to line up on the sides of the streets in an organised way to get a glimpse of him and greet him. Special pavilions were swiftly erected all along the road to offer shelter for his retinue. My father asked Vidura to organise for the costliest of gifts to be presented to Vaasudeva and his retinue, including elephants, cows and horses of high pedigree, precious gems, processed wool, deerskin, silk and more. The cooks at the royal kitchen were given orders to prepare the best dishes and sweetmeat. It was decided that Vaasudeva would be accommodated in Dushasana's mansion as it was more spacious and grand than mine. A special temporary pavilion with all facilities was constructed at the town of Vrikasthala where Vaasudeva was expected to break his journey on the way to Hastinapur. The best of my hospitality staff was stationed there. It was decided that Grandsire Bheeshma would personally go to the city outskirts along with Acharya Drona and Dushasana to receive him.

The frenzy and excitement over Vaasudeva's visit reached a feverish pitch. Citizens thronged the streets with flowers and rose water waiting to greet him. I was also excited as this was the first time I would actually be getting to spend some time with him. However, Uncle Shakuni remained aloof and thoughtful.

Vidura cautioned my father that he would not be able to sway Vaasudeva with all the riches and gifts in the world. The only thing that would make Vaasudeva happy would be our acceptance of his proposal for peace. Of course, peace was what I was also rooting for, but the only way I would want it was on my own terms, and there would be no compromise on this...be it Vaasudeva or Lord Indra himself.

Vidura's words rang true. Vaasudeva ignored all the hospitality that we had arranged for him at Vrikasthala and headed straight to Hastinapur. Our citizens gave him a rousing welcome as he entered the city in his golden chariot with the eagle banner driven by his famed charioteer Daruka. Grandsire Bheeshma personally welcomed him at the city gates. There was loud blaring of bugles and conches. Men, women and children crowded the streets and their balconies, hurling flowers and sprinkling rose water at him, ecstatically. The guards had a difficult time holding them back and Vaasudeva smilingly greeted them all. He had a small retinue accompanying him, flanked by the Yadava heroes Satyaki and Kritavarma on either side. Also accompanying him was a host of sages including the illustrious Bhargava and Narada. Why were they there? What was their business? This got me curious and suspicious. Uncle Shakuni also became alert. He whispered, "Son, this visit of Vaasudeva seems more than just a peace mission. You have to be extremely cautious while dealing with him. You must be careful about every word and gesture of yours. He is a master of deceit as much as he is a master of detecting one."

On reaching the royal assembly, my father welcomed Vaasudeva with the customary rites. Vaasudeva also offered his greetings to my father and the other elders according to their seniority. Bhanumati stood next to me as I welcomed Vaasudeva with my arms unfurled for an embrace. However, Vaasudeva held back and greeted me with folded palms. This gesture on his part in the presence of my wife and everyone else gathered was an open insult to me. Bhanumati was also taken aback. I swallowed my pride and decided to ignore the slight as I thought of my daughter Lakshmanaa.

After the exchange of formal pleasantries, I advised Vaasudeva that all arrangements had been made to host him in Dushasana's mansion. I also invited him to attend the special royal feast I had arranged in his honour in my mansion that night. But Vaasudeva curtly declined the offer. He said, "O Duryodhana, as much as I appreciate the offer of your hospitality and feast, I am afraid I have to decline. I am here as an envoy. I cannot feast with you until the mission of my visit is successful. Besides, feasting is something that's done between friends or between those dear to each other. I am neither your friend nor am I dear to you. So I will retire to Vidura's palace where Aunt Kunti awaits me."

This open snub in front of all was uncalled for. Here was a man who in the not so distant past said that I was as dear to him as Yudhishthira. I had utmost regards for Vaasudeva, not just as the father-in-law of my daughter, but also as the younger brother of my master Balarama. His rudeness was initially baffling not just to me but to Uncle Shakuni as well. But when he said that he would be staying at Vidura's palace, things became clear. Perhaps there was some channel of communication between him and Vidura and his mind had been poisoned with prejudice against me.

Later that evening, Vaasudeva casually walked into my chamber unannounced while I was in some discussion with Uncle Shakuni, Radheya and Dushasana. Although it was unexpected, I welcomed him and once again invited him to join us in our feast. To this, Vaasudeva replied, "Duryodhana, I am on a mission. I will execute it tomorrow in the royal assembly. The success of my mission lies in your hands. If your invitation for me to join your feast is not laced with deceit and comes from a genuine fondness for me, then make this mission of mine a success tomorrow and help spread my fame and glory to all quarters. We then shall dine together and make merry tomorrow night and many more nights after that. Until then, know that anyone who considers the sons of Pandu as foes is a foe to me as well."

"Very well, Vaasudeva...," I said, gritting my teeth, "if that is the way you deem it right, we shall wait for tomorrow. If what you propose tomorrow appeals to my judgement as right, I certainly shall oblige. You had better leave now since the journey to Hastinapur may have been tiring. Vidura would have also laid down supper for you and should be waiting for you to join. I am sure that you two will have 'plenty' to discuss."

He gave a half-grin, understanding my sarcasm. He said, "Very well, then, we will meet tomorrow."

"Yes, of course." I said, "I will personally come to bring you to the royal assembly in the morning. Sleep well. We have a long day tomorrow."

35

The royal assembly hall was filled with the silence of anticipation. Vaasudeva greeted my father and the other elders according to seniority and took his seat by the side of Vidura. I took my seat next to Radheya as always. The hall was filled with the various ministers, office bearers and nobles of Hastinapur. This was a pivotal day in their lives and for Hastinapur. All eyes were on Vaasudeva as he surveyed the hall. The half-smile that was his trademark never left his face. In spite of my inviting them inside, Satyaki and Kritavarma chose to stay outside the hall along with their retinue of the Yadava soldiers as per the instructions of Vaasudeva.

Then Vaasudeva spoke to the Grandsire, "O Son of Ganga, we are fortunate today that we have the presence of great eminent sages amongst us. They have accompanied me to Hastinapur to provide their valuable counsel to the decision-makers of this assembly, if required. They wait outside the hall. Please arrange to welcome them with due honours and have them seated here."

The Grandsire was thrilled when he heard this. He immediately set out himself to bring in the sages with all appropriate honours and worship. The entire assembly rose to receive them as they strode in offering their blessings. My father also got up to welcome them. I wondered what it was about me and the sages that I never quite seemed to get enough of them and their unsolicited counsel in my life.

After everybody was seated once again, my father broke the silence. He said, "O Vaasudeva, it is an honour and privilege that we have you in our midst today. Although you are tied to us through familial bond, you have come to Hastinapur as a messenger. Please let this assembly know what message have you for us from Yudhishthira."

Vaasudeva rose from his seat and addressed my father, "O gem of the Bharata race, know you that I have come not as a messenger as you have understood. I am here on my own free will as a monger of peace. Today, the world is standing on the edge of a bottomless abyss waiting to be tipped off by your son. The only one in the world who could prevent this calamity is you, my Lord."

Turning to the assembly he continued, "Everyone assembled here knows the truth. Despite being the rightful heir to the throne of Hastinapur, Yudhishthira never staked his claim. Duryodhana contemptuously treated him and his brothers to untold hardship with the evil counsel of the Lord of Gandhara. Need I mention how he tried to drown Bheema in the river after poisoning his food? He, along with his evil counsellors Shakuni, Radheya and Dushasana, attempted to burn the Kaunteyas in the palace of wax at Varnavrat. When the Kaunteyas came back from the dead by divine grace earned through their meritorious deeds, instead of installing Yudhishthira back as the heir apparent, the Kaunteyas were given just a portion of the kingdom, a kingdom that was rightfully theirs in entirety, and that too that portion which was just a wasteland. The Kaunteyas were expected to be satiated by that. They tamely submitted to all this not out of meekness but out of respect for the elders of the family and their desire for peace. When the Kaunteyas with their toil, converted this piece of land into the grand Indraprastha, instead of taking pride in their success, the evil Duryodhana allowed himself to be overwhelmed with envy and avarice. Resorting to deceit, with the help of the evil Shakuni, he coveted the kingdom and all the wealth of the Kaunteyas and still not happy with that, he tried to covet their fairly wedded Queen Draupadi. He made them all his slaves. This assembly hall has been a witness to the ugliest face of mankind when forgetting all codes of Kshatriya conduct, Draupadi was dragged to this hall by her hair during her period and humiliated in the very presence of her husbands and the elders of the Kuru clan including His Majesty. Radheya addressed her as a woman of low morals and attempts were made to disrobe her in this open assembly. Drunk with arrogance, Duryodhana and his set of evil counsellors have brought the entire Kuru clan to disgrace. The Kaunteyas bore all this silently."

Turning to the King, he continued, "My Lord, the Kaunteyas, who had the earth at their command, spent twelve years in the forest living in the harshest conditions just to honour their commitment to your son, who we all know, won the game of dice through cheating with the help of the deceitful Shakuni. Even this did not satisfy your son as he went along with his friends to the Kamyaka Forest to make merry and mock the Kaunteyas for their living conditions in the forests. However, the Gandharvas taught them a lesson in humility and, if not for Yudhishthira's magnanimity, your son would not have been alive today. The great Emperor Yudhishthira who has performed the Rajyasuya sacrifice spent the last year of exile along with his brothers and his queen in servitude of King Virata, all the while protecting their identity, just to honour the conditions laid down by Duryodhana. Now that the stipulated period is over, it behooves you to return Indraprastha to them and they will be willing to forget the bitterness that they have been carrying all along in their hearts. Also, my Lord, this will be beneficial to Hastinapur because, with Indraprastha as an ally, the sway of Hastinapur will reach beyond the confines of all borders. With Arjuna and Bheema ready to take up arms under your banner, standing side by side with the mighty Son of Ganga, Acharya Drona, Radheya, Ashwatthama, Somadatta, Bhurishravas and others, which army in the world would be foolhardy enough to challenge Hastinapur in battle? With Emperor Yudhishthira, who sees none as his enemy, ever ready to be your diplomatic ambassador at your bidding, all the monarchs in this world would be under your sway. Your sovereignty would be supreme. Therefore, please evaluate favourably my plea with the sages here as witness and take such a decision that peace, prosperity and progress may prevail."

Vaasudeva took his seat after the lengthy tirade. My father was silent and so were the others. I was furious. Here was a man whom I always held in high esteem insulting me in the presence of my own people and not one of them spoke a word. Grandsire Bheeshma finally broke the silence. He addressed my father, "Your Majesty, Vaasudeva has echoed the thoughts of the wise men in this assembly. The Kaunteyas are to be seen as your own children. It is in the best interest of Hastinapur that Vaasudeva has spoken. It is indeed our good fortune that we have somebody like the wise Vaasudeva, well-versed in the knowledge of Dharma to counsel us in this matter. Please listen to him and follow his counsel implicitly."

Similar implorations followed from Vidura and Kripacharya.

My father then turned to Acharya Drona and said, "O Acharya, you have been silent on this matter. Since you have been governing over Indraprastha for the last thirteen years, what is your view?"

The Acharya said, "My Lord, whatever decision that you may take as the Lord of Hastinapur, know that my son Ashwatthama and I are duty-bound to stand with you. However, as the Acharya under whom your sons as well as the sons of Pandu trained, it is my foremost duty to tell you that today, there is no one in this world who can withstand Arjuna in battle. The son of Ganga and I may have the knowledge of all the missiles, but we do not have age on our side. Ashwatthama, though my son, neither has the skill nor the temperament to combat Arjuna. As for Radheya, he is no doubt a hero in his own right but is no match for Arjuna as we have seen twice before, once at Draupadi's swayamvara and more recently at the duel in Matsya. Duryodhana is dear to me and it is my duty to warn him that he is living in a delusional world if he thinks he can win a war with the Kaunteyas. Therefore, I suggest that we accept Vaasudeva's proposal, which is in the best interest of everyone."

My father addressed me, "Son, you have heard what the elders in all their wisdom have counselled us to do. You have also heard the wise Vaasudeva speak. There is no better alternative for peace. Now, speak your mind in this assembly."

I rose from my seat and addressed Vaasudeva, "O Vaasudeva, you have come here with a prejudiced mind. You have accused me of so many wrongdoings without knowing full well the truth behind them. I do not blame you. It is perhaps in my destiny that I would suffer the prejudice of even the wisest of men...some of them who wanted to put me to death the day I was born." I turned and looked at Vidura who maintained a straight face as I said this.

Once again turning to Vaasudeva, I continued, "You accused me of trying to drown Bheema in the river...an incident that happened in our childhood when we were yet to discern right from wrong, but you conveniently failed to mention all the innumerable sufferings that we brothers endured at the hands of Bheema. How can I ever forget watching that big bully swim to and fro across the river clutching Dushasana by his neck, immersing his head in the water?"

There was total silence while I spoke. I continued, "By virtue of being the eldest son of the King, I was in line for succession to the throne of Hastinapur and yet, my father out of a sense of misplaced fairness, crowned Yudhishthira as the Crown Prince. I graciously submitted to his decision although the lordship of Hastinapur was a dream that I had been fed right from my childhood by the very same elders of the Kuru clan seated here. The Kaunteyas were not satisfied with this. They wanted to turn the people of Hastinapur against me and get me completely out of their way through false propaganda that I tried to burn them down in the house of wax at Varnavrat, when it was they themselves who set it on fire and escaped through a tunnel they constructed during their one-year stay there. It was a deviously well thought out plan in which an old woman and five innocent men were burnt alive just to mislead us into believing that it was Aunt Kunti and her sons who perished. When they finally resurfaced from hiding at the swayamvara of Draupadi, my father, instead of punishing them for these criminal acts of murder, absconding and propagating vicious false news, called them back and gave them Khandavaprastha, and also offered our resources to help them build it up to what it became."

"Well spoken, well spoken..." applauded Uncle Shakuni. My father also gently nodded in agreement, as there was a murmur across the hall.

I continued, "As if all this was not enough, we were invited to Yudhishthira's Rajyasuya and there I, the Crown Prince of Hastinapur, was assigned the job of receiving gifts that poured in from all the quarters for Yudhishthira. Did you not see that it was just an attempt to flaunt their opulence to trigger my envy? What does your sense of dharma say, O Vaasudeva, about Draupadi's mocking laughter at my expense at the Maya Sabha or her addressing me as the 'blind son of a blind king' in the very presence of her husbands? Did the 'righteous' Yudhishthira admonish her? That one incident alone offers enough justification for me to go to war with the Kaunteyas in the true spirit of Kshatriyas but my father wouldn't approve of that. You accuse me of winning the game of dice through cheating and deceit. Tell me, Vaasudeva, I ask you and everyone else in this assembly...how is it possible to cheat in the game of dice? It is not a game that is played in the dark. Yes, Uncle Shakuni played on my behalf, but that was only after Yudhishthira agreed to it. Blaming the opponent of cheating is the easiest way out for a loser to cover his own incompetence. Everything that I ever won from Yudhishthira was won fairly. Otherwise, do you honestly believe that the galaxy of heroes in this assembly including Grandsire Bheeshma and the venerable Acharyas would have remained silent? It was Yudhishthira who staked his kingdom, his brothers and his queen and yet you do not condemn his actions. Instead, you condemn me. You also falsely accuse me of going to the forests to mock the Kaunteyas' living conditions there, when in reality, we were there to survey and tally our wildlife count. There again, conspiring with the Gandharvas, the Kaunteyas took the opportunity to humiliate me. I bore that in silence. During the thirteenth year, Arjuna was discovered in the Kingdom of Virata by us before the stipulated exile period was over and as per the conditions laid down at the time of the game of dice, they were to go back for another thirteen years in exile. However, since Grandsire Bheeshma is of the opinion that the exile period was over much earlier, I will not debate that out of my respect for him. I am willing to spare the Kaunteyas from another thirteen years of exile, but the Kaunteyas should be wise enough not to expect anything beyond that concession from me. What claim do they have to Indraprastha? Indraprastha was fairly won by me in the first game of dice. When my father offered to honour Draupadi's wishes, she only requested for the Kaunteyas' freedom from bondage and the return of their weapons, chariots and banners, which we have obliged. Do you think that it was not obvious to us why she never asked for Indraprastha to be returned to them? She wanted to win it back from us through war. At the time we played the second game of dice, Yudhishthira was not the Lord of Indraprastha anymore. So be it technicality or be it morality, on what ground does Yudhishthira seek to reclaim Indraprastha? Therefore, Vaasudeva, listen to my stand on this as I speak loud and clear. Indraprastha will never be returned to the Kaunteyas for it never belonged to them in the first place. If they want to fight for it, nothing would give me more pleasure than an all-out war with them. After all, isn't that what they desire in their hearts too?"

My chest was heaving in anger as I took my seat. The hall was filled with silence. The half-smile that always played on Vaasudeva's face was now missing. He turned to the sages with a silent expression of helplessness in his eyes and urged them to speak up. It was now the turn of the sages and I knew that once they start, they would go on forever. Unfortunately, we were obligated to listen as they gave their lengthy sermons on right conduct, folly of pride and obstinacy and so on, citing boring ancient tales as examples. Sage Bhargava started by citing the example of an ancient king by the name Dhambodhava who made the mistake of seeking combat with the great seers Nara and Narayana famed for their rigid austerities and was defeated, and had his pride humbled in the process. He added that Arjuna and Vaasudeva were the reincarnation of these great sages. I was not sure whether to be annoyed or amused. Sage Kanwa spun a long tale of how Garuda's pride was humbled by Lord Hari. Garuda, the eagle who served as the vehicle of Lord Hari was supposed to have claimed that since he bore Lord Hari on his back, it was to be construed that he was stronger than Lord Hari himself. Lord Hari lightly pressed Garuda's wings with a single arm. Unable to bear the weight and pressure, Garuda was grounded and forced to shed the feathers of his wings. Thus was his pride subdued. Sage Narada narrated the story of Galava, an ancient sage who obstinately insisted to offer the mighty sage Vishwamitra his preceptor's fee. When Vishwamitra politely declined to accept any fee, Galava repeatedly pestered him till he relented and when he finally stated his fee, Galava realised that it was beyond him to offer that and was thus disgraced because of his stubbornness. The fee that Vishwamitra demanded was eight hundred white steeds, each of them with one black ear.

The sages went on and on with their absurd stories with no sense of time or occasion whatsoever. They were so absorbed in their own storytelling that the assembly completely digressed from the main issue at hand, which was about returning Indraprastha to the Kaunteyas. When the sermons went beyond a point, I lost my patience. I rose abruptly and interrupted, "I have heard enough of these ridiculous tales from you sages. I see no relevance in them whatsoever. This is not a platform to express what you think of me. This is about the propriety in the Kaunteyas' claim for Indraprastha. I remain firm in my conviction that Kaunteyas have no right whatsoever even to dream of such a thing. I will hear no more of this." So saying, I stormed out of the hall followed by Radheya and Uncle Shakuni.

A little while later, Dushasana also came out and joined us outside. I asked him what was happening inside. He said, "Brother, Vaasudeva is imploring our father and the elders of the court to have the four of us chained and thrown in prison to avoid war and save Hastinapur from destruction."

I was enraged at the sheer audacity of Vaasudeva to come in the guise of a messenger and attempt to turn my own people and their opinion against me. I said, "If he continues his drama, I will put an end to it. I will have him chained and thrown in prison instead." Uncle Shakuni signalled me to lower my voice as he pointed out to Satyaki and Kritavarma who stood at a distance. I hadn't noticed their presence. I was not sure if they had heard us.

Just then, an attendant came and informed us that I was asked to report to the hall immediately as my mother wished to speak to me. What was my mother doing there? Why was she getting involved? I reported to the hall. I saw my mother there alongside my father. My father had called for her to advise me. She said, "Son, your behaviour is not appropriate and does not befit a Kuru prince. Vaasudeva is not only our guest but a relative and well-wisher as well. Whatever he has spoken, he has spoken out of his commitment to peace and harmony. The Kaunteyas are your brothers and you must see them that way. Return Indraprastha to them. What do you lack here in Hastinapur? Your stubbornness will cause the destruction of the entire Kshatriya race that has taken sides in this dispute and your father as the King would not only be answerable to his forefathers for bringing the Kuru clan to disrepute but to the future generations as well. So please listen to Vaasudeva and do as he says."

My father also spoke, "Son, I know that I have limited influence on you. But I am sure you will not disrespect your mother's advice. Listen to Vaasudeva and return Indraprastha to the Kaunteyas."

For the first time, I started to get the feeling that I was alone in the world. This man, Vaasudeva, had succeeded in turning everyone against me including my parents. I looked at everyone of them as they anxiously awaited my response.

I was beginning to lose my strength and resistance, and my breathing started to get heavier. Then I turned around...and there I saw Radheya, steady and reassuring as always and suddenly I felt my strength coming back.

I addressed my mother, "Mother, if that is what you wish, I will obey you. But I need to know that your words come from a conscience clear of guilt that your son is being wronged here. I need to know that you advise me thus because you feel that it is the right thing to do and not because you fear any consequences. If that is the case, I shall be happy to obey you implicitly. Else I would request Vaasudeva to place forward any other proposal he may have which I may consider other than returning Indraprastha."

My mother remained silent. In her silence, I found the answer that I sought. Vaasudeva got up to address my father. He said, "My Lord, Duryodhana has asked me to place forward any other proposal. I do have an alternate proposal and I am sure that it should be agreeable to one and all here. The Kaunteyas will also be satisfied with this. I seek five villages for the Kaunteyas...Avishthala, Vrikasthala, Makandi, Varnavrat, and any other village of your choice as the fifth. Five villages are all that I seek for the Kaunteyas as the price for peace."

I laughed aloud. "Ha, Vaasudeva, so now the beggars want to be choosers? Let me once again say this loud and clear so that everyone here, including the sages who have accompanied you, know my mind. *I will not part with the Kaunteyas even that much land that can be covered by a needle.* Of this, let there be no doubt or further discussion."

After a few moments of silence, Vaasudeva slowly rose from his seat and addressed the assembly, "You all have witnessed the happenings here, today. You have seen my efforts for peace going in vain. If your King desires peace, it can be achieved only if this haughty Duryodhana and his evil set of counsellors are immediately chained and put in prison. Else you will be forced to seek consolation that it is in the destiny of this land to be cleansed by a catastrophic bloodletting...of a scale never witnessed before in the history of mankind."

I said, "Ha, Vaasudeva, my guess was right. You come here not as a messenger but as a mischief-maker trying to cause strife amongst us. Your plan will not succeed. I could imprison you this very moment if I want."

Grandsire Bheeshma interrupted, "Duryodhana, don't forget that Vaasudeva is our guest. He stands for truth. In fact, he is the embodiment of truth. Trying to imprison him means trying to confine space. Your foolhardiness will cause nothing but ruin. Can't you see that Vaasudeva is Lord Hari himself in human form? We should consider ourselves blessed that he is in our midst counselling us. Please desist from such thoughts."

I was now convinced that the Grandsire was on the edge of senility. Just then, Satyaki and Kritavarma entered the hall. Outside the hall, I could see Daruka ready with the horses yoked to Vaasudeva's chariot. The small retinue of the Yadava soldiers also stood prepared and on guard.

Vaasudeva spoke to my father, "O King, I came here as a messenger of peace. It is apparent that my mission has failed. Without further delay, I take leave of you. However, if Duryodhana, forgetting all code of conduct seeks to imprison me, I welcome him to give it a try."

So saying Vaasudeva stormed out of the hall accompanied by Satyaki and Kritavarma. Daruka was waiting for him and the moment he stepped on his chariot, it was off at wind speed.

My father became anxious. He addressed Grandsire Bheeshma, "This is inauspicious. Vaasudeva's abrupt departure thus does not augur well for us. Please go after him. Appease him and bring him back. Let everyone present here accompany you. He wouldn't have gone far. He would be in Vidura's house to bid farewell to Kunti. I am sure you will find him there. Please go and bring him back immediately."

Everyone present there including Radheya and Dushasana set forth immediately to Vidura's palace. I, however, refused to budge. Later in the day, Dushasana reported what happened. My father's guess was right. When they reached Vidura's palace, they saw Vaasudeva's chariot outside. Satyaki and Kritavarma were also waiting outside as Vaasudeva was engrossed in a private conversation with Aunt Kunti inside. Later, when Vaasudeva came out, he saw everyone led by Grandsire Bheeshma waiting for him patiently. He gently declined their request to come back to the assembly hall. He took their leave, paying his personal respects to them individually, promising that their next meeting would be at the battlefield. He then did something that surprised everyone. He suddenly caught Radheya by his arm, took him into his chariot and rode away followed by Satyaki, Kritavarma and their retinue at a distance.

36

Where did Vaasudeva take Radheya? What business did he have with him? That was a mystery. When Radheya returned in the evening, he went straight to his mansion. I expected him to come to me and tell me whatever transpired between him and Vaasudeva. However, that did not happen. The next day, when I met him, he was a little aloof and distracted. He spoke nothing of his interaction with Vaasudeva. Uncle Shakuni goaded me to ask him about it, but my self-respect got the better of my curiosity. If it was something important, I was sure that as a true friend, Radheya would tell me about it. Nevertheless, the truth was that I was disturbed by his silence.

It was now time to prepare our strategy for the great task ahead...war. We ordered our troops to move towards the holy battlefield of Kurukshetra situated near the Samantapanchaka Lake made famous by Sage Bhargava who did his rituals of expiations there after slaughtering generations of Kshatriya heroes...so goes the legend. I had the eleven Akshauhinis divided into infantries and cavalries and ordered their camping in specially designated evenly layered areas with sufficient shade and access to water. Separate teams were created for all the support required for the soldiers. Each unit was provided with its own set of physicians, cooks, animal caretakers, messengers, musicians, bards and more. Now came the most crucial part, which was appointing the Surpeme Commander. I had already chosen Radheya for this role and there was not the slightest element of doubt about this in my mind, but when I spoke to him about this, to my surprise and disappointment, he did not seem very enthusiastic. He said that it would be difficult for him to lead the army with Grandsire Bheeshma and Acharya Drona fighting under his banner because of their seniority to him as students of the great Bhargava. I was willing to go to battle without the Grandsire and Acharya, as I knew that they would not put in their best because of their fondness for the Kaunteyas. All I needed was Radheya, but his indifference was perplexing. However, my father was also of the opinion that the Grandsire was the right person to be the Supreme Commander...not just because of his seniority, but also for the fact that he was a master in the knowledge of divine missiles and was feared across the world. Uncle Shakuni also felt the same but for a different reason. He felt that the Kaunteyas' reverence for Grandsire Bheeshma would weaken their resolve to fight when they see him at the head of our army. Therefore, after much discussions and deliberation, we decided to request the Grandsire to take charge as the Supreme Commander.

Choosing an auspicious time, I went along with my brothers to the Grandsire's chamber and after offering appropriate worship and respects, I officially requested him to take charge and lead our forces as our Supreme Commander. The Grandsire remained silent for a while. Then with a deep sigh, he spoke, "Son, it is truly unfortunate that things have reached this far. It is ironic that this kingdom that you seek to fight for with your brothers, is the very same kingdom I had forsaken for my brother Vichitravirya. It is my ill fate that I have had to witness its partition and all the unfortunate incidents that followed...and now when I am tired of this life, you come to me with this request. If this is the will of the Creator, so be it. I shall lead the Kaurava forces. However, I must tell you there is a certain condition that I have."

We all looked at each other not knowing what to anticipate.

He continued, "I assure you that I will use all the means at my disposal to fight and the enemy forces shall be slaughtered by thousands every day by my shafts. I shall strike terror in their camps and burn them up like a forest fire...but...I will not kill any of the Kaunteyas. They are as dear to me as you are and, therefore, this will be an impossible task for me. So killing Yudhishthira and his brothers is a task that you must entrust to someone else."

I was at a loss of what to make of this. However, killing the Kaunteyas was something that I was depending on Radheya to oblige me with and so I agreed. Grandsire Bheeshma was officially appointed the Supreme Commander of our army of eleven Akshauhinis in a ceremony presided over by the royal priests of Hastinapur.

After the ceremony, the Grandsire called for a meeting of all the great warrior chiefs who were to play important roles in the war. He individually appointed the various chiefs as heads of the various divisions, based on their prowess and experience. He also formed a core leadership team that would play an important role in the strategies. The team was a good blend of experience, energy and enthusiasm. Acharya Drona, Acharya Kripa, Shalya, Ashwatthama, Kritavarma, Bhagadatta, Bhurishravas, Jayadratha, Uluka, Uncle Shakuni and I with all my brothers were briefed about our responsibilities. However,

Radheya was ignored. He remained silent like a simmering volcano about to erupt. I could not brook the deliberate insult to my friend. I asked the Grandsire, "O Grandsire, what about Radheya? You have not spoken your mind on what his role is."

The Grandsire said, "Son, I have assigned the leadership roles at various levels to these warrior chiefs whom I know as worthy and responsible heroes who will never back away from battle. As for Radheya, I am afraid I don't see him fit to lead at any level. He is just a braggart who will not hesitate to run away from battle, and that would be demoralising for any team or unit under him. Did this not happen at the Kamyaka Forest with the Gandharvas? How, then, do you expect me to entrust him with any important position in this army? However, since he is dear to you, he is welcome to fight in my army as any other ordinary soldier."

All eyes turned to Radheya as an embarrassing silence filled the hall when Grandsire Bheeshma spoke those harsh and insulting words. Suddenly Radheya exploded, "O Son of Ganga, I have lost count of the number of times you have needlessly insulted me and I bore them all not out of fear or respect for you or your reputation, but out of love for my dear friend Duryodhana. But you have now overstepped the line. When Duryodhana asked me to take charge as the Supreme Commander, it was I who advised him that the first consideration for this position be given to you, and yet you speak such harsh words. Perhaps age has made you forget that it was I, unaided, who brought all the kingdoms in the land of Bharata under Hastinapur's subjugation to enable my dear friend to perform the great Vaishnava sacrifice. However, if you consider me unworthy to hold a position under your banner, so be it. I shall not take part in this war as long as you are at the helm. I shall take up arms if and only if I get the news of your fall. However, if you are able to deliver to Duryodhana his most cherished victory in this war without my help, none would be happier than me. I shall then retire to the forests satiated with the sight of Duryodhana seated on the golden throne of Hastinapur."

Speaking thus, Radheya got up and walked away from the assembly. I immediately rushed after him. I tried my best to calm him down but no amount of appeasing helped. I pleaded with him to overlook the slight from the Grandsire for my sake. But Radheya was adamant. His decision was firm and final. Somehow, things were just not going the way they should have been. Here I was, waging a war with a commander whose heart was clearly not in the fight and the one hero on whom I was banking on, and who was my main source of strength and courage, was backing out at the last moment due to a bruised ego. It was the beginning of a feeling that all was not going to end well.

I did not sleep well that night. I tossed and turned in my bed reflecting upon the events that unfolded in the last few weeks. When I turned around, I found that Bhanumati was not by my bedside. I looked around and found her in our prayer chamber offering her worship to Lord Hari with tears in her eyes. I asked her why she was awake at that late hour. She said, "Lord, I am unable to sleep. The dream keeps recurring...the hundred serpents and the mongoose...my heart is gripped with fear. I know no peace. I fear for you. I fear for our father, the King. I fear for Hastinapur."

I turned around and walked back quietly to my bed. This time I spoke nothing as I left her alone to deal with her fears.

37

Before setting out for Kurukshetra, I went to meet my mother. She was alone, immersed in prayer. I touched her feet in reverence and sought her blessings. She touched my head and said, "May the Lord of Kailash protect you and bless you with all the glory."

I was disappointed. I said, "Mother, I came to seek your blessings for victory and nothing less."

She said, "Son, victory will ultimately favour the just... this is the universal law. But at this moment, my judgement on justice is clouded and therefore I am unable to pray for your victory with a clear conscience. I see no difference between you and Yudhishthira. He is as dear to me as you are. If either of you is wronged, I feel the pain. In this war, the perception of justice and truth hinges on who the victor is. Therefore, if you feel firm in your cause, then fight like a true Kshatriya, fight fair and fight without care for victory or defeat, for in that lies the pathway to your glory."

She held me close for a long time before she let me go with a heavy sigh. Though she denied me her blessings for victory, it was the inspiration drawn from her words that kept me going these last eighteen days. Bhanumati never gave our son Lakshman or me the ceremonial farewell that the women of our land give the warriors in their families for a victorious return from battle. Instead, she took up a ritualistic fast, as she remained in the prayer chamber praying for our safety. I let her be. I then took the blessings of my father who hugged and kissed me on my forehead. Vidura and Sanjaya remained by his side as per his instructions. Vidura was required to remain in Hastinapur for administrative reasons. As for Sanjaya, he was not only my father's charioteer but his personal attendant as well. My father assigned him the responsibility of giving him the updates of the happenings at the battlefield. Every other adult male in Hastinapur, except the very aged and physically incapacitated set out to Kurukshetra to play his part in the battle.

It was the eve of battle. As evening approached, I was getting restless. I was not sure of the reason. Somehow, Vaasudeva's visit had an unsettling effect on me. Radheya was not very helpful as he remained in his tent, aloof and indifferent. Uncle Shakuni sensed my uneasiness. He said, "Son, when you go to battle tomorrow, it is important to go with a free mind. The battlefield is a place to express your skill and valour, not your emotions, for emotions can cloud your thinking. On the battlefield, what the mind requires is clarity under pressure. Therefore, if your hatred and bitterness towards the Kaunteyas is weighing you down, this is the time to get it off your chest."

I looked at him questioningly. He continued, "Son, be it a war of words or weapons, the last round should belong to you. On this eve of battle, send your messenger to the Kaunteyas' camp. Express through him everything that you wanted to convey to the Kaunteyas all these years and make sure it is done in front of their chief allies. Hold nothing back. Let your words disintegrate their mental strength and moral facade. Let your words show them a mirror that reflects them in their true shameful light. This is also an approved strategy in diplomacy that serves as a prelude to war."

I reflected upon Uncle Shakuni's advice that came from a lifetime of experience in such matters. The idea appealed to me. However, the big question was whom to send for such a mission? Uncle Shakuni had the answer for that, too. He offered the services of his son Uluka for the purpose. I summoned Uluka to my tent and asked him to go and personally deliver the following message to Yudhishthira and his brothers in the presence of Vaasudeva and the other chiefs without missing a word in content or expression in intent: "O Yudhishthira, that day of reckoning that we looked forward to all these years, dawns tomorrow. When you gave me the option of war or peace, I welcomed war for I knew that it was also what you brothers wanted in your hearts. Did you not realise that I could read your intentions when you requested for five villages? You are a warmonger disguised in the cloak of a peace lover. Although there were genuine doubts over the legitimacy of your birth, they never stood in the way of your accession as the Crown Prince of Hastinapur. Instead of showing gratitude for my father's misplaced magnanimity, however, you brothers conspired to spread false propaganda against me that I tried to burn you all down in a palace of wax. Well, let me indulge you in your schemes today and let's say that I was indeed guilty of the accusation. Come tomorrow, show the world what you are going to do about it. You accuse me of having usurped your kingdom through deceit when it was you who had pledged it of your own free will. Once again, let me indulge you. Yes, let's say I employed deceit. Come tomorrow, show the world what you are going to do about it. All these years, you have been successful in fooling your friends and allies by hiding your shameful dark self with this veil of righteousness but you don't fool me with your hypocrisy. What man will ever look with eyes of desire upon the wife of a younger brother, who should be seen as a daughter? Yet using your mother's words as an excuse, you brothers shared the daughter of Drupada as a common wife just to avoid strife amongst yourselves. This shows how thin the thread is that holds you brothers together. Then, as if that was not enough, you pledged her too in the game of dice. What my brother Dushasana did to Draupadi pales in comparison to what you have inflicted on her. You and your mighty brothers who brag so much of the capabilities of your arms and armaments sat as mute impotent spectators while your Queen was humiliated in public. Could anything be more disgraceful for a Kshatriya? You roamed around in the forests for twelve years like wild beasts when you should have been ruling the earth. You shamefully laboured as slaves in the Kingdom of Matsya. The gluttonous Bheema toiled as a cook in the smoke-filled kitchen of Virata, while the effeminate Arjuna, spent his days in Virata's inner chambers, singing and dancing with the womenfolk. The twins slaved in the stables and cattle sheds while your common wife and Empress Draupadi served as a maid to Virata's Queen. And you, O mighty Emperor and performer of the exalted Rajyasuya, had no qualms in spending your days as a sycophant in Virata's court. Would you all have done this if you were genuinely of a royal Kshatriya lineage? You brothers are a blot not just to the Lunar Dynasty but to the entire Kshatriya race. All those years in the forests in the company of the sages who feed off others' generosity has perhaps taken away all your sense of Kshatriya pride and dignity. But tomorrow is the day to redeem yourselves. I have heard loud and clear, the message that Arjuna had sent for me through Sanjaya–that he would engulf my Hastinapur in flames. I am also aware that Bheema has vowed to drink Dushasana's blood on the battlefield. Now listen carefully: Come tomorrow, show the world that you brothers are capable of supporting your words with action. If you have embarked upon this foolhardy mission of battling us relying on Vaasudeva who has refused to take up arms in the battle, please know that he has earned his victories and fame in the past by resorting to his illusory tactics. We too have many such magicians in our camp. If it is the strength of Drupada and his sons or Virata or the skill of Satyaki and Abhimanyu that has emboldened you, this sense of false security will be shattered once you see the white palmyra banner of Grandsire Bheeshma's chariot. These heroes that you rely on to fight for you will find it hard to hold their ground once they see the advancing chariot of the Grandsire. I hear that Arjuna has mastered the use of fourteen divine missiles. Come tomorrow, show the world how well these missiles fare against Grandsire Bheeshma, Acharya Drona or Ashwatthama who have all mastered the esoteric knowledge of the divine missiles. Perhaps, they may not employ them fully out of their fondness for you Kaunteyas, but remember...there is Radheya. When Radheya enters the battlefield, it will be like witnessing the dance of Rudra at the time of dissolution. Let us see who is there amongst you heroes who can withstand his fury. His chariot driven by the mighty Shalya will mow its way through your army promising nothing but death and destruction. I say all this now, so that history can record that I, Duryodhana, gave you Kaunteyas one last chance to step into the real world. Keep in mind, O Yudhishthira, you have seven Akshauhinis at your command gathered to fight for your cause and their annihilation will be on your hands for if you think you can win back Indraprastha through battle, you are deluded."

Uluka registered every word I spoke in his mind. He took leave of us and left for Yudhishthira's camp. He returned later that evening to report about his mission. The mission had met its objective. Uluka had delivered my message in front of the Kaunteyas and their chief allies including Vaasudeva exactly the way I had wanted him to, and sure enough, he got them all provoked. It was a verbal onslaught that they never expected. They fumed with fury and for a moment, Uluka feared for his life. However, Vaasudeva pacified them all and sent a message for me through Uluka. He said, "O Duryodhana, you have spoken so much of the Kshatriya's dignity, code of honour and conduct. You seem to know so much about it. So now prepare yourself, prepare for death on the battlefield...in the true glorious way of a Kshatriya."

38

The rules of the battle were drawn and agreed upon by the supreme commanders of both the camps–our Supreme Commander Grandsire Bheeshma, and Prince Dhrishtadyumna, whom the Kaunteyas had chosen as their Supreme Commander. It was mutually agreed upon that the battle would commence every day at the break of dawn and continue till sunset. All fighting would seize at sunset and there would be no hostilities after that till the next daybreak and during this time, members of either camp were free to mingle with each other and even share a meal. Those who were not directly involved in the fighting like charioteers, physicians, musicians, messengers, the chariot-wheel protectors, cooks, mahouts and such were not to be attacked. All single combats must be between warriors of the same class and equal stature. Chariot warriors were to challenge only chariot warriors for single combat, and likewise foot soldiers were to challenge foot soldiers and so on. A warrior was not to be attacked without first alerting him to be on guard. He was not to be attacked from behind or when on retreat. A warrior was not to be attacked if he was disarmed or stripped off his armour. He was to be given time to rearm himself. A warrior who lost his chariot was to be given time to get into a new chariot before resuming combat. A warrior who accepted defeat and pleaded for mercy was not to be harmed further. There was a long list of such rules that Grandsire Bheeshma and Dhrishtadyumna decided to agree upon in good faith after consultations...and I have lived to see each one of these meaningless rules broken by both the camps in the past eighteen days.

39

The eleven Akshauhinis on my side were arrayed on the eastern side of Kurukshetra, well before dawn. I personally moved amongst the ranks trying to motivate and inspire the galaxy of heroes and warriors who had assembled to fight for my cause. The Grandsire had arranged the army in an unconventional array facing all sides, with the elephant cavalry positioned in the outer periphery and the horse and chariot chariot warriors flanking the sides and nodal points. The Grandsire stood in his chariot looking like a demigod, tall and majestic in his silver-white armour and headgear with the palmyra flag banner swaying atop the magnificent chariot, pulled by the finest of white steeds. He stood at the head of the legion from Hastinapur that led the eleven Akshauhinis from the front. Acharya Drona, Acharya Kripa, Ashwatthama, Shalya, Bhurishravas, Somadatta, Bhagadatta, Kritavarma and Susharma were all stationed strategically at the head of various divisions. The Grandsire instructed me to guard the centre along with my son Lakshman and Uncle Shakuni while Dushasana along with my other brothers and Jayadratha guarded the rear. I gave instructions to Acharya Drona who was second in command to ensure proper cover and protection for the Grandsire, especially while combating the Kaunteyas as he had asserted he would not personally kill any of them.

The Kaunteyas had arranged their forces in the 'Vajra' formation. The formation got this name as it was believed to resemble the 'Vajra' or the thunderbolt, which was the weapon that was used by Indra to kill Vritra, an asura in the shape of a dragon, as per ancient Vedic legend. It was an effective formation normally deployed to fight enemies larger in number. The neck of the army would be thinly layered. The outer periphery comprising the foot soldiers and horse-mounted soldiers fought with their swords, javelins, maces and clubs. The chariot and elephant warriors who fought with weapons of longer ballistic range gave them cover from the inner ring.

Yudhishthira's chariot stood in the centre and the chariots of Dhrishtadyumna, Arjuna, Bheema, Shikhandi, Abhimanyu and Satyaki took up various strategic positions, in the array, in such a way that at any time, they could retreat to Yudhishthira's aid if required. Nakula and Sahadeva guarded the rear along with Virata, Drupada and the sons of Draupadi.

The huge battlefield was filled with silent anticipation as all eyes were turned to the eastern horizon awaiting the first rays of dawn. Suddenly we heard the chirping of birds from the distant trees as the first trace of the golden hue appeared on the eastern skies. The Grandsire blew his famed conch 'Shashanka' lustily to welcome the Sun God followed by loud cheers and blaring of drums, cymbals, horns and bugles. Following the cue, Acharya Drona and the other heroes too took out the conches and blew them with vigour and enthusiasm. In response, strangely, it was not Dhrishtadyuma but Vaasudeva who first blew the conch, famed across the world by the name of 'Panchajanya'. This was followed by Arjuna and Bheema who blew their conches named 'Devadutta' and 'Paundra', respectively. Soon the others followed. The atmosphere was charged as the thin, cold air reverberated with the noise of the conches, war drums, bugles, roars and war cries from the soldiers. The elephants trumpeted, horses neighed, asses brayed and jackals howled in the distance as the birds took flight from their branches in fear, and the birds of prey hovered above us in circles in expectation of the sumptuous feast to be served to them. The earth seemed to tremble as the sun slowly rose through the dark, cloudy eastern skies as if in reluctance to witness the impending holocaust. As everything quietened, I saw Arjuna's chariot move forward. It was headed in our direction. This alerted me as the protocol demanded that the privilege of the first strike belonged to the Grandsire by virtue of his seniority. However, Acharya Kripa told me to calm down as the chariot stopped midway. We were perplexed as we watched Vaasudeva and Arjuna deeply engrossed in an animated conversation in the middle of the battlefield, unmindful of others. This went on for some time while all others waited with bated breath and in silence for the Grandsire to give the clarion call for battle. But the Grandsire himself seemed to be waiting for something. I was geting impatient. In that moment, a pleasant breeze suddenly swept the battlefield as the skies opened up to a gentle drizzle. A strange emotion engulfed me in that moment and for some unknown reason, I felt gripped by an inexplicable euphoria. It felt surreal... like the Gods had come together in a celestial assembly to bless the moment...to confer glory on all the heroes gathered on the battlefield...be it through their victory or through their death.

When the drizzle stopped, what happened next was something that perhaps, for the first time, made me grudgingly respect Yudhishthira, if not for anything else, for his sheer genius and cunning. He suddenly laid down his arms, got off his chariot and walked towards us. Following his cue, his brothers followed him. Surprisingly, as soon as Arjuna alighted from his chariot, I saw Vaasudeva taking off alone with the chariot in another direction. He got me wondering where he was headed. Meanwhile, the Kaunteyas, led by Yudhishthira walked towards our direction. For a moment, I thought that they had changed their mind about waging the war. But from the look on the Grandsire's face, it seemed to me this was the moment he had been waiting for. I ordered my chariot to move to the front as the Kaunteyas came and stood before the Grandsire with folded palms. Then Yudhishthira addressed the Grandsire, "O pride of the Bharata race, O Grandsire, destiny has ordained that we, the sons of Kunti have to engage you in this fight for justice. I seek your permission to wage war with you and also your blessings for victory."

I waited anxiously for the Grandsire's response. The Grandsire got down from his chariot and stood in front of Yudhishthira who touched his feet in reverence. The Grandsire then spoke knowing full well that I was watching and listening. He said, "O Yudhishthira, you have pleased me with this gesture. If you had not come to me thus, you would have invoked my curse. But you have acted true to your reputation. You have earned my blessings. May you be victorious in this battle."

I stood there in disbelief as I heard my army's supreme commander blessing the enemy for victory. Suddenly this war was not making any sense to me. It seemed like I had lost even before it began. Yudhishthira then walked up to Acharya Drona and sought his blessings too. The Acharya said in my very presence, "O Son of Kunti, I am fully aware that in this battle, the truth is on your side, and yet fight I must for Duryodhana, for I am bound by my obligations to my King and Hastinapur. Know that I cannot be conquered in battle and as long as I stand with my bow, victory can never be yours. However, you have Vaasudeva on your side and more importantly, you have truth on your side. Therefore, fight without fear or guilt. You are assured of your victory."

Yudhishthira repeated the charade with Acharya Kripa, Shalya and the other elders assembled. They all blessed him and assured him of victory in battle in my very presence. I felt my strength leaving me. Tears swelled in my eyes as I realised that the loyalty of the very people on whom I depended for victory was with the enemy camp. For whom was I fighting this war? It was a farce. I felt all alone. I never missed my Radheya as much as I missed him at that moment. Even if he did not fight, his mere presence on the battlefield would have been enough to keep my spirits from sagging. But he was sulking in his tent with his bruised ego which seemed to weigh on him more heavily than his commitment to me. Uncle Shakuni could read my mind. He sent forth a messenger immediately to Radheya's tent to ask him to make himself present on the battlefield. He need not fight. He just needed to be there by my side offering moral support. No sooner had Radheya received the message, than he rushed to my side and once again, on seeing him, my spirits were lifted.

Meanwhile, after taking the blessings of the elders, the Kaunteyas returned to their side. Yudhishthira then made an announcement for all to hear, "This day, we have all assembled here to wage a righteous war for truth and justice. Truth is sacrosanct, but as we all know, it runs in layers and its perception may change with the uncovering of each layer. In this war, if there is anyone in my army who feels they are fighting for an unjust cause, this is the time to move over to the enemy camp. Likewise, if there is anyone in Duryodhana's camp who feels that he belongs to my army for this is where justice lies, he is most welcome to join us. This is the moment of truth for all of you heroes assembled here to decide where you belong."

Yudhishthira's announcement was relayed across the battlefield by the official messengers of both the armies who were stationed on special posts on poles erected across the battlefield at intervals for the purpose of relaying commentary on the happenings at the various areas of the battlefield. Suddenly, Yuyutsu, my step-brother, born of my father to one of my mother's maids called Sughada, moved his chariot forward and requested the Grandsire's permission to defect to the enemy camp. The Grandsire embraced him and said, "Son, you have truly made me proud of you today and yet I am ashamed of myself. You have done what I neither had the courage nor the conviction to do. Proceed without fear for you have chosen the right path." Avoiding my gaze, Yuyutsu turned around and headed to the opposite camp where he was welcomed by Yudhishthira. I do not entirely begrudge Yuyutsu for what he did, for he grew up with a lot of resentment towards me and my brothers. Although he was my father's son and of the same age that I was, he was born out of wedlock and to a Vaishya woman. For these reasons, he did not enjoy all the privileges that my brothers and I did. This had developed a sense of inferiority in him. I do not know to what extent the Kaunteyas had a role in his resentment towards us. But I always noticed that he used to spend a lot of time with Bheema in our younger days, and to that extent, this made me develop some resentment towards him as well. Over the years, the gap between us got wider and now finally, when it mattered, I was happy that he, at least, was clear where he stood, quite unlike the others including...as I was to discover seventeen days later...my own Radheya!

40

The midday sun was hidden behind the battle dust as the two armies clashed. The warriors fell upon each other as deafening war cries filled the air and in no time, the battleground was strewn with severed heads and limbs. Personal combats were fought on various fronts as the heroes from both sides displayed their valour. Kritavarma took on Satyaki, my brother Dhurmuka engaged Bheema in combat, Shalya targetted Yudhishthira, Dhrishtadyumna was attacked by Acharya Drona while his brother Shikhandi accosted Ashwatthama. The combats were evenly matched and none turned their back. Arjuna's chariot was not to be seen at the forefront. It took me a little time to realise that he had penetrated our formation even before we could realise and had ploughed through our army all the way to the rear end where Susharma along with Dushasana and Jayadratha intercepted him. Meanwhile, his son Abhimanyu took on the Grandsire himself and put up an impressive show. However, I found that the Grandsire was going easy on him much to my dislike. The maximum damage in the forenoon was caused by Bheema as he fell upon my army like an unchecked storm, destroying everything in its path. He was joined by a band of rakshasas–a demonic, cannibalistic tribe from the forests, proficient in the art of illusion and sorcery, which they used effectively while fighting their battles. They were led by

Ghatotkacha. He was the son of Bheema, born of Hidimbi, a rakshasa woman with whom Bheema had spent some days of his youth in the forests during the time the Kaunteyas had gone into hiding after the fire incident at Varnavrat.

The rakshasas fought unconventionally from the ground as well as the air using boulders, uprooted trees, fireballs, venomous snakes and such weapons that they hurled at us from a height and it was difficult to counter them with conventional warfare that we Kshatriyas were trained to employ. They also used their gift for creating optical illusion to mislead the enemy. They were specifically proficient in using this gift against animals, especially the elephants and horses, causing them to get agitated with fear and go out of control. Like the Gandharvas, their strength grew with the onset of darkness. Acharya Drona had given a select few of us the training to counter them but not all of us had mastered the skill. It was not considered honourable for Kshatriyas to use the help of rakshasas to fight their battles and, therefore, Ghatotkacha's unexpected presence on the battlefield came as a bitter surprise to all of us. Aided by Ghatotkacha, Bheema wreaked havoc amongst our ranks. Unable to withstand this further, I rushed to the Grandsire's side. The Grandsire was engaged with Abhimanyu, who had just brought down the Grandsire's flagstaff with a well-aimed shaft. The Grandsire was in full admiration for this stripling of a lad. He said to me, "Behold this boy, a mere child, and yet a worthy hero no less than his father."

I was furious. I said, "O Grandsire, my army is being burnt up in hundreds by Bheema and his son while you indulge in this combat as if it were an exhibition. Need I remind you that you are the Supreme Commander of my army? Pray tell me, what is my crime that I have earned such insincerity from you? If your heart is not in this battle, please stay away from the field and allow my Radheya to take charge."

My words had the desired effect as the Grandsire was touched to the quick. With a series of swift shafts, he struck Abhimanyu's charioteer and covered him with a relentless stream of arrows. Watching Abhimanyu's predicament, several other heroes came to his rescue on the command of Dhrishtadyumna. Soon the Grandsire turned his attention to them. Meanwhile, Shalya was engaged in a fierce combat with Prince Uttara of Matsya. They were both mounted on their elephants. The valiant Uttara fell as he was struck fatally by a javelin hurled at his chest with deadly accuracy by Shalya. Seeing Uttara's fall, his brother Shweta, full of wrath, led an all-out attack on Shalya and his forces. Shalya, exhausted from his combat with Uttara, tried to hold up against the onslaught but was soon losing ground. I urged the Grandsire to do something fast. The Grandsire sped his chariot to the aid of Shalya. He intercepted Shweta's chariot and engaged him and suddenly, it was not the same Grandsire anymore... So this was the real Bheeshma whom the world feared. He destroyed Shweta's chariot and killed his charioteer as well as the protectors of his wheels. Shweta now stood on the ground but continued to fight. Watching his situation, Bheema, Dhrishtadyumna and Abhimanyu rushed to his help but the Grandsire kept them at bay. He continued his attack on Shweta who was now slowing down with fatigue. Then, the Grandsire took out a special shaft, charged it with an incantation and shot it at Shweta. The shaft blazed its way through and pierced the armour of Shweta, taking away his life. Great was the joy in our camp as our forces danced around the dead hero. The Grandsire did not stop there. His chariot moved across the battlefield like a forest fire scourging up the dry woods. By sunset, the Kaunteyas' camp was enveloped in a cloud of gloom. They lost their troops in large numbers and more importantly two of their important heroes fell on the very first day of the battle, and both of them, the sons of King Virata.

The day undoubtedly belonged to us. The Grandsire had inflicted great destruction on the enemy forces. Later that evening, the Grandsire and the Acharyas retired early after giving the necessary briefings and instructions to the various unit heads for the next day's battle plans. As I sat in my tent reflecting over the day's events, it occurred to me that all those rules of fair fighting that were agreed upon were broken by both the sides on the very first day.

So much for the rules.

Just then, my guard informed me that I had a visitor outside my tent who sought an audience. He was a rakshasa named Alambusha. He had come with a small band of followers to offer his help in the war. He had been nursing an animosity towards Bheema in his heart for several years. Bheema had killed his brother Baka in an encounter in the forests years ago and ever since, Alambusha had been waiting for a chance to extract revenge. I thought over the matter. I knew that the Grandsire would never allow Alambusha, a rakshasa, in his army as his Kshatriya honour would not permit him to accept a rakshasa's help. At the same time, there was Ghatotkacha fighting for the Kaunteyas and wreaking havoc amongst our forces. We needed someone to counter him from our side employing similar methods of fighting. After carefully reflecting on the matter, I decided that we needed Alambusha to fight for us. I told him that he and his troops were welcome to join us, but on the condition that they remained in the background and ensured that the Grandsire was not aware of them. I told him that he would report to me directly and that his primary responsibility would be to take on Ghatotkacha and his forces. Alambusha thanked me and left.

I walked around our camp along with Radheya and Ashwatthama trying to keep the morale of the soldiers high. Some were fast asleep from exhaustion, while some sharpened their weapons preparing for the next day's battle. Others were tending to their horses and elephants. The physicians moved about the tents attending to the wounded. A separate area was cordoned for cremating the slain heroes. The musicians sat around a bonfire rendering soft, soothing music to ensure that the fatigued soldiers were relaxed. As I reached my tent late in the night, I found Uncle Shakuni waiting for me inside with a pair of dice. Radheya and Ashwatthama took leave and retired to their tents. I told Uncle Shakuni that I was not in the frame of mind for a game. I wanted to get some sleep as we had a long day of battle awaiting us the next morning. But what he told me next ensured I did not get a wink of sleep that night. Uncle Shakuni told me that the soldier whom he had sent to summon Radheya to the battlefield that morning had some disturbing information to share. I wondered what this was all about. He said that when the soldier approached Radheya's tent, he saw Vaasudeva there, outside the tent, conversing with Radheya though he could not gather what they spoke as they were at a distance. Curious, he hid behind a tree and observed. After their discussion, Vaasudeva hugged Radheya and took leave.

So that explained where Vaasudeva took off alone that morning, when the Kaunteyas came to seek the elders' blessings for the fight. I would be lying if I said that I was not disturbed. What was going on between Radheya and Vaasudeva? Radheya was not the same ever since Vaasudeva's visit to Hastinapur. He had been aloof too. When I looked forward to him taking up the leadership of my army, he declined it recommending the Grandsire for the position instead, and then refused to fight under his leadership. The zeal for battle he had been showing all along was now missing. What was Vaasudeva up to? I spent the night reflecting whether I should confront Radheya on this and ask for an explanation. But there was a serious risk of offending him by letting him know that my trust in him and our friendship was not above suspicion. That was something that I never wanted. I pacified myself with the thought that if there were something of importance, Radheya would share it with me. Radheya's friendship was too dear for me to lose, especially when I was finding myself increasingly being isolated in my cause.

41

The next day, Dhrishtadyumna had arranged his forces in the formation known as 'Krauncha.' The army arrayed in the shape of a heron with outstretched beak and wings spread wide. At the beak were Arjuna and Drupada along with their forces. Bheema and Dhrishtadyumna positioned themselves at the neck while Yudhishthira, Sahadeva and Abhimanyu guarded the wings. Shikhandi and Virata guarded the rear.

The 'Krauncha' was a rarely used formation, with not many who had the knowledge of either breaking through it or using it effectively. This formation surprised us. However, the Grandsire and Acharya Drona were up to the task. They stood leading the attack from the front with Uncle Shakuni, Dushasana, Lakshman and I along with our forces following right behind them and offering cover for their attack. Bhurishravas, Shalya and Bhagadatta positioned themselved on the left side with their forces while Somadatta, Susharma and Jayadratha were positioned at the right. Ashwatthama, Kritavarma and Acharya Kripa along with a large force guarded the rear.

At dawn, the Grandsire gave the call for battle. He led an all-out attack causing the enemies to fall in great numbers. We had made significant progress when the Grandsire was checked midway by Arjuna. The forenoon witnessed a magnificent duel between the Grandsire and Arjuna. Their chariots made excellent, delightful movements as their shafts met, neutralising each other's effect in mid-air. The duel went on without either of them backing down or giving a quarter. The Grandsire shot sharp arrows at Vaasudeva too, causing him to bleed. This infuriated Arjuna as he struck the Grandsire's bow with a special shaft, breaking it at the centre. The Grandsire picked up another bow and continued to fight. Time stood still as these two foremost warriors in the world, went at each other.

Despite all the intensity, it was evident that the Grandsire treated this like a sport rather than a combat to death. He kept praising Arjuna every time his shafts were effectively countered or whenever Arjuna baffled him with one of his own. It didn't seem to occur to him that this was a battle, and in battle, the foremost duty of a warrior was to kill or die honourably. I took my chariot towards the Grandsire and spoke my mind to him. I directly questioned him on his commitment. He looked at me in anger and said, "Son, I promised you I would slay the enemy forces in thousands for you on each day of the battle, but I had also told you I would not kill any of the sons of Kunti. Today, let me also tell you it's not just my affection for them that is stopping me. Can't you see they are under the protective umbrella of Vaasudeva? So stop blaming me for whatever is happening and allow me to continue the fight."

So saying, he resumed his fight. He sent a volley of arrows covering Arjuna and Vaasudeva. The arrows left his bow without respite as his chariot moved across the battlefield with great speed and skill. Suddenly, a shaft came out of nowhere striking his charioteer. It was Satyaki who had rushed to the assistance of Arjuna, his master. With the charioteer fallen, the Grandsire's chariot lost control of the steeds as they bolted away taking the Grandsire far from the battle.

That afternoon, Bheema led an attack on the forces of Kalinga. Great was the damage he brought upon them killing several heroes, some of them who were the kith and kin of my dear Bhanumati. One of her brothers, Bhanumat, had his body severed into two halves with a single stroke of the sword by Bheema, in the full view of the Kalinga army. They also lost their leader Srutayush who fell to Bheema's arrows. This had a terrible demoralising effect on the Kalinga army. The Kalingas were one of the firsts to offer to fight for me in this war considering the family ties I had with them and I was duty-bound to ensure their protection. All this happened at the southern end of the battlefield. When I got the news of these incidents, I rushed towards the south with my forces. Fearing for my safety, Acharya Drona followed me. I led the attack on Bheema's forces and I personally took on Bheema. Alambusha, who mingled with my army, discreetly took on Ghatotkacha. Meanwhile, Abhimanyu and Satyaki came to Bheema's rescue. The battle soon became scattered. Great was the loss on our side that day and we were relieved when we heard the Grandsire blow the conch signalling the end of hostilities for the day.

42

The Grandsire arranged our army, that by now had reduced by a tenth in numbers in the 'Garuda' or eagle formation with himself leading it from the beak and Acharya Drona and Kritavarma positioned at the eyes. The Kaunteyas arrayed their forces in the formation known as 'Ardhachandhraka' or the crescent formation with Bheema leading from the right horn and Arjuna from the left. As soon as the sun was up in the eastern skyline, the eagle tore into the moon scattering the enemy forces and rendering them in disarray and chaos. Great was the carnage that followed as the Grandsire spread terror all around the battlefield. He roared like a lion as he led our forces, infusing them with a fresh gust of energy. As per our plan, while the Grandsire led from the front, breaking Dhrishtadyumna's array and rendering it ineffective, Acharya Drona along with Kritavarma, targeted Yudhishthira who was protected by Nakula, Sahadeva and Satyaki. I led my forces against Bheema's unit and there ensued a deadly battle between us. Ghatotkacha came to Bheema's help and immediately Alambusha engaged him. The duel with Bheema was intense as we dispatched long-range shafts at each other. However, we both managed to withstand each other's onslaught. My charioteer was clever enough to ensure that our chariots never got close enough as he was aware that if Bheema got a chance to get an enemy within his physical reach, he would use his bare arms to grab him and suffocate him to death with his iron arms and python-like grip. During the combat, a javelin out of nowhere hit me suddenly with such force that I reeled under its impact. My charioteer immediately drove me away from the combat area to the safety of our army tents where our physicians could attend to me. Meanwhile, news was being relayed that Arjuna had checked the Grandsire's progress. The Grandsire had made significant inroads into the enemy ranks using special missiles capable of mass destruction. Now Arjuna engaged him and a great combat ensued between them. Similar combats were being fought between Acharya Drona and Dhrishtadyumna, Kritavarma and Satyaki, and various others at different fronts. As noon progressed, there was a disturbing message that was relayed across the battlefield as the fight too came to an abrupt halt. The message was that Vaasudeva had taken up arms and joined the battle and he was headed towards the Grandsire. Fear spread across our army and there were loud cries. "Alas, the Grandsire is no more."

I got on to my chariot and asked my charioteer to rush to where the Grandsire was. When I reached there, a baffling sight greeted me. The Grandsire was very much alive as he stood in his chariot with folded palms. He had laid down his weapons. His eyes were filled with tears as he seemed to be waiting for something. And there, standing on the battleground was Vaasudeva holding the unhinged wheel of a broken chariot lying nearby. His eyes were red with wrath and his chest heaving as he stood ready to hurl the wheel at the Grandsire. Clutching his feet was Arjuna, imploring him to desist and promising him to fight like a true Kshatriya, giving no concession to the enemy, no matter who it was or who stood against him. All the warriors around watched the drama on the battlefield, silently. The Grandsire stood in poised reverence, welcoming death at the hands of Vaasudeva while Arjuna begged Vaasudeva to get back to his role as charioteer. Vaasudeva, pacified after a lot of persuasion, returned to the chariot and once again took up the reins. The Grandsire seemed disappointed as he took up his bow. Arjuna took out his conch Devadutta, blew it with renewed vigour, and began a deadly attack on the Grandsire and his supporters using special shafts. I immediately arranged additional forces for the protection of the Grandsire. The Grandsire being the master that he was, managed to counter the attack. Fortunately, the sun had set before much damage could be done. That evening, my informers narrated to me the details of the episode. I was told that Vaasudeva was not happy about the way Arjuna was combating with the Grandsire. He felt that Arjuna's love and reverence for the Grandsire was stopping him from fighting to his full potential. His instinct was dampened by familial bond and hence, Vaasudeva took it upon himself to kill the Grandsire to fulfil his obligation to Yudhishthira. With this intention, he dismounted his chariot and advanced towards the Grandsire. Seeing Vaasudeva rushing towards him, the Grandsire put down his arms and welcomed Vaasudeva to put an end to his life as he felt that it would be his greatest honour to meet death at Vaasudeva's hands.

43

I set out to the battlefield the following day, with my mind seriously disturbed about the way things were moving forward. Here I was, fighting under a supreme commander whose blessings for victory lay with the enemy. A supreme commander who indulged in killing the enemy forces by thousands and yet who refused to kill the ones who really mattered…a supreme commander who put down his arms and invited the enemy to come and take his life. How could this old man bordering on senility and blinded by his admiration for Vaasudeva be trusted with my army? I kept my thoughts to myself as it was too late to change the leadership with Radheya playing reluctant.

It was during the afternoon of that fateful fourth day of battle that, for the first time, my Bhanumati's recurring dream began to actually disturb me...for it was on that day that eight of my brothers–Senapati, Jalasandha, Sushena, Ugra, Birabahu, Bheema, Bheemaratha and Sulochana–were dispatched to the heavens…and all of them by Bheema. Bheema and Ghatotkacha had caused massive destruction to our elephant cavalry. They had particularly targeted the elephants, hurting them at their vital organs and causing them to run amok amongst our own forces. Fourteen of my brothers came forward to check Bheema's advance and eight of them met with their end. When I heard this news, my bow slipped out of my trembling hands and I sat down in my chariot, my head buried in my arms. I was despondent as tears welled up. My thoughts went to my mother. How would I answer her? Would she not hold me responsible for my brothers' deaths?

Then I heard a voice, "Yield not to such feebleness, Son. Your brothers died fighting valiantly for your cause. Your duty now is to see that they get the justice and honour they deserve for their sacrifice. The only way to go about it is to fight. Go after Bheema and his son. Don't let them get away with this."

It was Uncle Shakuni.

The tears of grief were now replaced by tears of rage. Aroused by his words, I let out a loud war cry and hearing that, my forces got excited. We launched an aggressive assault on Bheema and his cavalry. Simultaneously, Alambusha and his troops fell upon Ghatotkacha. Ghatotkacha was using his illusory skills against our elephants, causing them to panic. However, Alambusha was able to counter them with his own. Great was the fight that ensued. We used all weapons at our disposal. The battlefield soon turned into a river of blood as lifeless severed heads, limbs and torsos fell all over. Meanwhile, upon hearing about the death of my brothers and my fight with Bheema, the Grandsire rushed to our support along with the great elephant warrior Bhagadatta and his unit. Seeing the Grandsire approach from afar, Alambusha, quietly retreated from the battlefield without being noticed. Bhagadatta shot a deadly shaft at Bheema, causing him to swoon in his chariot. Satyaki and Abhimanyu rushed to his rescue and took on the Grandsire and once again, the fight became dispersed. Soon, Acharya Drona joined us and consequently Arjuna too joined the fight. The losses were heavy on both sides. However, with the skies getting darker, Ghatotkacha's attack became even more powerful. Without Alambusha to check him, our troops suffered heavily at his hands. All eyes kept turning to the west awaiting the sun to set. As soon as the sun began its descent, the Grandsire sensing the mood of the soldiers, ordered the troops to withdraw for the day.

That night, after cremating my brothers, we returned to our tents. The news of the tragedy by now would have reached Hastinapur. How would my father and mother have taken it? How would Bhanumati have taken the news of the death of her near and dear ones the previous day? The more I thought about this, the more agitated I became. Unable to find peace, I went to the Grandsire's tent. He was immersed in silent meditation. I waited patiently by his side. When he opened his eyes, he was surprised to find me there. He gestured me to come and sit by his side. I sat on the floor next to his seat and broke down. He gently pacified me, "Son, you are a hero and it does not befit a hero to weep thus in battle. The true mark of a Kshatriya is to take responsibility for his thoughts and actions. Your brothers fought for your cause of their own free will and now have attained the glorious heaven meant for those killed in battle. You have lost only eight of them. You still have the others and all of us. You have refused to listen to the repeated advice of the elders to make peace with the Kaunteyas. Therefore, you should be prepared to face the consequences of that like a true Kshatriya. Take heart, the battle is long from over. You still have me, the Acharyas, Kritavarma, Ashwatthama, Shalya, Bhurishravas, Bhagadatta and a host of other excellent heroes, not to mention your own Radheya, ready to lay down our lives for you. So why do you despair?"

I looked up at the Grandsire and asked him, "I hold what you say as true, O Grandsire. These heroes that you just mentioned, with yourself at the helm are capable of giving fight to even Lord Indra and his army. Yet, the Kaunteyas dare to challenge us and they have gained significant ground in the last three days. Great are the losses that our forces have suffered when compared to theirs. How is this possible, O Grandsire? Are our heroes underperforming deliberately? Are they of questionable integrity?"

The Grandsire looked at me with benevolence and said, "Son, what you say about the prowess of our warrior chiefs is true. Each one of us on any given day is capable of destroying the enemy single-handedly, but the Kaunteyas are protected by Vaasudeva. Know that Vaasudeva is none other than Lord Hari in human form. He has manifested himself in the race of Yadu to rid the earth of all evil and darkness and establish Dharma. I have been told about this by the sages Narada, Markandeya, Vyasa and even my preceptor Bhargava himself. When Vaasudeva is on the Kaunteyas' side taking up their cause, victory would never settle elsewhere. Therefore, listen to my plea once more and make peace with the Kaunteyas before it is too late."

I stood up, enraged. I had enough of this. I said, "O Grandsire, now I understand...as I had suspected, it is these good-for-nothing sages who have muddled up your mind with all this nonsense. If Vaasudeva is indeed Lord Hari in human form, he must favour me the most for there is none more devoted to Lord Hari than me and my Bhanumati. Even as we speak now, Bhanumati must be in her prayer chamber offering worship to Lord Hari. I have even performed the exalted

'Vaishnava' sacrifice. This man, Vaasudeva, whom you worship and glorify is just a stooge of Yudhishthira, and a clever one at that, who knows how to manipulate people to take care of his own interests. Being the father of my son-in-law and the brother of my teacher Balarama, I had held him in high esteem once, but not anymore. I will wipe out the Kaunteyas along with this man Vaasudeva from the face of the earth with or without your help. I will not let the sacrifice of my brothers go in vain. There is no question of a peaceful compromise with the Kaunteyas. Therefore, O Supreme Commander, please prepare for tomorrow's battle with an uncluttered mind and clarity of intention. Don't let the sages confound you with their meaninglessness. We are here not just to fight but also to win...and win decisively. Victory is what I seek from you. Nothing else would be acceptable. Bring me victory."

Saying thus, I stormed out of the Grandsire's tent. I had gone to the old man seeking solace...and came out seething instead.

44

The battle continued in the same vein for the next five days, with the advantage oscillating between the Kaunteyas and us. Great were the losses on both sides as the battlefield was strewn with mangled carcasses of soldiers and the animals used in the battle. It became increasingly difficult in the dark of the night to identify the dead as the soldiers moved around with torch flames to find their dead kith and kin on the field, and to perform their cremation rites. The single combats fought on various fronts were non-conclusive as the chiefs on both the sides were evenly matched. The Grandsire moved about in the battlefield like the deity of death causing large-scale destruction wherever he went. Only Arjuna was capable of checking him but the Grandsire ensured that he attacked those divisions that were not in the proximity of Arjuna's chariot. By the time Arjuna came to the rescue, severe damage would have already been inflicted by the Grandsire. Similarly, our forces suffered severe damage from Ghatotkacha and Bheema, who were covered well by Abhimanyu, Satyaki and Dhrishtadyumna. Bheema searched for my brothers, every day, and slew them one by one in single combat. I was told that he had vowed to personally kill each one of my brothers and he seemed to pursue the fulfillment of his oath with steely determination. Each night, I sat alone in my tent with tears in my eyes, grieving over my brothers killed by Bheema that day, and the numbers only kept growing. This war was heading nowhere. Soldiers were dying on both sides by thousands. Both armies by now had reduced to half in strength. Yet the main actors on both sides were alive. Grandsire stood between us and defeat, and yet his decision to not kill any of the Kaunteyas made it difficult for us to progress. The sons of Dhritarashtra had reduced by a third in number while all the sons of Pandu remained alive. I did not want to lose any more of my brothers. I decided that if things had to change, the Grandsire had to step aside and make way for Radheya. If not, he should change his decision about not killing the Kaunteyas. I decided to have a serious talk with him that night. I took Dushasana along with me. As I approached his tent, I saw Yudhishthira and Arjuna emerge out of it. They did not see us as they got on to a chariot and rode away towards their camp. What were they doing in our camp and that too in the Grandsire's tent that late in the night?

When we went in, the Grandsire welcomed us with a smile. He seemed to be relaxed and a strange glow emanated from his visage. I do not recall seeing him thus since a very long time...so much at peace with himself. I questioned him about Yudhishthira and Arjuna's visit to his tent. He said, "Son, as per the rules, all hostilities must seize at sunset. The Kaunteyas are as dear to me as you are and they are welcome to come and pay their respects and courtesies to me if they wish to. So your questioning me in this regard is not only inappropriate but an affront to my integrity."

I remained silent but he knew that I was not happy with his response. He then held me by my shoulder and said with a smile, "Son, this childlike nature of yours is your biggest curse and yet your biggest gift. I am unable to remain angry with you when I see you sulk. Instead, you bring out the protective instinct in me. Rest assured that you will not lose this battle as long as I have my bow in my hand. This is my promise."

Dushasana interrupted the Grandsire and spoke, "O Grandsire, no disrespect was meant. It was just a natural curiosity when we saw the enemy in our Supreme Commander's tent. There should be no blame in this."

The Grandsire smiled and said, "Very well then, if you must know, I will tell you why they were here. They were here on the advice of Vaasudeva, seeking my counsel on how to defeat me."

Dushasana let out a hearty laugh. "Those fools..."

I lifted my hand to interrupt him and asked the Grandsire, "And what was your response, O Grandsire?"

The Grandsire said, "I told them that there is no man in their army or in the entire world, capable of defeating me in battle. So if they must remove me from their path, let them bring their womenfolk to fight...for I am bound by oath to fight with only those born as males."

We remained silent not knowing what to make of the Grandsire's advice to the Kaunteyas. On the surface, it seemed to me that he had just mocked them for trying to be clever. But then again, the Kaunteyas have a history of being rescued out of a precarious situation by a woman. Did the Grandsire just intentionally give them something to think and act upon?

As we took leave of him, he hugged us both tight for a long time and kissed our foreheads, something that we were not used to from the Grandsire even as children. His countenance that night did not give me the heart to offend or upset him and so I let him be. However, the Grandsire's advice to the Kaunteyas kept me awake that night. How seriously would the Kaunteyas take it? What would be the response to this advice from Vaasudeva who was their guide and counsellor?

45

The answer came to me the next day. The Kaunteyas led an all-out attack against the Grandsire with a formation known as 'Sura'. It was a formation that was used by Indra's forces while combating the Asuras as per Vedic folklore. Shikhandi led the attack and Arjuna, Bheema, Abhimanyu and Satyaki followed closely behind. I ordered Dushasana and Susharma to hasten towards the Grandsire and help him combat the combined onslaught as Dronacharya, Ashwatthama and Kritavarma had penetrated deep into the enemy camp to the rear where Yudhishthira was stationed along with Dhrishtadyumna, Drupada and the twins. Dushasana rushed to the Grandsire's aid. Great was the destruction witnessed that forenoon. The Grandsire stood blazing like the scorching sun drying up the ocean with its heat. Deadly shafts left without respite from his bow, that remained bent in a complete circle, as heads rolled from their bodies in thousands. Neither Arjuna nor Bheema could check his progress as he broke their formation, scattering the forces around. Knowing the Grandsire to be in control of the situation, I moved towards the unit of Dronacharya that was being harassed by Ghatotkacha. Angered by the death of his cousin Iravan, a few days earlier, Ghatotkacha was causing havoc in our ranks. Iravan was the son of Arjuna, born of a Naga Princess named Uloópi whom he had taken as wife during one of his 'pilgrimage' travels. Like Ghatotkacha, Iravan was well-versed in the art of illusion and employed it effectively in war, causing major havoc. He had single-handedly destroyed an entire unit from Gandhara brought in by Uncle Shakuni. Unable to check him by conventional warfare methods, I ordered Alambusha to take him on. Alambusha did the needful and brought him down with a powerful shaft spreading gloom across the Kaunteyas' camp. Seeking to exact vengeance for the loss of his dear cousin, Ghatotkacha sought out Alambusha for combat. Late afternoon, suddenly, we heard the loud and shrill blowing of the Devadutta and Panchajanya from the northern end. This was followed by celebratory blaring of kettledrums, horns and bugles. This was inauspicious and did not augur well for us. We were anxious as we waited for the commentators to relay the news. Just then, we saw Dushasana rushing towards us in his chariot, cheerless and despondent. He had bad news...our Grandsire, the Great Bheeshma had fallen.

I felt numb as the news struck me. The Acharya collapsed in grief in his chariot. Dushasana narrated to us what transpired at the northern end of the battlefield. Arjuna, Bheema and the others, positioning themselves behind Shikhandi for cover, made a combined attack on the Grandsire. Shikhandi himself had attacked the Grandsire repeatedly with his knife-edged darts. However, the Grandsire refused to be provoked into battle with Shikhandi. He kept avoiding him as he tried to parry all the shafts aimed at his vital parts by Arjuna and the others. The reason for the Grandsire not reciprocating the attack was that he would have had to first take down Shikhandi who was being used as a human shield by Arjuna who had forgotten all etiquettes of fair fighting.

But Shikhandi was born a female named Shikandini, who got herself transformed into a male with the help of a Gandharva. Since the all-knowing Creator had created Shikhandi as a female, the Grandsire refused to see or accept him in any other way. His oath to not fight with women was leveraged by the Kaunteyas to their advantage. Using Shikhandi as a shield, the warriors on the Kaunteyas' side led by Arjuna, dispatched sharp and deadly shafts at the Grandsire, piercing his armour in several places. His horses were killed and so were his charioteer and caretakers of his flanks. His bow was broken into two and his chariot was also destroyed as the Grandsire stood on the ground with his sword and shield in hand which he kept swishing in the air trying to fend off the stream of arrows. The relentless attack continued as the long and sharp arrows pierced him all over his body leaving not enough space for even a finger in between them. Then, a well-aimed shaft from Arjuna broke the sword and another smashed the shield to pieces. The Grandsire stood tall and unarmed on the battleground as hundreds of arrows pierced through his body from his neck down to his feet. All the warriors around had stopped their fight as they watched the drama unfold in utter shock and disbelief. Then, Arjuna aimed a well-aimed shaft, charged with a special incantation, that found its mark on the Grandsire's chest. It struck with such force that the Great Bheeshma whom the world feared and revered–the master of all divine missiles, the student who even surpassed his master, the Great Bhargava–fell to the earth under its impact. As he fell, dark clouds gathered in the skies and a gentle breeze blew across the battlefield. Great cries of woe filled the air.

Dronacharya immediately ordered the withdrawal of troops and halt of all hostilities. We rushed to the spot where the Grandsire lay. The most terrible sight greeted us as the Grandsire lay there on his back, supported by the hundreds of arrows that pierced him and came out through his back. The arrow tails stuck out of his body like quills of a porcupine. The sheer horror of the sight had a severe demoralising effect on our forces.

All the warriors of both the camps stopped fighting as they quietly gathered around the Grandsire to pay their respects. The Grandsire was in great pain. He attempted to say something but his voice was feeble. I ordered for my team of physicians to attend to the Grandsire immediately. I ordered them to ensure that every arrow on his body is removed and the wounds are treated with the best of pain-killing balms and healing herbs. However, the Grandsire forbade them to touch him. He said, "Son, what need do I have of these physicians? Today, I am blessed that I lie on a bed that even the best of Kshatriyas could only aspire for. On this bed of arrows shall I cast away my body as I leave for the other world. However, the time has not arrived yet. I shall wait for that auspicious moment when the sun begins its journey in the northward solstice. I will hold on to this body until then by the power of my will."

There was not a warrior gathered there who did not have tears in his eyes except Shikhandi who stood with an air of indifference and of course, Vaasudeva who stood watching everything with that half-smile of his...even at that moment. The Grandsire requested for a headrest to support his head that hung low over the arrows. I immediately dispatched my soldiers to get pillows for the Grandsire from his tent. However, the Grandsire rejected them. He then called for Arjuna and requested him, "Son, you have given me a bed befitting a warrior. Now please provide me with a similar pillow."

Arjuna placed two long arrows crossing each other on either side of the Grandsire's head and another smaller one with a feathered handle between them, holding them together. This supported the Grandsire's head. He then said, "Yes...that feels better, Son. I just need to ask for one thing more. My throat is parched and dry. I wish to have some water to quench my thirst and cool my body that burns with these wounds."

Before any of us could react, Arjuna took an arrow and charged it with an incantation. He then shot it to the earth and there emerged a fountain of fresh and clear spring water. Collecting the water with his palms, Arjuna poured it into the Grandsire's mouth and quenched his thirst. He also collected some water in an empty quiver lying around and washed the Grandsire's wounds.

The Grandsire then looked in my direction and said, "Son Duryodhana, behold this wonderful feat of Arjuna. This was the astra called 'Parjanya'. There is none in the world other than Arjuna capable of this feat that you have just witnessed. Let this convince you that no good will emerge out of this war that you have waged against the Kaunteyas. With Vaasudeva to protect them, they cannot be defeated even by Indra. If the hostilities end with my death, I shall consider that as my greatest blessing. It is still not too late. Make peace with Yudhishthira and his brothers for the good and welfare of the Kuru race and humanity at large. Let there be no more bloodshed. The road you have taken will bring nothing but annihilation. Please do not be obstinate in this matter and lead all those who have rallied behind you to their doom."

There was absolute silence when the Grandsire spoke. Everyone looked at me in anticipation for my response. Here I was, once again, being admonished and humiliated publically. I spoke, "O Grandsire, you make it seem like I am responsible for this war. Need I remind you that the call for this war has come from Yudhishthira. All I have done is that I refused to entertain his unjustified demand for Indraprastha, which he had willingly pledged to me, a demand for which he had no reasonable ground. Please do not seek to make me submit to them out of fear. I know no fear. Why should I fear these cowards who caused your fall through deceit? What heroes would do what they did, forgetting all codes of Kshatriya honour? Seeking cover behind a transgender, they attacked you and you call them heroes. When the entire Kaurava forces relied on you for leadership, you in your misplaced magnanimity gave the enemy the advice on how to bring you down and they took your advice to the word. Else, would they have achieved what they have? And what chances of victory do I have when my Supreme Commander counsels the enemy? I have come this far, firm in my resolve and with no regrets. Now I will see the war to its very end."

After I spoke, there was once again a deafening silence. The Kaunteyas seethed with rage but restrained themselves as they saw the teardrops roll down from the corners of the Grandsire's eyes. Then Vaasudeva came forward and wiped those tears with his upper garment and said, "O Son of Ganga, do not be saddened. When a dying man refuses medicine, there is little that anyone can do to help him. Seek consolation in the truth that you have played your role in the impending destiny of Hastinapur. Lying here on this bed of arrows, you will soon witness the day that is not far off, when the earth drinks the blood of this haughty Duryodhana and his evil supporters."

As Vaasudeva spoke thus, the Grandsire's moist eyes remained gazing at me. What was the emotion behind the gaze? Was it a gaze of helplessness, frustration, wrath or pity? Or was there a trace of grudging admiration in it, too? I was unable to ascertain. However, I couldn't remain there any longer. I folded my palms, circumambulated the Grandsire with respect and walked away.

46

There was no further fighting that evening as the troops withdrew to their tents. Both the sides were tired and cheerless at heart. I ordered a trench to be dug up around the area where the Grandsire lay and also for a canopy to be erected to shelter him from the heat and rain. I stationed some guards to protect him at all times. I ordered for maids to attend on him every night and shower him with sandal powder and flowers. After giving all the neccassary instructions, I rode my chariot back to my tent. As I rode back, I reflected upon the events of the last ten days. I was overcome with melancholy. Why was I fighting and for whom was I fighting? Those very heroes who fought for me, wished for my defeat. They were ready to die for me but refused to kill for me. However, this was no time for introspection. My army needed a leader…a Supreme Commander who led with no constraints and whose commitment was beyond aspersions. I went straight to Radheya's tent. There he was, fastening his quivers filled with the best of shafts of all sizes and designs to his chariot. His magnificent chariot was well stacked with maces, swords, lances and other shiny weapons and of course, his mighty bow–'Vijaya'.

I am unable to describe the sense of relief when I saw him. His tall, dignified presence and comforting embrace was like a soothing balm for my restless and burning soul. He welcomed me inside. I discussed the war with him and the way things were going for us. Now with the Grandsire out of the way, the time had come for him to take charge of my army. With him leading from the front, it was time for the world to see why my faith in him was not misplaced. I told him that the Kaurava army stood at his disposal awaiting his command.

Radheya, however, had other thoughts. He said, "Dear friend, this army of yours has a galaxy of high born monarchs and heroes. Although it may never be expressed, they would feel slighted fighting under the banner of a low-born son of a charioteer. This would cause dissension amongst our ranks. However, Acharya Drona is not only a high-born Brahmin well-versed in the Vedas but also a master in the knowledge of war and use of divine missiles. He is also a disciple of the Great Bhargava no less proficient than me or the Grandsire himself. Besides, he is well-respected amongst the various chiefs we have at our command as he has been the preceptor to most of them. They will be happy to do his bidding. The Kaunteyas, especially Arjuna, hold him in high reverence and this will weaken their resolve when they see him leading our army. Therefore, it is my suggestion that we request the Acharya to take up the mantle of the Supreme Commander and lead us to victory. However, if he falls, then I will take charge of our forces and personally lead them to victory. This is my promise to you. So let us hasten to the Acharya's tent."

That very night, the Acharya was appointed the new Supreme Commander with appropriate rituals. The first thing he did after his investiture was welcoming Radheya to join the camp. Radheya's presence infused fresh energy and life into our camp. Much of the impact of the Grandsire's fall was neutralised by Radheya's arrival. However, the Acharya did not designate an attacking position to him in the front, which the Acharya assumed for himself, Ashwatthama, Susharma and Kritavarma. He explained that he required Radheya, his son Vrishasena, Kripacharya and Jayadratha to remain by my side at the centre, guarding the rear to check the advance of the enemy forces. Since Acharya himself would be leading the army from the front, there would be no need for Radheya there. Instead, he would be more useful in the rear where we required someone of equal competence to hold us together. Radheya submitted to the Acharya's decision gracefully and added that since he would not be at the frontier in charge of the attack, he would have no need for Shalya as his charioteer for now. Shalya would be more useful as a chariot warrior assisting the Acharya in the front. However, he would use Shalya's services as the charioteer when the need arrived. This was agreeable to all.

Later that night, while discussing strategy in my tent with Radheya, Uncle Shakuni and my brothers, we decided it would be best to take Yudhishthira captive rather than having him killed. If Yudhishthira was killed, his brothers and supporters would take up his cause upon themselves and continue the war. Alternately, if he were taken alive, that would make him our slave, which would mean that his army, along with all their chiefs, would come under our subjugation in a single stroke. That would end the war. This suggestion came from Radheya and was instantly backed by Uncle Shakuni. The thought made sense to me too as continuation of war would not be good, no matter who won. Early next morning, before both the armies arrayed on the battlefield, I went up to the

Acharya and spoke to him about this. He was pleased with the thought. He said, "Son, this is a good decision. I was hoping that you would come up with this. This way, the cursed war would end. But I need you to promise me that when I capture Yudhishthira and place him in front of you, you will give him all the respect and honour that an elder brother deserves and you will spare his life."

I looked at him straight in the eye and said, "Yes, Master. I promise. If you capture Yudhishthira alive for me, I shall spare him his life. This despite all the brothers I have lost so far in the battle, this despite witnessing my revered Grandsire laid to rest on a bed of arrows. I swear on all that I hold sacred to spare Yudhishthira's life,"...and I meant every word of it.

"Very well, then. I shall spare no efforts to make a gift of Yudhishthira to you this very day." Great was the joy on the Acharya's face as he took out the conch and blew it forcefully, lifting the morale of the troops. The Acharya led a ferocious attack tearing through the enemy formation with Shalya, Kritavarma and Susharma, along with their troops close behind him. The ease with which the Acharya broke into the enemy's army thrilled our forces. We shouted and cheered in joy as we received the periodic news updates on his advance deeper and deeper into the enemy camp, causing heavy destruction. He easily defeated all the heroes who came his way. Shalya engaged Bheema while Susharma and his troops engaged Arjuna. Acharya gained sufficient ground as he single-handedly defeated Drupada, Shikhandi, Dhrishtadyumna, Virata, Dhrishtaketu and a host of other warriors, compelling them to retreat. We eagerly awaited the news of Yudhishthira's capture any moment. However, that was not to be as the day soon made its way to the evening and the sun finally set in the western skies.

Later that night, we met at Acharya's tent. We found him cheerless as he administered medicinal balm over his bare wounds. He said, "Son, it appears that we have Yudhishthira's spies amongst us in our camp here. The manner in which Dhrishtadyumna had arrayed his forces today was indicative that he was aware of our plans. He had Yudhishthira so well-protected and almost unreachable in the rear. The Creator is witness to my exertions on the battlefield to please you. I had broken every formation that stood in front of me and none could withstand my attack. I had penetrated till the very end and Yudhishthira was within my reach. I had disarmed him and was on the verge of capturing him, but then out of nowhere came Arjuna's chariot speeding through the carcass-strewn battlefield. He checked my advance with his swift shafts and halted my progress while Yudhishthira managed to get away."

I listened with rapt attention. He continued, "Son, I have heard that Dhrishtadyumna was born out of the sacrificial fire to hasten my death. Even then, I fear him not for he will not be able to withstand my missiles. It is true that there is none in this world who could stand against me in battle save Arjuna with Vaasudeva as his protector and guide. He is the ultimate testimony to my success as a preceptor and now he has advanced far ahead of his preceptor too. I can single-handedly take on the entire army of Yudhishthira if Arjuna is not a part of it. Unfortunately, that is not the case. As long as Arjuna is alive, it is impossible to capture Yudhishthira. However, if by some means, Arjuna is kept engaged by someone, then be assured that I will capture and deliver Yudhishthira to you."

"Lay your worry on this matter to rest, Acharya." It was Radheya. "I will take on Arjuna in battle tomorrow. This is what I have been waiting for all these years..."

"Not yet, Radheya. Remember that you are not fighting for yourself but for Hastinapur. I need you to be right where you are, next to Duryodhana. Just as we plan to capture Yudhishthira alive, it is possible that similar thoughts are entertained in their camp as well to get Duryodhana captured. Hence, I need you to remain by his side to protect him. I cannot trust anyone else to do this but you."

Turning to me, the Acharya continued, "Son, spread word in our camp seeking volunteers to challenge and engage Arjuna in battle."

I did as instructed and the volunteers arrived from the least expected quarters. It was the Narayana warriors provided by Vaasudeva. The Narayanas were extremely fierce and fearless warriors who always relished a challenge. They had a natural flair and passion for fighting. But their commitment to my cause was still not above aspersions as I feared there might be spies amongst them as Uncle Shakuni had once warned me. To what extent would they be committed to the fight when they see their Master Vaasudeva along with Arjuna facing them? Would they be stage-managing a fake war? I had realised by then that with Vaasudeva, nothing could be taken for granted. I was in a dilemma. Then to my relief, came forward King Susharma of Trigarta along with his brothers. He had an old score to settle as he had previously suffered humiliation at Arjuna's hand when Arjuna was on a conquest seeking the supreme sovereignty of Yudhishthira in order to perform the Rajasuya. He promised me that he and his brothers along with their army and the Narayanas would take on Arjuna the next day. I embraced Susharma. He was someone I could rely on. My heart was filled with hope as I could not wait for sunrise. Victory was finally in sight.

The next morning, Acharya arranged our forces in the eagle formation while Dhrishtadyumna once again reciprocated by arranging his in the crescent formation. Yudhishthira, as expected, was nowhere to be seen in the front. A host of warriors led by Satyajit, one of the sons of Drupada, and Satanika, the younger brother of Virata, stood protecting him. Arjuna also positioned himself close to Yudhishthira. Acharya, Bhagadatta and Shalya led a three-pronged attack on the enemy, once again, making deep inroads. Bheema once again checked Shalya and a great battle ensued between them with neither giving a quarter. On the northern end, Bhagadatta and his troops wreaked havoc on the enemy. Mounted on his notorious elephant Supratika, he sent down missiles crushing the enemies in large numbers. On Yudhishthira's instruction, Arjuna rushed to the rescue of the army on the northern front. There ensued a fierce battle between Arjuna and Bhagadatta and, several times, Arjuna narrowly escaped from being fatally struck by Bhagadatta's shafts, largely due to the skilful manoeuvring of his chariot by Vaasudeva. We listened with bated breath as the commentary of this great battle was relayed across the battlefield. Then, once again, was heard the familiar blare of the Devadutta followed by celebratory sound of cymbals, horns and kettledrums. My heart skipped a beat as the news was relayed...the mighty hero, Bhagadatta had fallen to a fatal shaft from Arjuna. The news came as a shock and was met with mournful silence amongst our troops. This was followed by further bad news that my cousins Vrishaka and Achala, sons of Uncle Shakuni had also fallen to Arjuna's arrows. Uncle Shakuni was devastated. He swooned in his chariot and had to be taken away. Meanwhile, the Acharya had penetrated deep and was locked in combat with Drupada and his sons. He sent word through a messenger that he was closing in on Yudhishthira and that the time was right for Susharma and his troops to take on Arjuna and keep him engaged. Susharma did the needful. He challenged Arjuna who had no choice but to accept as per the Kshatriya tradition. His brothers and the Narayanas joined Susharma as they collectively attacked Arjuna and Vaasudeva, covering their chariot with arrows. Arjuna was, however, up to the challenge as he used missiles charged with special incantations to counter them. The battle thus raged on at various fronts and was evenly matched. Towards the evening, the Acharya had advanced deeper into the enemy ranks. He had put to death both Satyajit and Satanika. The other heroes were no match for him and sped in all directions at the very sight of his mighty chariot, driven by fiery chestnut-coloured steeds. But just as he was closing in on Yudhishthira, yet again his plans were ruined by a shower of arrows from Arjuna who rushed to his brother's rescue. Yudhishthira fled the scene, in his chariot, while Arjuna engaged the Acharya till the sun went down in the western horizon.

The discussions in our camp that evening went late into the night. I spoke to the Acharya at length recounting the loss we suffered at our end that included Uncle Shakuni's sons and several of Susharma's brothers to Arjuna's arrows. "O Acharya, this battle could have been over today as we had planned. We had everything going for us. Yudhishthira was well within your grasp and yet you let him get away. Surely, you fight for us but favour the enemy. Else, you would not have let him get away. You are the preceptor to most of the heroes assembled on either side. There is nobody who can withstand your arrows and this is known the world over. How then could Yudhishthira have escaped from your clutches? When you blessed him to be victorious, I saw it just as a gesture of an elder and a preceptor. Now it seems to me that your loyalty and commitment indeed rest with the Kaunteyas and not Hastinapur. You restrain Radheya and hold him back in the rear out of fear that he might accomplish what you are unable or perhaps unwilling to do."

There was a brief silence after I spoke as no one expected the Acharya to be addressed thus. But at the same time, everyone knew that I was not the one to hold back and always spoke my mind. I may have been accused of many shortcomings, and perhaps guilty of most of them but putting up a facade was never one of them. This was one of my traits that perhaps the ones who mattered to me the most found endearing. The Acharya was most certainly one of them. He looked at me kindly and said, "Son, the words coming out of your mouth hurt me more than the shafts proceeding from the Gandiva. Know you that I entertain no partiality towards the Kaunteyas although Arjuna was my best student. I blessed Yudhishthira with victory because the truth is on his side. Where there is truth, there is Vaasudeva and where there is Vaasudeva, there is victory. But I assure you that you will not lose this war as long as I am alive. My efforts to capture Yudhishthira today were thwarted once again by Arjuna, but that was because he was very much in the proximity. He was able to hold back

Susharma and his army and make them retreat, and rush to Yudhishthira's aid. If Susharma and his men could somehow take Arjuna far away from Yudhishthira on the battlefield and keep him engaged for the whole day tomorrow, then I shall present Yudhishthira, bound in chains, in front of you before sunset. You have my word."

After the Acharya spoke, Susharma, grieving over his dead brothers, came forward and said in a voice steeled with resolve, "O Acharya, I along with my remaining brothers and army will take a vow with the sacred fire as our witness that we will challenge Arjuna and engage him in this war till we kill him or get killed by him. Come tomorrow, we will draw him as far away from Yudhishthira as possible to help you accomplish your mission. This is our solemn vow."

Saying thus, Susharma and his brothers took the sacred 'Samsaptaka' vow. This was a solemn pledge taken with the sacred fire as witness to attain victory or death in their mission. Those heroes who took up such a mission were called 'Samsaptakas'. The Samsaptakas are so firm in their resolve that they leave nothing to chance. Before embarking on their mission, they even have their own funeral rites performed in advance while still alive to ensure a glorious afterlife in the event of their death. To many heroes across the land of Bharata, challenging Arjuna was as good as a suicide mission.

Everyone congratulated and hailed Susharma and his Samsaptaka army. Flowers were showered on them as Susharma fell at the Acharya's feet and sought his blessings. The Acharya embraced him and turning to the various chiefs assembled, he said, "O best of heroes, you have witnessed the sacred pledge undertaken by the Trigartas. Their sacrifice has assured them their auspicious place in Hastinapur's glorious history. We now have no excuse. This battle must end tomorrow. Array yourselves in battle in the impenetrable 'Chakravyuha', tomorrow. Let Duryodhana, Radheya, Lakshman, Dushasana, his son Durmasana and the Lord of Gandhara guard the centre. Let Shalya, Ashwatthama, Bhurishravas, Kripa and Jayadratha station themselves at equal measure of distance to guard the sides at the outer periphery with their troops, while I lead from the front. This formation is bound to baffle the enemy. There is no one in their camp save Arjuna and Vaasudeva who know how to successfully penetrate this formation and scatter it. But with the Samsaptakas promising to lure them and engage them far away from the centre of the battleground, neither Bheema nor Dhrishtadyumna or any of the other heroes on their side will be able to resist our advance. We will capture Yudhishthira tomorrow and end this war."

The words of the Acharya were met with loud cheers of joy and celebrations. The mood in the camp was upbeat.

47

The thirteenth day of the battle dawned. As instructed by the Acharya, our forces had arrayed in the 'Chakravyuha' or the wheel formation. This is a multi-tiered formation in the shape of a set of concentric wheels when viewed aerially. The tiers were designed in such a way that the best of warriors guarded the outer tier in groups covering equidistant peripheral area and if it were to be broken by the enemy forces at any weak link, the breach could be sealed immediately by the adjacent groups on either side, trapping the enemy inside. Once inside, the enemy troops were allowed to proceed with minimal resistance till they would reach the inner core where then they could be trapped and hemmed in from all sides offering them virtually no chance to come out alive.

As the sun came out again on the eastern horizon on the thirteenth day, we fell upon the Kaunteyas' forces, baffling them with our formation. The Samsaptakas, as planned, sought out Arjuna for combat. By noon, they had lured Arjuna to the southern end of the battlefield, sufficiently far away from the centre. The Acharya decided it was time to forge ahead with his mission. Just then, we felt a sudden ripple-like movement through the layers of our forces as our troops at the front were scattered. It was the young Abhimanyu. He led a ferocious attack on our forces with Bheema, Satyaki and the other chief warriors following close behind his heels. He broke and entered the wheel formation even as the Acharya looked on. However, as soon as he entered, and his troops rushed to the spot and effectively sealed the breach trapping Abhimanyu alone before Bheema and the others could follow him inside.

Surrounded from all sides by our warriors, Abhimanyu stood unfazed like a lion in the middle of a herd of bison. Being trapped alone inside did not seem to bother him in the least. He fell upon our forces like a twister letting out continuous unending streams of shafts in all directions. Even the Acharya stood mesmerised by this young lion, as he took on the best of our heroes single-handedly by turns and together, and made them all retreat. His swift shafts pierced the armours of the great Bhurishravas, Dushasana, Kritavarma, Kripacharya, Ashwatthama, and other veterans who came in his way, bruising with his sharp arrows, not just their bodies but their egos as well. Even Radheya and his son Vrishasena were not spared from his onslaught and were forced to retreat. To lift up the morale of the troops, I personally led an attack on him but was baffled by his fighting skills. He appeared to be at many places at the same time and his arrows seemed to come at me from all directions. One of them hit me on my chest and I reeled under its impact. The bow slipped from my hand. My charioteer immediately rode me away to safety. Seeing my condition, Shalya rushed to my help but he too faced a barrage of shafts and was compelled to retreat. Rukmaratha, the son of Shalya, seething with rage, rushed at Abhimanyu to avenge his father's humiliation but in a matter of moments, he was dispatched to the other world by a special shaft well directed at his neck. The soldiers around stood in shock. Acharya Drona watched in admiration and remarked, "Truly, this boy has inherited the best of both, his father and his Uncle Vaasudeva. Even Indra cannot withstand him in a head-on battle."

Hearing the words of the Acharya, my son Lakshman was infuriated. He said to me, "Father, the words of the Acharya just show how partial he is to the enemy. Instead of fighting the enemy, he admires them and sings their praise. It is futile to depend on such heroes who wish well for the enemy, however reverential they may be in stature. If he is blinded by admiration for his favourite pupil's son, let him enjoy the battle as a mute spectator as I take Abhimanyu on. Today, you will see what I can accomplish."

In a rush of blood, he ordered his chariot towards Abhimanyu before I could react. I tried to pull him back but it was too late as he had advanced too far ahead. I was tired and recovering from the blow on my chest but I went behind him and also asked Radheya, Dushasana, Kritavarma, Dumarsana and the others to hasten to his protection and give him cover. As we caught up with him, he was already engaged in battle with Abhimanyu. Then, in my very presence, a shaft with a crescent-shaped arrowhead left Abhimanyu's bow and in a flash, it severed my son's head causing it to fall to the earth and roll down to where my chariot stood. Abhimanyu roared and slapped his thigh in exaltation. I was numb as my world stood still. This could not be happening. My young son, the future of Hastinapur, who grew in my arms, for whom I nurtured great dreams, was now lying lifeless on the battlefield. Alas...alas, not thus...If Bhanumati should see this? I had failed her. Her pride and joy, raised in comfort and luxury, that smiling face that was ever the source of solace and inspiration in the most trying times, that little one with the moon-like face and tiny limbs who grew up to be the fine young man who would make any father proud, was now lying in a pool of blood with his head separated from his body. Had I known it would come to this, perhaps I would have taken Vaasudeva's advice. Of what use was Hastinapur when the promise of its tomorrow lay shattered on the battlefield? I got down from the chariot and picked up my son's head with trembling hands. My voice refused to come out as I choked. I carried his crowned head and placed it next to his trunk, and how beautiful and alive did he look in that blissful sleep. The Acharyas, Radheya, Uncle Shakuni, Kritavarma and the others stood around me, dry of consolatory words to offer. Shalya too joined them, eyes filled with wrath and tears over the loss of his own son. They all stood in silence as I tried to speak but my voice failed me. I held back my tears and refused to cry. I promised myself that I would not shed a tear until my son's death was avenged. I thought of all those times that I was wronged by the Kaunteyas over the years. They played in my mind in sequence, and this was the pinnacle. The rage inside me grew and finally expressed itself through a loud roar that shook everyone up. "Kill, kill the evil Abhimanyu and then show me your faces, you all." This was followed by loud roars from everyone there as they took up their arms, ready to charge. Then the Acharya reined them back and said, "O valiant heroes, do not charge in haste or you will all meet with the same fate as this young prince. I do not say this to undermine your prowess or valour. Please do not feel belittled that you have not been able to conquer the Son of Arjuna. You will not be able to do so in a straight combat. He seems to have specialised in a special esoteric Gandharva warcraft that helps him to empower his shafts through certain incantations to cause optical illusions and confound the enemy. He has obviously inherited this knowledge from his father who was taught these incantations by a Gandharva named Tumvuru. Arjuna himself has spoken about this to me in the past. This explains how he has been single-handedly countering all of you today. The only way I see to conquer him is to attack him collectively. Attack him from all sides including from the rear. Somebody should disarm him by attacking him from behind."

The heroes did not relish the suggestion. Attacking someone from behind was not the approved way for Kshatriyas. The Acharya being a Brahmin perhaps found it agreeable, but not the others. Then Radheya spoke, "O Acharya, I will take up this unpleasant task upon myself for the sake of my dear friend. I cannot bear to see him in grief. I will attack Abhimanyu from behind and disarm him. "

"Very well, then", said the Acharya, "let us proceed".

Abhimanyu, meanwhile, was on a rampage destroying our forces in great numbers. Jayadratha had successfully kept Bheema and the others at bay, not allowing them to enter the formation. But Abhimanyu did not seem to require any reinforcement. He was trying to breach the formation to allow Bheema's forces to enter the formation. However, Jayadratha proved a formidable foe as he and his forces resolutely defended the breach from the inside as well as the outside.

If Abhimanyu were allowed to continue, he would have perhaps single-handedly won the war for Yudhishthira.

Then, Shalya, grieving over the loss of his son, rode up to him seeking single combat. He sent a shower of arrows in his direction. Just as Abhimanyu took out a shaft from his quiver and took aim at Shalya, a sharp-edged arrow from behind cut his bow. It was Radheya. This took him by surprise. Before he could react, Kritavarma shot down his charioteer and the caretakers of his wheels while Acharya Kripa killed his horses. Undaunted, Abhimanyu alighted from his chariot with his sword and shield in hand but two swift shafts from Acharya Drona broke his sword and shield to fragments. Abhimanyu, unarmed, looked around and realised that mighty chariot warriors were attacking him from all the sides. In desperation, he took up the wheel of a broken chariot nearby and started to whirl it around to protect himself from the well-directed arrows that came rushing at him from all directions. He hurled the wheel towards the Acharya but a shaft from Ashwatthama intercepted it and smashed it. Picking up the mace of a slain warrior on the field, Abhimanyu rushed towards Ashwatthama and swung hard at him. Ashwatthama jumped out of his chariot just in time to avoid the blow and his chariot was smashed to pieces. Ashwatthama then took refuge in Dushasana's chariot. Abhimanyu hurled the mace at Dushasana's chariot destroying it. Dumarsana, who could not brook the humiliation of his father, now jumped out of his chariot and struck Abhimanyu with his mace. Abhimanyu collapsed. As the fatigued Abhimanyu attempted to rise, Dumarsana brought down his mace with immense force, cracking his skull in a single blow, saying thus, "This one is for my brother Lakshman".

The warriors let out loud cheers of celebration as they lifted Dumarsana and danced in joy around Abhimanyu's body. This was perhaps the first day since the war began when we had tasted some success worthy of mentioning but the cost of it was too dear to bear. I hugged Dumarsana as I finally shed the tears I had been holding back. While the warriors celebrated, there were only two amongst us who did not join. One was Radheya, which was understandable as for the first time he was forced to do something dishonourable not befitting a hero, which was attacking someone from behind. He had compromised on his dignity for his friend and for him dignity was paramount. The other was our Supreme Commander who watched in silence with tears rolling down his face...and it was obvious to all that these tears were being shed for the son of his favourite student Arjuna, and not mine.

48

I stood alone in front of the funeral pyre of my son. I preferred solitude at that moment for I knew that if my men found me in that mournful condition, it would adversely affect their morale. Besides, I needed to be by myself at that time as I watched the smoke from the pyre rise skyward and merge with the infinite sky. The night was cold, still and dry and I could hear the sound of thunder reverberate in the emptiness, followed by streaks of lightning. The sound of thunder in a cloudless sky was considered a bad omen and a harbinger of inauspiciousness. But what could be worse for a father than lighting the funeral pyre of his son? The flame from the pyre raged, so did the fire inside me as I heard the cracking of my son's bones and joints that held his youthful, shapely sinews in the heat of the fire, sinking my heart into the depths of despair and grief.

Then I felt an arm on my shoulder. It was Uncle Shakuni. He said, "Son, remember that you are not alone in your loss. I too have lost my sons and so have Shalya and many others in this battle. But know that they have all attained those auspicious regions in the heavens meant for heroes. Many more will lose their sons, fathers, brothers and kin on both sides, but they have all given up their lives willingly, fighting for what they felt was right. Therefore, do not give way to grief. Your son had earned himself a glorious death on the battlefield that every Kshatriya aspires for. A glorious end on the battlefield is more welcome to a Kshatriya than death on the bed caused by disease or age. And don't forget that there have been losses on their side too."

I remained silent. He then took me by the arm and said, "Come with me now. Everyone is waiting for you at the Acharya's tent. There is some news that my spies have brought me from Yudhishthira's camp. There has been a development."

As I entered the Acharya's tent, I was greeted by silence. The Acharya was seated on his special seat and seated on the floor by his feet was Jayadratha. Radheya, Ashwatthama, Shalya, Dushasana, Dumarsana, Vikarna, Bhurishravas, Uluka and the other chiefs all stood quiet waiting for someone to speak up. Then Dushasana spoke, "Dear Brother, an excellent opportunity has presented to us by itself without exertion on our part. We have information from our spies that Arjuna, grieving over Abhimanyu's death, has taken an oath that he would take the life of Jayadratha before the sun sets tomorrow failing which he would end his life by self immolation."

This was some development indeed. I looked at Jayadratha and he appeared all shaken up.

"But why him?" I asked. "He was nowhere around Abhimanyu when he was killed. It was us who collectively attacked him. If Arjuna must seek personal vengeance in this battle for a higher cause, then he should be looking to kill the Acharya for ordering the collective attack on Abhimanyu. If it is his reverence for the Acharya that is stopping him, then there is Radheya, Ashwatthama, Shalya, Dushasana, Kripacharya and myself who are all equally responsible for the death of his son, not to mention Dumarsana who dealt the fatal blow. Why is he not targeting us? Or even Susharma, who has been engaging him away from the centre of the battle for the last two days? Why Jayadratha? Is it because he thinks out of arrogance that the King of Sindhu is a soft target?"

Radheya said,"No, my friend. It is because it was Jayadratha who effectively sealed the breach created by Abhimanyu in the 'Chakravyuha' and trapped him inside. If not for him, our formation would have been broken by enemy forces led by Bheema and Satyaki. It behooves us to ensure that Arjuna fails in his mission tomorrow, not just to watch him self immolate... but to fulfil our obligatory duty to the Lord of Sindhu. We must protect him at all costs."

The Acharya said, "What Radheya speaks is true. We must focus on how to protect Jayadratha tomorrow. It will not be just Arjuna that we shall face tomorrow. He will have the entire force to back him in his mission. Besides that, I have information that Vaasudeva has asked his charioteer to keep his own chariot ready. If my conjecture is right, this would mean that if Arjuna fails in his mission, Vaasudeva may take up arms to accomplish it for him."

Jayadratha looked nervously at the Acharya and said, "O Acharya, I exerted myself today on the battlefield and succeeded in holding the Kaunteyas' army at bay by the grace of Mahadeva. But pray, tell me, come tomorrow what should be my course of action? You are the preceptor for all of us and you know our strengths and weaknesses. Arjuna has sworn to hunt me down to the very end of the earth tomorrow to realise his promise and Vaasudeva has pledged to spare no efforts in seeing him succeed. Please advise if

I should retreat from battle tomorrow. Surely, Arjuna will not fight someone who has retreated from battle."

I was furious. I said, "O great hero, has all shame taken leave of you? Have you no honour left that you speak like a coward? It is out of consideration for my sister Dushala that I spare you for such cowardly talk of retreat. Let Arjuna come tomorrow with Vaasudeva and the entire army behind him. Come sunset and we will make sure he is united with his dear son in the other world."

The Acharya interrupted, "Duryodhana is right. You are a hero and a mighty one at that. Today you have taken on Bheema, Satyaki and the other great warriors on their side and yet held your fort. So this kind of cowardly talk does not befit your stature. Fight and earn glory, be it through victory or death on the battlefield. You have no reason to fear when you have these heroes here to protect you. I personally will station myself to guard the front. As long as I stand there with my bow in hand, know that Arjuna will not be able to get to you without first getting past me. This is my promise. Tomorrow, I will array the army in three formations and place you at the very end. It will be impossible for Arjuna to reach you before sunset, leave alone killing you. So go in peace and get some well-deserved rest for a battle well fought today."

49

As the sun rose reluctantly to witness the bloodiest day of this cursed battle, that fateful fourteenth day, the Acharya arranged our forces in three formations. At the outer tier was the 'Shakata' formation, which was a square block guarded on the front by the elephant cavalry. This was a formation normally used to protect someone important like the King. At the head of this formation, leading the attack, stood Dumarsana and his father Dushasana. At the second tier was the 'Padmavyuha' or lotus formation, which was a slight variation of the 'wheel' formation and resembled a blooming lotus when viewed aerially. The Acharya stationed himself at the rim. Finally, there was the 'Suchimukha' or needle formation at the end of which stood Jayadratha under the protection of our chief chariot warriors including Radheya, Ashwatthama, Susharma, Shalya and myself. The formation was formidable and Jayadratha was assured that Arjuna would not be able to get to him without divine intervention. He, however, stood on guard.

The Acharya had given all the necessary instructions to the chiefs. We had two objectives. One was to stall Arjuna's progress towards Jayadratha at any cost and the other was to capture Yudhishthira alive, a plan that was thwarted by Abhimanyu the previous day.

The Acharya was firm in his resolve to protect Jayadratha and so were all the heroes as they stood proud in their chariots awaiting the battle call. The confidence they exuded filled me with hope as I surveyed the array of formations. Even Jayadratha seemed calm and composed and that by itself was a big relief. But all hopes were rattled towards the noon as we kept getting the updates on Arjuna's progress. He had stormed into the 'Shakata' formation, forcing Dumarsana and Dushasana to retreat. As he approached the Padmavyuha, the Acharya challenged him and halted his progress. They engaged for some time as we eagerly listened to the updates. Then came that great act of treachery from the Acharya as we listened to it happen from the commentators. Arjuna had abruptly stopped the fight and saluted the Acharya with folded palms as Vaasudeva steered the chariot around the Acharya, circumambulating him, and then entered the Padmavyuha with no resistance whatsoever from the Acharya. We looked at each other, baffled, and with a loss of reaction. Jayadratha came up to me and said, "O Prince, our Supreme Commander has betrayed our trust. It would have been more honourable if he had chained me up and offered me as a gift to his Arjuna."

"Do not show haste in drawing conclusions, O King of Sindhus," said Radheya. "The Acharya would not do something without evaluating all consequences. Why do you fear when we stand guard here? Even if everyone else fails, I, Radheya, will protect you."

The words from Radheya were reassuring. However, the Acharya had a lot to explain. Meanwhile, inside the Padmavyuha, Arjuna was unstoppable. It was not the Arjuna that we knew for the past thirteen days. Heads rolled off their necks in hundreds as our forces fled in all directions. Watching the army suffer the heat of Arjuna's wrath, Kritavarma came forward to check him but he too had to retreat. Then Sudakshina, the Lord of Khambhojas came forward to meet Arjuna. A well-aimed shaft from the Gandiva pierced his heart, sending him to the other world. Every now and then, we could hear the blaring of the Devadutta followed by the relay of the announcement of yet another hero of ours surrendering to Arjuna. Arjuna was on a rampage, using all the special missiles at his command. I could hear this no more as I rushed my chariot towards the Acharya.

I said to him, "Today, Arjuna has made a mockery of your army formation. And you, O Acharya, have made a mockery of our trust in you. Today, when the Lord of the Sindhus has placed his life in your hands and when the fortune of the entire Kaurava force hinges on you, we stand betrayed. How could you allow Arjuna to break into the Padmavyuha without resisting him? Did he have your consent and blessings? It appears to be so." I was hissing like a snake as I spoke.

The Acharya calmly replied, "Son, I have said this before and I say it again. Arjuna with Vaasudeva as his charioteer is unstoppable even by the Gods. I did my best to keep him engaged. But realising that they were losing time, Vaasudeva convinced Arjuna to retreat and even before I could react, got his chariot past me. When I asked him to return to combat, Arjuna paid no heed as his chariot moved further in. I could have gone after them but I felt this was a good opportunity for me to go after Yudhishthira. I need not worry on account of Arjuna when all you heroes, younger in age and swifter of limbs are available to tackle him."

He got me thinking. How genuine was his explanation? I said, "Very well, Acharya..." I said, "Please go ahead with your plan but return with Yudhishthira in chains. Meanwhile, I will personally go and take on Arjuna."

The Acharya said, "Son, don't be hasty. Arjuna, today, is like a turbulent river in spate, crushing everything in its path. You will not be able to withstand him in battle."

I said, "Acharya, you have taught us many things but fear is not one of them. Even death does not scare me in the least. So I will fight Arjuna today."

The Acharya said, "Son, fear is important for a warrior for it is fear that keeps him alive and his faculties sharp. It is running away from fear that one should refrain from. If you must fight Arjuna, then wear this armour on your person. This is an armour that has been consecrated with special incantations to protect its wearer."

So saying, the Acharya took out a shiny black-iron armour from his chariot and gave it to me. It gave full protection to the body and arms from neck downwards, exposing only the fingertips. Clad in that armour, I went forth seeking Arjuna for battle. All this while, I had an eye on the progress of the sun's journey westward.

Meanwhile, Bheema and Satyaki had broken into the Padmavyuha and were slaughtering our forces by hundreds. Bheema had hurled his mace at the Acharya's chariot smashing it to pieces and while the Acharya was trying to mount another chariot, the two of them penetrated the vyuha. Bheema was once again singling out my brothers for combat.

It was well into the afternoon when I found Arjuna and the sight that met my eye baffled me out of my wits. He stood there on the ground under the shade of a tree. Next to him was a fountain of fresh spring water. It was obvious that he had used the 'Parjanya' missile to create it. His horses were unyoked and drinking from the water while Vaasudeva was relaxing in his chariot with his eyes closed. They seemed to be least mindful of the time and in no hurry to get towards Jayadratha who was still quite a distance away. I shot a few sharp arrows at Arjuna who intercepted them with ease. He shot back a set of sharp razor-edged arrows that struck my armour but hardly causing me any discomfort. The Acharya's armour was indeed excellent. Vaasudeva now woke up and I sent forth a set of arrows in his direction too, but Arjuna intercepted them all, midway. He continued to shoot his arrows at me but they just fell off my armour. Then after a brief consultation with Vaasudeva, he sent ten sharp needle-headed shafts that pierced me on all my fingertips that were the only exposed part of my body. The bow fell off my grip as my hands trembled with pain. Sensing my discomfort, my charioteer immediately steered the horses away and took me to safety.

The battle raged on with fierce intensity at various fronts. We suffered a major setback when Alambusha who engaged Ghatotkacha was overpowered and slain. This spread panic across our forces. Satyaki and Bheema had, meanwhile, advanced deep into our forces, destroying the legions that stood in the way and had almost caught up with Arjuna. A great combat ensued between Satyaki and Bhurishravas. These two heroes had a history of a bitter family feud. The reason for their rivalry was that Bhurishravas's father Somadatta had desired the hand of Vaasudeva's mother Devaki against her wishes when she was a maiden, and Satyaki's grandfather

Sini fought against him to help her unite with his dear friend Vasudeva, the father of Vaasudeva. That caused a rift between their families and that bitterness carried over generations. Now, when the opportunity arrived to settle scores, Satyaki challenged Bhurishravas for single combat. The battle between them was evenly matched until Satyaki began tiring. Bhurishravas disarmed him, destroyed his chariot and killed his charioteer. Satyaki fell on the battleground in exhaustion. Bhurishravas got down from his chariot and grabbed him by his long tresses. He drew his sword and was ready to behead Satyaki with a single blow. We were thrilled as we listened to the news relayed. Satyaki was one of the foremost and dangerous warriors on their side. He was the student of Arjuna and no less than his master. His passion for fighting was matched only by his reverence for his teacher, Arjuna. His loss would be a major blow to the Kaunteyas. Then suddenly, to everyone's shock, as Bhurishravas lifted his sword, a shaft struck him from behind chopping his right arm off his shoulder. Falling to the ground and wriggling in pain, Bhurishravas turned around to see who it was that struck him from behind. It was Arjuna, who had rushed to the aid of his student. Before the news of this cowardly act could sink in, the next we heard was that lay slaughtered in a pool of blood on the battlefield, his head severed by Satyaki, even as he was trying to rise from the ground with the help of his one arm. This cowardly and treacherous act of Arjuna and Satyaki was condemned across the battlefield. It was a highly dishonourable act for a Kshatriya to interfere unsolicited, and without alerting, during a single combat between two heroes when one of them has challenged the other. It was against all codes of ethical warfare. It was that one similar act that had sullied the fair name of Rama, the famous Prince of Ayodhya, when he killed Vali, the King of Kishkindha, who was engaged in a single combat with his brother Sugriva who had challenged him. This was different from Abhimanyu's case, where there was no personal call for combat or challenge between anyone. That battle was more general with Abhimanyu going on a rampage like a wild elephant in a sugarcane field using Gandharva warfare, and we had no option but to collectively check him. By and large, the opinion of everyone was that Arjuna, hailing from the reputed lineage of the Kurus, by himself, was incapable of such a dishonourable act unless it was prompted by Vaasudeva himself.

Suddenly, we heard the shrill sound of the Panchajanya blown in the 'Rishaba' note. This was Vaasudeva calling for his charioteer Daruka who arrived with Vaasudeva's chariot. Satyaki mounted and the fight continued. Dhrishtadyumna, Drupada and the Panchala forces, who stood between Yudhishthira and the Acharya, held the Acharya in check at the forefront. Meanwhile, at the rear, our forces were reeling under the three-pronged attack of Arjuna, Satyaki and Bheema. That afternoon, the count of my brothers who fell to Bheema rose to fifty-six. By now, I had become numb and devoid of reaction each time the news of death of yet another one of my brothers was relayed. However, the last one was what upset me the most. Vikarna, that brave and yet naive brother of mine...all his bravado in the assembly hall when he took a stand against me and spoke for Draupadi, did not help him when it mattered the most. Bheema strangled him to death with his bare hands, denying him the death from a weapon which is the more honourable way for a Kshatriya to die. Filled with wrath, I turned to Radheya and asked him to attack Bheema. I wanted Bheema dead at any cost. Radheya hesitated for a moment, as he was reluctant to leave Jayadratha unprotected. But with the sun journeying fast towards the west and Arjuna still quite a distance away, I told him that Jayadratha would be safe. Radheya ordered his chariot towards Bheema. Watching him go alone, Ashwatthama decided to join him and take on Satyaki.

Great was the cheer in my army as these two unrivalled bowmen arrived in time for battle. Ashwatthama took on Satyaki and kept him at bay using his special missiles charged with incantations. Bheema, meanwhile, charged at Radheya like a gusty wind. All those sharp, insulting words of Radheya in the assembly hall were perhaps still fresh in his mind. Radheya, on the other hand, was calm and composed. We were on the edge as we listened attentively to the narration of the battle by the news carriers. They hurt each other several times, causing each other to swoon, but recovered soon and resumed the fight with renewed vigour. Radheya was clever enough to stay out of Bheema's reach for he knew the danger of being caught in his arms. The contrast in their styles of fighting was evident as we listened to the narration. Bheema was a savage as always, with only one intention, which was to destroy anything and everything in front of him using any means that was in front of him. Radheya, on the other hand, had a definite plan and method. He skilfully wore down Bheema by parrying and countering his attack, exhausting him of all the shafts in his quiver. He then began disarming him methodically with his own special shafts. He broke his bows, maces, javelins and all the other weapons in his arsenal. He then injured his charioteer Visoka and killed the caretakers of his wheels. Then with a special shaft, he destroyed his chariot and Bheema now stood unarmed on the ground. Radheya now proceeded towards him. The hairs on my body stood at their ends as I listened to the proceedings. This was the day that we waited for. This bully who was the main cause of animosity between us cousins, the scourge of us brothers, who tormented us all through our childhood now stood at the jaws of death as my Radheya closed in on him. The faces of my fifty-six brothers flashed past and they seemed to smile at me from the heavens above. My ever-dependable Radheya would avenge them any time now. As I waited for the good news, the next I heard was that Radheya let go of Bheema without killing him. He, instead, turned his attention to Satyaki who in the meantime had forced Ashwatthama to retreat to the rear. This was unbelievable. Surely, there must have been some mistake. I rushed to the spot and there was Radheya, now engaged with Satyaki. Although Radheya was a superior archer, they seemed to be evenly matched, shaft for shaft and missile for missile, primarily because Satyaki had the advantage of having the skilful Daruka as his charioteer. Daruka was no less than his master in the art of handling the horses and manoeuvring the wheels. Meanwhile, Arjuna had proceeded further and was now at the mouth of the 'Suchimukha'. Dushasana, Ashwatthama, Vrishasena and Susharma engaged him, all of them defending Jayadratha like a fort. The sky had taken a crimson hue. I asked Radheya to abandon the combat with Satyaki and rush to the help of

Jayadratha as the sun was only a few moments away from setting in the western hills. Together we rushed to the rear end. There we saw Arjuna, single-handedly countering the collective onslaught of all the heroes. Radheya and I joined in the attack. Shafts flowed in a continuous stream from the Gandiva as Arjuna shot them tirelessly using both his hands alternatively. He showed that evening, why he was known the world over as 'Savyasachin' or the ambidextrous one. All the while, I kept an eye on the sun as it seemed to take an eternity to set. Jayadratha, who we all knew was essentially a hero at heart, could not sit idle while we warriors defended his life with ours. He too came out to fight. Then it happened. A sudden darkness enveloped the battlefield. We looked westward. The sun had disappeared. Loud cheers and roars of celebration erupted. Conches and bugles blared in the air. Arjuna was crestfallen. Perhaps the Sun God had not approved of his oath. The bow slipped from his hand as he stood downcast, before us, in his chariot. Vaasudeva too was silent. Jayadratha, now came cheerfully forward in his chariot to accept our congratulations as he stood next to us. He took out his conch and blew it to signal our victory for the day. But suddenly, that was drowned by even louder blaring, this time of the Panchajanya. We turned and saw Vaasudeva blowing it forcefully in a haunting note. It was a siren call to welcome the God of Death as behind him we saw Arjuna, with the Gandiva in hand bent to a circle and its string stretched to the full. On it was placed a crescent-headed shaft. The shaft began to glow as he charged it with incantations. Ashwatthama immediately recognised this as the Pashupata Astra, the divine missile blessed by Lord Shankara himself.

Until then, we had only heard about this. The legend of this missile was that it was capable of rendering just about anything that its master desired...even if it were the annihilation of the entire world with all the life in it. So the talk about Arjuna being in possession of the esoteric knowledge of this weapon was not mere gossip after all. Arjuna carefully took aim and released the shaft as it headed straight towards Jayadratha. We all watched the drama, dumbfounded and in awe, as the divine missile of Lord Shankara lit up the evening sky and blazed its way and even as we watched, it severed the head of Jayadratha with such an explosive impact and swiftness, that none of us who witnessed it understood what happened. It was only when we saw the headless body of Jayadratha lying on the battlefield, did we realise what had just occurred.

50

I sat alone in my tent with a heavy heart with tears of despair flowing from my eyes. I felt enveloped by darkness and the world crumbling around me. Jayadratha's face haunted me. One moment he stood tall and triumphant in his chariot and in the next moment, he was a headless body on the battlefield. How would I face my sister Dushala? How could I tell her that she was widowed because of our incompetence? Jayadratha had chosen to retreat from the war, but it was I who forbade him. It was my responsibility to ensure his safety.

The truth set in. For the first time, I felt in my heart that we would lose the war...for my 'real' enemies were in my own camp. My eleven Akshauhinis had reduced to three. Fifty-six brothers of mine had fallen in the war thus far. The Grandsire was rendered invalid. My Supreme Commander was simply going through his motions. His fight was just cosmetic and his heart was not in the war. The mighty Radheya, relying on whom I waged this war, was indifferent too. He had his own secrets to keep. His secret interaction with Vaasudeva was still a mystery to me, though I never brought it up with him. There was something going on of which I was completely unaware. His letting go of Bheema when he could have easily killed him made me doubt his commitment. When Uncle Shakuni questioned him about this, he said he was merely following the rules laid down for the war as per which, he was not to strike an unarmed person shorn of his weapons and chariot. That was absurd. The rules of war had been broken right from the first day. Radheya himself was party to the collective attack on the unarmed Abhimanyu just the day before. But he justified that action by saying that the Acharya was responsible for that as it had happened under his command and supervision. I remained silent. Although Arjuna broke his vow and killed Jayadratha just moments after the sun went down, the fact that he could reach the very end of our formation that day made me realise that he was indeed deserving of every bit of his reputation. He killed Jayadratha right under the watch of Radheya, Ashwatthama, Shalya and the other heroes. There was nobody in both the armies who could be considered his equal...not even Radheya. Between Satyaki, Bheema and him, they had reduced our army more than by half, and all this while our Supreme Commander was preoccupied with a never-ending mission of capturing Yudhishthira. What was his excuse this time? Arjuna was away from Yudhishthira the whole day and yet the Acharya failed in his mission. He was the one who allowed Arjuna to enter the Padmavyuha in the first place. If not for that act, Jayadratha would have been alive.

While I was being ravaged by my thoughts, the Acharya entered my tent. On seeing him, I lost control over myself and spoke my mind to Acharya on what I felt about his superficial involvement in this war, especially as the Supreme Commander. I held nothing back as I hurled a volley of accusations momentarily forgetting that he was my preceptor. Hearing the commotion, the others rushed to the tent. The Acharya bore the humiliation in silence but I could sense his mounting rage. Finally, after I stopped, he said, "O Prince, your accusations are more hurtful than any shaft. But I am obligated to bear them out of my binding duty towards Hastinapur. I promise you that I shall never remove my armour till I see the destruction of the Kaunteyas or die in that attempt. Today, Arjuna broke the rule by extending the fight beyond sunset. Therefore, we are not bound by that rule anymore." He turned to the chiefs around and said, "O heroes, rally your forces. We will attack the enemy right now."

Although the soldiers were weary from the day's battle, the Acharya's orders were met with loud war cries and the blaring of bugles and conches. The soldiers set out with torch-flames and fell upon Yudhishthira's forces that were taken by surprise. A great battle ensued in the dark. The birds of prey were denied their descent for supper as the battlefield was a terrible sight with thousands of torch-flames lit up and the dazzling streaks of the shafts from either side filling up the skies like a shower of meteors. Thousands were killed on either side as everything broke loose and mayhem prevailed.

The Acharya, stung by my words, suddenly looked like the fiery Rudra himself on the battlefield. He repeatedly let loose special missiles charged with deadly incantations on the enemy causing large-scale destruction. Radheya joined him, and together, they looked like they would vanquish the enemy and finish the war that night. Sahadeva confronted Radheya, who lost no time in disarming him, killing his charioteer and causing him to retreat. Just as the Kaunteyas' forces were reeling under the onslaught, there began a ferocious counter attack led by Ghatotkacha and Bheema. Bheema killed another twenty of my brothers, taking the count to seventy-six. But that night, he was surpassed by his son. With Alambusha out of the way, Ghatotkacha now seemed invincible. The rakshasas became more powerful with the onset of darkness. Ghatotkacha used his powers of illusion to spread panic and terror across our army. He killed Alayudha and Jatasura, two important accomplices of Alambusha. He destroyed our forces in thousands. He seemed to exceed his father in prowess. The Acharya meanwhile had charged ahead towards Yudhishthira. However, Arjuna, who now engaged him, halted his progress. Back at the centre of the battlefield, Ghatotkacha tormented us by hurling huge boulders, uprooted trees and powerful shafts from the skies. Dushasana, Ashwatthama, Shalya, Kripacharya, Kritavarma, all tried to contain him but were forced to retreat with grievous injuries. I charged forward to tackle him but he hurled a huge rock at me. I jumped out of my chariot in the nick of time avoiding the rock that smashed my chariot and killed my charioteer. It seemed like Ghatotkacha would single-handedly annihilate our forces before daybreak. The forces were reeling under his relentless onslaught. I rushed to Radheya and said, "Radheya, if we don't do something about this rakshasa, none of us may live to see the sunrise tomorrow."

Radheya was hesitant. He then took on the rakshasa himself. There ensued an intense battle. Radheya was able to counter the shower of shafts and boulders hurled by the rakshasa and neutralise them midway in the air. However, I found his approach defensive, which was not his style. His son Vrishasena joined him in battle. Then all of a sudden, a powerful shaft struck Vrishasena, knocking him down unconscious. Seeing his son hurt, Radheya was now furious. His eyes reddened as he took out a golden casket from his arsenal. He opened it. Inside was a luminescent silver lance alongside which were placed some fresh flower petals, indicating that this was a special lance that Radheya worshipped ritualistically. He touched the lance to his head and chanted some incantations. The night sky was suddenly illuminated by the glow of the lance as the soldiers around stopped their fight and watched in awe. Radheya slowly and surely took aim and let it fly at Ghatotkacha. The lance found its mark and in a flash, Ghatotkacha was struck dead. Great was the joy amongst our soldiers as they danced in celebration, hailing Radheya. This was a decisive blow to the Kaunteyas. They had no business to bring in a rakshasa into our battle in the first place. The fact that it was Bheema's son added to my joy. I rushed towards Radheya and embraced him. So did the other heroes. But amidst all the joy and celebrations, Radheya remained gloomy. When I asked him the cause, he said, "Dear friend, in the heat of the battle, I just used the most precious weapon I had in my arsenal–the 'Shakti'. This is a divine missile blessed by Lord Indra himself that kills whomsoever it is used against, but it can only be used once. I had reserved it all these days for Arjuna."

51

The night's battle ended with the fall of Ghatotkacha. The generals on both sides recalled their weary troops. Ghatotkacha's death was a small consolation in what was otherwise a day of irreparable loss. Yet again, I went to the Acharya's tent. He was outside, attending to his horses. I greeted him with folded palms and said, "O Preceptor, great is the injustice that you are rendering to me and my Hastinapur. It is now four days since you promised to capture Yudhishthira alive and yet you return empty-handed at the end of each day. Under your leadership, our forces have shrunk in size and our heroes have fallen in great numbers. I have lost seventy-six brothers so far to Bheema. I have lost my son. I have lost my Uncle Bhurishravas. I have lost my brother-in-law who had placed his life in your hands. Yet, all the Kaunteyas are alive. I am aware that even the Gods are incapable of stopping you from attaining what you've set your mind on. Then why do you let us down like this, we, who have committed to do your bidding in this war?"

The Acharya spoke, "Son, the Kaunteyas live because they are protected by Dharma. I have said this many times before, where there is Dharma, there is Vaasudeva, and where there is Vaasudeva, there is victory. This is my firm conviction. And yet I will exert on the battlefield till the very end for you and for Hastinapur, for I am duty-bound."

At that moment, I hated the Acharya with all my heart. Here was a man as insincere as can be found and yet adept at camouflaging it with the cloak of loyalty...and I had to endure him as my Supreme Commander. I lost my patience. I said, "Very well, O Acharya, come tomorrow, I release you from your obligation to Hastinapur. You and your son Ashwatthama may fight if you like or stay aside and watch while I, along with Radheya, Shalya, Uncle Shakuni, Dushasana and the other remaining heroes on my side, take down the Kaunteyas along with Vaasudeva."

The Acharya smiled and said in a voice full of sarcasm, "Well spoken, like a true hero, O Prince. Now you must walk the talk. Let the army be divided tomorrow. I shall lead one unit and endeavour to keep my promise to you and capture Yudhishthira. You, in the meantime, can lead the other independently, along with your dear Radheya, your Uncle Shakuni and the others. This will be a great opportunity for your coterie to show the world that you are as good on the battlefield as you are on the gambling board."

Saying thus, the Acharya went inside his tent leaving me outside, fuming in fury.

The next morning, the Acharya divided our forces in two halves, positioning himself at the right along with his forces. The rest including Radheya, Uncle Shakuni, Uluka, Shalya and my brothers stood on the left along with our forces. The Acharya left us with no particular instructions. It dawned on me that he had indeed meant every word he spoke the previous night. At the break of dawn, he tore into the enemy forces like a storm. As if to balance this, Arjuna and Satyaki led an attack on us. A great carnage ensued on either end of the battlefield. Arjuna massacred our troops in great numbers before Radheya checked him.

Meanwhile, Satyaki positioned his chariot right against mine. As we alerted each other for a duel, my mind was filled with the memories of the days of our youth. We were good friends who spent a lot of time together during my days of training under Balarama at Dwaraka. We used to hunt, feast and train together. All those days flashed past as I remarked, "Alas, my friend, how despicable is fate that we must find ourselves on opposite sides of this wretched war. How I wish that the times were different and we never had to fight this war. But, cruel is destiny that makes the best of friends turn foes. Fight you I must, against the will of my heart."

Satyaki was shaken with emotion for a moment as he replied, "Duryodhana, we have come past all those sentiments and reached this far in battle. This is no place to reminisce about the old days and better times. We are Kshatriyas and our duty on the battlefield is to fight. So set aside these emotions and fight like a Kshatriya and earn glory."

His words roused me as I sent a volley of shafts in his direction. He countered them with great difficulty. Then with a swift arrow, he broke my bow. Before I could take another bow, he asked his charioteer to steer him away from the combat. He shouted, "O Prince, I could kill you right now, but I refrain from doing so just for Bheema's sake. I do not want to deny him the pleasure of breaking your thighs and keeping his pledge." But while he said that, I noticed he was unable to hide the tears that flowed from the corners of his eyes. I realised that my friendship did mean something to him after all.

Meanwhile, Arjuna had to discontinue his combat with Radheya and rush back to the aid of his troops that were being scourged by the Acharya. The Acharya fought as if he were possessed by a demon that afternoon. He began to use the 'Brahmastra', one of the most potent missiles that could kill the enemy in thousands. He repeatedly used it to deadly effect. Three of Dhrishtadyuma's sons rushed to stop him but he dispatched them all to the other world in no time. When Drupada rushed to avenge the killing of his grandsons, a well-aimed shaft from the Acharya pierced him through his chest, killing him instantly. Virata too fell to a sharp javelin from the Acharya. Arjuna, soon, engaged the Acharya and there ensued a great battle with the use of divine missiles. We listened with bated breath to the narration as the advantage oscillated with every volley of shafts.

And then came the shocking announcement... the Acharya had laid down his arms.

I ordered my chariot to rush to the front. There, at a distance, I saw the Acharya seated cross-legged on the battleground with his eyes closed, as if in a deep trance. His bow and quiver lay next to him on the field. The Kaunteyas were all around him. The fighting had stopped as everyone around watched in anticipation of what was to happen next. Then I saw Dhrishtadyumna's chariot come forward, slowly, towards the Acharya. Before I realised what was happening, he jumped out of his chariot, grabbed the Acharya by his long hair and in a single stroke of his sword, beheaded him, realising the prophecy.

The horrific sight of the Great Preceptor lying on the battlefield, head separated from the trunk, caused panic our forces that began to flee in retreat. I went after them trying to bring them back to the battle. However, Ashwatthama stopped them in their tracks. Great was their surprise when they saw him as they proclaimed, "He is alive... is alive!" I was lost as to what was happening. Just then, Uncle Shakuni joined me. He narrated to me what had happened as reported by his informers in Yudhishthira's camp. With the Acharya burning up Yudhishthira's army using the Brahmastra, they hatched a devious plan to get him out of the way. Bheema announced in the full hearing of the Acharya that he had killed. The Acharya was well-known for his fondness for his son. His very existence revolved around his son. The news of Ashwatthama's death was unbelievable for the Acharya. He knew that there was none in either of the armies capable of killing Ashwatthama in battle except Arjuna. Therefore, he verified the truth of the matter with Yudhishthira who was perceived to be the epitome of honesty. When Yudhishthira affirmed that Ashwatthama was indeed killed by Bheema, the Acharya was devastated. He lost all interest in the battle and in life as such. Then, Bheema approached him and hurled a verbal volley of accusations at him. He addressed him as a butcher, condemning him for deviating from the duties of a Brahmin, which was to impart knowledge, and indulging in warfare, ordained for Kshatriyas.

Duly admonished by Bheema, the Acharya decided that he had had enough of this battle. He put down his weapons, alighted from his chariot and sat down cross-legged on the battlefield with his eyes closed in a yogic trance. When he was in that meditative state did Dhrishtadyumna commit the heinous act.

Then I was given to understand that Bheema did indeed kill Ashwatthama...just that it was an elephant by that name that belonged to the King of Avanti.

And as I had expected, it was Vaasudeva who had hatched the dastardly plot.

Ashwatthama took the news of his father's death and the treachery of the Kaunteyas with a stony silence. His eyes turned blood red and his body trembled with rage. He stood like a volcano ready to erupt as he gathered the retreating soldiers and addressed them in a deep rumbling voice, "O heroes, why do you turn your back in fear? Know that today, my father, our Supreme Commander was killed by the Kaunteyas by deceit. There is no other way that they could have achieved this. It behooves you, O heroes, not to run from fear of such cowards. Today, before the sun sets, you shall see the end of this war. The world will witness the wrath of a vengeful Brahmin as it had once before when the Great Bhargava lost his father, the great-souled Jamadagni. In your very presence, shall I, Ashwatthama, send these cowards to the abode of Yama. Watch me as I deploy the 'Narayana Astra'".

A murmur spread across the troops and the air was suddenly filled with excitement. We had only heard about the 'Narayana Astra'. Like the 'Pashupata', this missile could never be countered. It was consecrated with incantations to invoke Lord Narayana to preside over it. The knowledge of this missile was limited to a very few. Even Radheya did not know the secret incantations to this. Ashwatthama took out a special star-headed shaft from his quiver and placed it on his bow. He closed his eyes and chanted the incantations to charge the shaft. Suddenly, the earth seemed to tremble and the mountains shook as a storm swept across the battlefield. Lightning and thunder occurred at various parts of the vast battlefield. Terror spread across both the armies as the world seemed to approach its doom. Ashwatthama released the missile skywards, to the west, in the direction of the Kaunteyas' army. The shaft suspended itself in the sky like a shining star and generated scorching fumes of smoke. From it emanated a multitude of glittering weapons...discs, maces, shafts, javelins and so forth in thousands that filled up the sky and descended at unimaginable speed towards the Kaunteyas' army. We watched in awe as the 'Narayana Astra' began its work. The Kaunteyas' army ran helter-skelter. Their leaders looked baffled. Some of them tried to resist but it was of no avail. It seemed to me that their entire army would be engulfed by the missile, sparing none. Then, suddenly, something strange occurred. We saw Vaasudeva stand up in his chariot and address the others. The entire army of the Kaunteyas then laid down their arms and prostrated before the Astra that shone above them with fierce intensity...all of them except Bheema who stood tall, prepared to counter the missile. He took the onslaught of weapons on his body as he tried to resist it. Suddenly, Vaasudeva and Arjuna forced him to the ground. The entire army lay prostrate with their arms folded as the flying weapons passed over their heads without hurting anybody and returned to their source. The 'Narayana Astra' was thus neutralised.

Ashwatthama looked crestfallen. I asked him the reason for his 'Narayana Astra' being suddenly rendered ineffective. Ashwatthama explained, "My Lord, it is true that there is no counter incantation for the Narayana Astra. But it is also true that this is an incantation that even Arjuna is not aware of.

My father had shared this knowledge only with me. The only way to counter the Astra is to not resist it. The more you resist it, the more powerful it becomes. However, the Astra will never harm anyone who humbly submits himself to it. We overlooked the fact that they have the all-knowing Vaasudeva on their side who knows this secret. What can the Narayana Astra do when Narayana himself is on their side?"

Ignoring his last comment, I said, "Well, if that be the case, deploy the missile again. And this time, while they submit themselves before the Astra, we will use the opportunity to capture Yudhishthira."

"No, Prince, that cannot be done," said Ashwatthama with a sigh. "This missile should never be deployed a second time. If it is deployed, it will turn back and annihilate our own forces. Perhaps, fate does not approve of our intentions. The only way forward for us is to fight for glory without care for victory or defeat."

So much for the Brahmin's wrath.

52

I dealt with the fall of the Acharya with mixed emotions. No doubt, I was indebted to him for the knowledge that he imparted to us. His tutelage had made Hastinapur famous the world over. At the critical time of the exile period of the Kaunteyas, he governed Indraprastha with remarkable efficiency ensuring that there was no insurgency. His partiality towards Arjuna not withstanding, he was worthy of the highest reverence. Hastinapur would miss his calming and reassuring presence. Yet, with his fall, hope once again filled my heart as the moment that I had been waiting for had finally arrived. Radheya kept his promise of taking up the leadership of my army if the Acharya fell. All the remaining heroes accepted his leadership unanimously. That very night, the royal priest of Hastinapur performed the ritualistic ceremony and placed a garland of forest flowers around his neck honouring him as our Supreme Commander.

Radheya stood tall and proud, radiant as the sun with the garland around his neck. Next to him stood his valiant son Vrishasena. The father and son were a sight to behold, like a proud lion with its cub. For a moment, my thoughts went to my Lakshman and I felt a tug at my heart. But that was not the right time. Great work lay ahead.

Radheya addressed all the chiefs, "O great heroes, at this moment, as your Supreme Commander, I have only this to say to all of you. I have pledged my life to the cause of my friend Duryodhana. Come tomorrow, the Kaunteyas will witness the true worth of my friendship to Duryodhana. We have reached so far in this battle witnessing many wrongs perpetrated from both the sides. But under my leadership, we will fight hard and we will fight fair. Fight by the rules. The fight will not be just for victory, but for glory as well. So retire for the night and get your well-deserved rest. At the break of dawn tomorrow, we will array ourselves in the 'Makara' formation."

The next morning, our forces arrayed as instructed in the 'Makara' or the crocodile formation with Radheya at the front. At the eyes were Uncle Shakuni and Uluka. And behind them was Ashwatthama. I was positioned at the centre with my brothers and flanking the sides were Kritavarma and Shalya with their forces. The formation was lean in strength. Our forces had reduced to a tenth of what they were at the beginning. That was the reason Radheya decided not to use Shalya's services as a charioteer yet as he was required more as a chariot warrior to lead his legion from Madra. It was a pity I could not provide Radheya a force of bigger strength. When I mentioned this to him, he laughed and said, "Dear friend, I do not require your forces to win this war. All I require is your trust and confidence, for that is my biggest force."

The Kaunteyas yet again arranged themselves in the crescent formation with Arjuna at the centre, Bheema and Dhrishtadyumna at the sides. The Samsaptakas under Susharma once again accosted Arjuna. The Samsaptakas too had dwindled in great number over the last four days, all falling to Arjuna's arrows. For the first time in the past sixteen days, we witnessed the battle being fought as per the rules laid down.

Radheya's approach to the fight was very unlike the Grandsire or the Acharya who seemed to forget themselves in the heady intoxication of battle. Here was a warrior fighting in a style and pattern that almost gave an artistic hue to his method. He strictly forbade our warriors to break the rules of fighting. To some extent, this was a relief to both sides, unlike the situation under the Acharya's leadership where chaos reigned.

The day belonged to Radheya, Kritavarma and Kripacharya as they ploughed through the enemy ranks. Kripacharya took on Dhrishtadyumna and struck him down with a powerful shaft, causing him to swoon. Kritavarma fought Shikhandi and soon forced him to retreat. Meanwhile, Yudhishthira led a charge on me and we had an intense exchange of shafts. I was amazed to watch Yudhishthira's expertise with the bow. I always knew he was an expert with the lance, but his skill as a bowman was a revelation. He repeatedly struck me with his sharp arrows, but I was protected by the Acharya's armour. With successive shafts, he killed my charioteer and horses. He also broke my bow with another shaft. Soon I was disarmed and just as he closed in on me; Ashwatthama came to my rescue and picked me up in his chariot.

Meanwhile, Nakula accosted Radheya and challenged him. He roared, "O low-born son of a charioteer, my brother Arjuna seems to have forgotten his oath to slay you. I shall fulfil it for him. Today, I shall make you pay for those insulting words you uttered in that assembly."

Radheya smiled in reponse as he sent a volley of shafts to which Nakula had no matching answer. One could not follow the movement of his arms because of the lightning speed at which he mounted his arrows and shot them one after the other. In no time, Nakula was disarmed and his chariot destroyed. I watched the duel in great joy. Radheya approached Nakula. I was excited and thrilled. Finally, after losing seventy-six brothers, I would get to see the first Kaunteya killed in the battle. Radheya removed the sword from his scabbard as he closed in. He raised his sword and just when I thought he would sever Nakula's head, he just touched his neck with the tip of the sword and said, "Go, Nakula, you are still a child. Learn to seek your equals for battle. There is nothing to be ashamed of in losing this fight. Some day, you will be proud that you engaged with the great Radheya in battle. Go now. Go, seek protection under the wings of your Arjuna." So saying, he steered his chariot away.

I watched in disbelief. What was Radheya up to? First, it was Sahadeva, then Bheema and now Nakula. That was three times in three days that Radheya let go of an opportunity to kill a Kaunteya.

Meanwhile, hearing of Nakula's humiliation at the hands of Radheya, Arjuna rushed to avenge his brother. There ensued a great battle between two of the best archers in the world. All the warriors in the vicinity stopped their fight just to watch the duel. Both the chariots made wonderful movements as we watched a great exhibition of fighting. Suddenly, Arjuna decided to take the intensity of the duel to a higher level by using special missiles charged with incantations. For every missile, Radheya had a counter missile that neutralised it midway. Arjuna was intense and I had never seen him exert so much on the battlefield. Radheya, on the other hand, was calm and collected as always, even occasionally applauding Arjuna magnanimously when he managed to pierce his armour.

Then Radheya sent a razor-headed shaft that broke Arjuna's bowstring, causing the great Gandiva to bounce off his hand. Radheya then took out a special shaft that was shaped like a serpent. It was called the Naga Astra. He touched it to his head and chanted the incantations to charge it. Soon, the shaft began to glow generating a hissing noise. Arjuna looked tense. It was evident he had no answer to this shaft.

Radheya said, "O Mighty Hero, take a good last look at the world around you."

He let go the shaft as it blazed its way towards Arjuna's neck. All the warriors watching on the field exclaimed, "Alas! Arjuna is dead!"

Then something happened that spoiled Radheya's plans. The ever-alert Vaasudeva, pressed the front of the chariot into the ground with his feet causing the horses to buckle and Arjuna to lunge forward. The shaft smashed Arjuna's silver white headgear causing it to fall. Great was the applause for Vaasudeva as well as Radheya from all the soldiers around. Arjuna stood humiliated in his chariot. Radheya took up another shaft and took aim. This time it was sure to find its target. Just then, from a distance, we heard Dhrishtadyumna blow his conch. The sun had descended in the western hills. Radheya put back his shaft in his quiver, took out his conch and blew it forcefully announcing the end of hostilities for the day and the withdrawal of troops. He said to Arjuna, "O Arjuna, you are indeed a great warrior worthy of your reputation. But you need to notch your skills higher to challenge this low-born son of a charioteer. You were saved today by the Sun God. But come tomorrow, this fight shall go to the very end."

Arjuna tore a piece of cloth from his lower garment and tied it around his forehead to keep his tresses from falling over his face and said, "O Radheya, today was your day. But tomorrow is another day. I swear on my Gandiva that I shall not wear my crown which you have knocked down today, this crown known the world over as 'Kiriti', till I sever that proud head off your neck."

All the while, Vaasudeva watched the exchange of words in silence...the mysterious grin never escaping his face.

53

That night Uncle Shakuni, Dushasana, Uluka and I held a long discussion in our camp. As much as we were encouraged by the fact that the day's battle undoubtedly belonged to us, Radheya's obsession with rules of fighting was bothering us. He had the opportunity to kill all the Kaunteyas except Yudhishthira and yet he let them get away. I decided to have a talk with him alone. I went to his tent and spoke my mind to him. I told him, "Dear friend, these rules have been broken several times before by either side. This war has come way past all those rules. I want the Kaunteyas dead. I have lost my son, my brothers, my relatives, my friends and well-wishers, and you still consider those meaningless rules more important than my losses. I have pinned my hopes on you. With you at the helm, I was relieved that I finally had someone who was as committed to seeing the end of the Kaunteyas as I was. But your actions confound me."

Radheya looked at me straight in the eye and said, "Dear friend, know that in your happiness lies the very meaning of my life. Your grief is my grief and your victory is my victory. You will some day realise the truth in my words. I intend to win not just the war for you, but eternal glory as well. That can never happen if we Kshatriyas resort to deceit. Although I have counselled you against the schemes of your Uncle

Shakuni many times, I have always stood with you in all your machinations against the Kaunteyas. However, I can absolve myself of all those wrongs, as they were not my decisions... even the ones committed in this war. But now that I am in charge, please understand I cannot bring myself or my army to disrepute by not honouring the warrior's code of conduct."

I was stunned to hear Radheya speak thus. "All those wrongs?" Did he actually say those words? After all these years, now suddenly when the moment of truth had arrived, he felt that the Kaunteyas were wronged by us? Tears welled up. I felt that familiar darkness enveloping me. That familiar feeling of loneliness came back. In a choking voice, I said, "My friend, if you feel that it is the Kaunteyas who have been wronged by us, if you feel that you are on the wrong side in this war, Yudhishthira had given everyone the opportunity to defect to his camp at the beginning of this war. But it is still not late. If you feel I have wronged the Kaunteyas, you have my approval to move to his side. Let that not come in the way of our friendship."

Radheya held my shoulders firmly and said, "Duryodhana, we have come way past that stage to discuss what was right and what was wrong. We are at war and our concern at the moment should only be about how to achieve victory. Today, Arjuna would have been sent to the abode of Yama, if not for Vaasudeva's presence of mind. As long as Vaasudeva is with Arjuna, I will be at a disadvantage. It is time for us to request the Lord of Madra to take up the reins of my chariot. Arjuna and I will meet again on the battlefield tomorrow and this time I promise you, only one of us would see the sun set in the western skies."

He embraced me reassuringly. I was pacified to some extent. Together we went to Shalya's tent and greeted him. I requested him to honour Radheya by taking up the role of his charioteer the next day. As already promised prior to war, Shalya agreed but with a condition that Radheya should not object to any counselling he may offer in the battlefield. Radheya said that on the contrary, he would consider that as a privilege and welcome it.

On the way back after the meeting with Shalya, we stopped at Uncle Shakuni's tent. He was not inside. The guard informed us he had gone to visit the Grandsire lying on his bed of arrows to pay his respects to him.

Radheya said, "Dear friend, I too need to meet the Grandsire. No matter his views on me, it is important to seek his blessings for the decisive battle tomorrow. You may proceed to your tent and get as much rest as possible. Tomorrow will be a historical day in this battle."

So saying, he took leave of me. I came back to my tent and settled down to catch some sleep. But sleep evaded me. I was disturbed. I had an intuition that something was just not right about Radheya's behaviour in the past few days. He preferred to be all by himself in his tent most of the times. Sometimes, it even seemed to me that he was avoiding me. I was still in two minds if I should confront him about his interaction with Vaasudeva. However, I decided I would keep that for another day, maybe after the war was won. I took the jar of wine placed next to my bed and drank from it till it numbed the pain from the bruises on my body and in my heart, as I closed my eyes and gently drifted off to sleep in the protective cloak of darkness.

54

The battlefield on the morning of the seventeenth day looked nothing like it was on day one. Both the armies had reduced by huge numbers. Radheya did not have enough forces to make a conventional formation. However, he divided the army into small groups led by Uncle Shakuni, Kritavarma, Kripacharya and Ashwatthama. Radheya, with Shalya as his charioteer, stood tall right at the front along with the remaining Samsaptakas under Susharma. The troops, though weary from the last seventeen days' battle, stood inspired and motivated by Radheya's majestic presence.

The Kaunteyas' forces had dwindled too. Of the many chariot warriors who stood against us on the first day, only a few remained and that included the Kaunteyas, Dhrishtadyuma, Satyaki, Shikhandi and the sons of Draupadi. No sooner was the call for battle given, than the Samsaptakas accosted Arjuna and kept him engaged. Bheema locked horns with Ashwatthama and there ensued a great battle between them. The savage assault from Bheema caused Ashwatthama to swoon and forced his charioteer to retreat. In the meantime, Yudhishthira once again sought me out for a duel, and I was up for the challenge. The duel was evenly matched until Nakula and Sahadeva joined him. Together, they launched a combined attack on me. I held them at bay but was slowly losing ground. They sent a shower of shafts at me when out of nowhere came Radheya with a volley of swift arrows to counter them. Radheya's arrival caused panic in the Kaunteyas' army. He was like a gigantic tidal wave causing terror and destruction in its path. Watching his forces scattered in all directions, Yudhishthira came forward to face Radheya. He taunted Radheya as he said, "O Great Bowman, it is banking on your strength that the wicked Duryodhana has embarked on this war. You have harboured hatred for us ever since you came into our lives on that fateful day in the arena. You were denied permission to fight then. Well now, the time has come, and you have your chance to prove yourself to the world that you are indeed who you claim to be."

In response, Radheya just smiled as he let loose a stream of shafts in his customary style. In no time, he had Yudhishthira disarmed and stripped of his armour. His chariot was smashed to the ground. Radheya advanced towards Yudhishthira. I watched from a distance as he closed in. Yes! This was it. The war would end now as Radheya was about to capture Yudhishthira alive. I knew he would deliver unlike the Acharya who could only make empty promises. I knew my Radheya would never fail me. As Radheya reached within an arm's length of Yudhishthira, suddenly, descending out of nowhere, a shaft struck me on my chest. So severe was the blow that I swooned in my chariot and had to be rushed off the field.

55

When I woke up in my tent, I realised I was all alone. Although my chest hurt from the blow, the balm applied over it by my physician helped to ease the pain to some extent. I realised that it was getting dark outside. My guard came in and announced that Shalya was waiting to see me. I asked him to be ushered in. The visual I had before I blacked out came back to my mind…Yudhishthira, disarmed and helpless in front of Radheya. My heart began to thump in expectation. Have we won the war? Did Radheya make good of his promise? Where was Yudhishthira now? What should be my next course of action? However, all my excitement dropped the moment I saw Shalya. He looked crestfallen as he narrated to me the events that occurred on the battlefield.

Radheya after having disarmed Yudhishthira, approached him and held his neck by the curved hook of his bow and said, "O Great Emperor, it takes more than mere talk to stand up to Radheya in battle. You are fit to be a Brahmin studying the scriptures and offering oblations to the sacred fire. Why do you engage in activities meant for Kshatriyas? Go now and send Arjuna to battle me." Humiliating Yudhishthira thus, Radheya spared him.

This was unbelievable. The war would have been over if Radheya had just captured Yudhishthira. Instead, he let him free. I was furious. I was certain now that all was not as it seemed with Radheya. How could he let go of such a golden opportunity? If this was not an act of treachery, what else would qualify? Seeing his brother thus humiliated, Bheema rushed to attack Radheya but was intercepted by my brothers led by Dushasana, and a terrible battle followed. Like moths rushing into the fire, my brothers rushed to their death at his hands. Only Dushasana remained and he fought on valiantly. The sight of Dushasana only charged up Bheema more. He broke Dushasana's chariot and bow. Dushasana took up his mace and then made the cardinal mistake of getting within Bheema's reach. Seizing the opportunity, Bheema knocked the mace out of his hand, pounced on him and threw him to the ground. He placed his feet on his neck and grabbed both his arms, dislocating them off their shoulders. He then sat on him and tore his armour from his chest. Then in the very presence of Radheya who looked on doing nothing, he tore my brother's chest with his bare hands while my brother was still conscious and plucked out his lungs and heart. Blood gushed out from my brother's chest like a fountain. Roaring like a wild beast, Bheema looked challengingly at Radheya while collecting the blood in his palms and drinking it with relish. He exclaimed to the terrified warriors, "This is sweeter than ambrosia, more intoxicating than the best of wine, more nourishing than my mother's milk, the blood of this wretch. Watch all of you as I fulfil my oath. Watch me fulfil my promise to Draupadi."

During his last struggling moments to hold on to life, Dushasana kept looking hopefully towards Radheya for deliverence. Radheya, however, remained unmoved like a statue as he watched Bheema dance wildly around my dying brother.

And then took place the great decisive duel that everyone had waited for years. Arjuna, hearing of the insult to his brother Yudhishthira, rushed to deal with Radheya. He was intercepted by the young Vrishasena. There, in the very presence of Radheya, Arjuna felled him with a fatal shaft. Filled with rage over the killing of his son, Radheya charged towards Arjuna and engaged him in a deadly duel. The continuous twang of the Gandiva and the Vijaya reverberated in the air. Arjuna, with a scarf tied around his forehead instead of the famed Kiriti, deployed divine missiles. Radheya skillfully countered and neutralised them with ease. Radheya cut Arjuna's bowstring repeatedly, but Arjuna fastened it back to the bow even before Radheya could reach his quiver to take the next arrow. This earned him the admiration of Radheya. Both their chariots made their movements on the field as if in anticipation of the next move of their opponent. And then it happened. Radheya's chariot wheel sunk into a soft portion of the ground filled with wet mud. Shalya got down and tried to lift up the wheel but wasn't able to by himself. Radheya got down to assist him. He requested Arjuna to hold the fight in all fairness as he tried to pull out the wheel.

At that moment, a loud booming voice was heard. "Ha, Radheya, it is so strange that you of all people should speak of fairness. Where was your sense of fairness when Draupadi was dragged by her hair into the assembly and her modesty outraged? Were you not present in that hall? Were you not the one who referred to her as a woman of low virtue? Was it not you who stood by the wicked Duryodhana when he said that he would not part even with land, enough to be covered by a needlehead, for the Kaunteyas? Where was fairness just three days ago, when a sixteen-year-old boy, alone and unarmed, was collectively attacked and killed?"

It was Vaasudeva. Turning to Arjuna he continued, "Arjuna, this man deserves no consideration whatsoever. He is the one person who has given Duryodhana the courage to wage this war. This is your opportunity. Kill him now and repay your debt to all those who have lost their lives in this war fighting for your cause including our own Abhimanyu. Think no further. Act now!"

Listening to Vaasudeva's tirade, Radheya said nothing. He once again began exerting himself to pull out his chariot wheel when Arjuna took out a special shaft from his quiver called 'Anjalika'. He took aim and released it even as Radheya was still engaged in pulling out his chariot wheel. The shaft headed towards Radheya's neck and even as he looked up, it severed his head causing great celebration in the Kaunteyas' camp. The fighting on both sides stopped. Vaasudeva and Arjuna blew their conches in celebration as Yudhishthira rushed forward to verify the news of Radheya's fall. On seeing the headless trunk of Radheya on the battlefield, Yudhishthira was filled with ecstasy as he hugged Arjuna and Vaasudeva. Our forces, rendered leaderless, scattered in all directions. Great was the gloom that enveloped our camp as the sun went down after witnessing yet another eventful day at the holy field of Kurukshetra.

56

It took time for me to take in everything that Shalya had just narrated. My mother's face came to my mind. How was I ever going to answer her? Even if I won the war now, was it worth sacrificing all my brothers? She had just two sons out of hundred left alive, my brother Sudarshana and me. Would my father have already got the news? He had assigned Sanjaya the job of keeping him updated on the war. My mind went to Bhanumati. Was she still in her prayer chamber? Did she know about the fate of her son Lakshman? Her dream was now haunting me more than it did her. And Radheya...for whom was he fighting? He died for me...but refused to kill for me. Would there ever be an explanation to his actions? He let me down when it mattered the most. Now what was there to fight for when the victory was stripped of all its charm? I was drained of all emotions.

Shalya sat silent by my side. Uncle Shakuni, Uluka, Ashwatthama, Kripacharya and Kritavarma joined him in my tent. Ashwatthama broke the silence. "O Prince, know that you are not alone. We are all in this together. There is not a single hero in the battlefield who has not suffered a personal loss. But even now, all those lives lost in this war can be justified if we can make peace with the Kaunteyas. It is still not too late. I will speak to Yudhishthira on your behalf if you approve. I am certain he will be favourable in his response."

I smiled at Ashwatthama. I was now beyond anger. I said, "O Son of my Preceptor, how can I seek truce with the Kaunteyas now and face my mother? What answer would I give to my father, the King of Hastinapur? How could I back out of the battle in fear of defeat after seeing the death of my preceptor and my brothers? How could I seek comfort in peace with the Kaunteyas, after seeing my Grandsire laid to rest on a bed of arrows? How could I seek peace with the Kaunteyas when I see my sister Dushala in the raiment of a widow? If peace with the Kaunteyas was an option, would I have lost my son in battle? My salvation today lies in this war and not in peace. Speak no more the language of cowards. Discuss amongst yourselves and decide on the foremost amongst you to lead from now on. All of you are equally worthy heroes and capable of beating the best. Tomorrow, we shall meet."

I dismissed them for the night. I called for my brother Sudarshana and we set out on our horses towards the area of cremation where the bodies of the slain heroes were stacked. The ones identified were being cremated by their next of kin and the unidentified ones were being given a mass funeral. Brahmin priests, knowledgeable in the cremation rituals, were brought in for the purpose by either sides. We went to where the bodies of my brothers were kept. I never shed a tear when my eyes fell on the mangled carcass of my dear Dushasana. And then, there was Radheya, radiant even in death, the proud but severed head separated from the trunk. Next to him lay his valiant son Vrishasena, of the same age as Lakshman. Alas, how cursed was I to carry the stains of their young blood on my hands? I oversaw the cremation of all of them and the other heroes on our side who had lost their lives for me that day.

After leaving Sudarshana at his tent, I wandered around in the misty night aimlessly. At a distance, the fire from the crematory pyre blazed as the smoke rose up to merge with the dark sky. As it rose, in the fogginess of that smoke, I could see, smiling at me, the faces of all my dead brothers and along with them, those great heroes who willingly gave up their lives for my cause. How could I repay my debt to them? My heart weighed down with grief and anguish as I roamed across the battlefield in the cold moonlit night seeking solace. Would I have done anything differently had I known it would come to this? Then I saw at a distance, the Grandsire lying there all alone like a fallen lion, on his warrior's bed of arrows. I alighted from my horse, walked up to him and stood silently at his feet. He lifted his head gently and when I looked at his tired face, I broke down. He said in his feeble voice, "Come closer, Son, for I cannot see you clearly."

I went and sat down by his head. He said, "Why these tears, Son? They are not befitting a hero."

I said, "O Grandsire, today I am all alone. I have nothing left to fight for in this war. My brothers are gone. My preceptor has left me for the other world. My Radheya has left me."

The Grandsire said, "Son, don't make the mistake of calling him Radheya. He was not Radheya...he was a Kaunteya."

I was not sure if I was hearing correctly.

He continued, "Son, there is a truth that you must know now. I have been told about this by sage Narada himself. Your dear friend Radheya whom you considered as your alter ego, relying on whom you embarked on this war was actually the first-born of your Aunt Kunti. She bore him out of wedlock before she was married to your Uncle Pandu. Fearing the censure of the word, she abandoned him as an infant. He was found by Adhiratha, your father's charioteer and counsellor in those days. He was adopted and raised by him and his wife Radha as their own child."

Hearing the Grandsire's words, a numbing shock overtook my grief.

"Does Aunt Kunti know about this?" I asked.

"Yes, Son. She recognised him the very first day when he proudly swaggered into that arena like a lion. She recognised him by the shiny earrings that he wore. She had left him with those earrings when she had abandoned him."

My mind went back to that eventful day at the arena... the day that changed the course of Hastinapur's history. Now it became clear why Aunt Kunti had fainted and had to be carried away when she saw Radheya and Arjuna preparing to face each other in combat that day.

I asked tearfully, "O Grandsire, why didn't you tell me this earlier? I would have willingly given away Indraprastha or even my Hastinapur to Radheya. This war could have been avoided."

"Son, it had to be kept a secret to protect Kunti's honour. Besides, Radheya wanted it that way. He wanted this to be a secret as long as he was alive. This was a promise that he had extracted from Kunti."

"Radheya knew about this? He knew that he was a Kaunteya? All along, he stood by my side against his own brothers?"

"Yes, Son. He came to know about this first from Vaasudeva, and then from his own mother. They both tried to lure him to their side. But he remained loyal to you. He made them both promise that this would be kept a secret as long as he was alive. He came to seek my blessings the night before he joined the war and that night he told me everything about it."

The reason for Vaasudeva's private meetings with Radheya was now clear to me. So that was what it was all about. He had weakened Radheya's will to fight by disclosing to him the truth behind his birth. But why did he not do that earlier? The war could then have been averted. It seemed to me that he, more than anybody, wanted the war to happen.

"O Grandsire, I now understand why Radheya desisted from killing the Kaunteyas in spite of getting the opportunities. Now I see clearly the reason he remained a mute spectator while Bheema tore open my brother's chest and drank his blood. He was bound by his new-found fraternal affection. After all, blood is thicker than water."

"Do not say that, Son. Do not misjudge him. Radheya was loyal to you. But he was bound by the word he gave to his mother Kunti that he would not attempt to kill any of her sons except Arjuna in battle."

The Grandsire's words struck me like a thunderbolt. "He gave her his word? How could the Supreme Commander of any army be bound by such promises? How could he do that when he was committed to fighting for me? Even if he did give her his word, he let go of a perfect opportunity to capture Yudhishthira alive. That would still have given me victory and ended this war. O Grandsire, it now appears that even Radheya wanted Yudhishthira to win this war. All along, he stood by my side like my very own shadow while it now appears that his only motivation was to prove to the world his superiority over Arjuna. It is now clear to me that my cause in this war meant nothing to him. How misled was I?" I broke down, sobbing.

The Grandsire said, "Son, you are judging him too harshly. Radheya's integrity was always above aspersions. Vaasudeva offered him Indraprastha and the acceptance of his lordship by the rest of the Kaunteyas. He even promised him that Draupadi whom he once aspired for would also accept him as her lord if he joined their camp. But Radheya remained loyal to you and refused to leave your side. He preferred to die fighting for you."

I said, "O Grandsire, he should have established his value for our friendship by killing the Kaunteyas for me, and not by dying for me. Fighting on my side, it now appears to me that he sacrificed his life for Yudhishthira's cause and not mine."

The Grandsire had no answer to that. He turned his gaze silently towards the dark sky.

I continued, "I am tired, O Grandsire, I realise now that I am truly all alone. I have no interest in this war. Even if I win this war now, there is no one left except Uncle Shakuni to share my victory. I have already lost all that I had hoped to gain through victory. Of what value is victory then?"

The Grandsire looked at me kindly and said, "Son, I must tell you this at least now. The biggest treachery that you have endured so far has not been from Radheya or anyone else. It has been from your Uncle Shakuni. The far-seeing Vidura was right when he had warned me about Shakuni's decision to come and settle in Hastinapur. Little did I imagine that he had such a devious ulterior motive."

I was perplexed at this new revelation. This was too much to take in a single day.

He continued, "Son, Shakuni took you under his wings and succeeded in moulding you to his will. He consistently nourished over the years, the seeds of hatred sown in your heart against the Kaunteyas. He made you an instrument to achieve his evil designs. And I heard them all from his own mouth just a couple of nights back, when he came to me to gloat that he was at the threshold of achieving the fruit of his lifelong penance...the complete ruin of the Kuru household."

"What are you talking about, Grandsire, I do not understand..." I said.

The Grandsire continued, "It is an old story, Son...dates back to the days when your Uncle Pandu ruled Hastinapur. I had led a northward expedition on his behalf and had brought all the kingdoms there under his subjugation, including Gandhara, which was then ruled by your maternal grandfather King Subala. I had imposed a heavy tribute on Gandhara to be paid annually to Hastinapur. When the Yadava King Kuntibhoja offered Pandu the hand of his foster daughter Kunti for marriage, Pandu insisted that your father Dhritarashtra being elder, should be married first. But being born blind, it was difficult to get him an alliance from any royal household. It was then that I heard that Subala had announced a swayamvara for his daughter Gandhari, your mother, who had come of age. I set forth to Gandhara and asked Subala for the hand of his daughter for Dhritarashtra. This was strongly resented by your Uncle Shakuni at the time. However, Subala was forced to accept and give in when I told him that being matrimonially allied with us would mean that his hefty annual tribute to Hastinapur would not be required to be paid anymore. Seeing his young sister get married to the blind prince was an insult and humiliation that your Uncle Shakuni couldn't brook for his Gandhara. He swore to make it his life mission to see the ruin of the Kuru household. He made you an instrument in his grand scheme of vengeance without you knowing about it."

The night had turned into an unending nightmare. Uncle Shakuni, who doted on me, who narrated all those stories while I dozed off to sleep on his chest as a child, whose finger I held while taking those early steps, whose counsel guided me when my spirits were low, my friend, philosopher and guide... who poured me my first cup of wine, who kept my darkest secrets...all the while was just using me as a tool to achieve his ends? Betrayed from all sides, fool that I was, I felt I had lost my right to live.

Seeing my plight, the Grandsire said, "Son, do not despair thus. Whatever is happening is the work of destiny. You and I are but pawns in its hands. But even now, I will advise you to cease all hostilities towards the Kaunteyas. Seek Yudhishthira's pardon. He is a man of virtue who will never forsake those who take his refuge. End this war. Let those who remain alive be and let peace prevail."

I got up and said, "O Grandsire, it is too late now. If peace must prevail, it can happen only in a world without Duryodhana or the Kaunteyas. As long as I am alive, and any one of them is alive, peace will never be an option. I take your leave. If I shall see you again, it will be as the victorious Lord of the Earth. If not, our next meeting shall be in the other world. I seek your forgiveness for all my faults and the harsh words I may have subjected you to...but this is me. What you see is what I am. I have no false visage."

I saw tears flowing down the Grandsire's eyes. He looked at me adoringly as he said, "Son, I may not have said this to you before. I have admired Yudhishthira for his virtues, Bheema for his strength, Arjuna for his heroism and many others for various reasons, but they were all just objects of my admiration. However, if there was anyone who has been the object of my unconditional affection and pride, that was you. This bed of arrows that I lie on is testimony to this. Not for a moment have I wavered from my fondness for you, even when you hurt me with the harshest words...for I knew that they came from a heart devoid of guile. I have always counselled you with your best interest in my mind and heart. Now that you have resolved on what should be your way ahead, be firm in it and earn your everlasting glory."

I did not return to my tent. Instead, I wandered around aimlessly, the whole night, a restless and agitated soul. Vidura's words of warning to my father when I was born came to mind. He had said that my life would spell doom for the Kshatriya race. How prophetic did his words turn out, and more importantly, how significant was his own contribution to that!

My horse stopped by the side of a tree. It was fatigued and badly wounded from the battle. I decided to give it a rest. I harnessed it to a tree and laid down to rest next to it. It was still dark but I could sense by the chirping of the birds that dawn was not far away. My mind was far from the battle. It lingered on all those good times in the past as I drowsed to sleep.

57

The golden-coloured serpent slithered alone in the vast desert. It had no place to hide as the eagle hovered above it. However fast it moved in the desert sand, it could not get past the encompassing shadow of the eagle's wings. The eagle swooped down on the serpent. It gripped it in its talons and carried it across the desert to a stretch of grassland where waited the fat mongoose. Next to the mongoose lay ninety-nine serpents, their heads bitten off. The eagle dropped the serpent right in front of the mongoose, which pounced on it even before it could raise its hood in defence. The mongoose held the head of the struggling serpent between its jaws, digging its teeth into the back of its hood as the serpent wiggled for its life...and then I woke up with a start, sweating profusely. My mind travelled to my dear Bhanumati. We had vowed that her dreams would be mine and my dreams would be hers to share...but alas, not thus...

I realised that the sun had reached the mid skies. I looked around and found myself next to a large lake, frozen in the cold winter at the edge of the forest. This was the lake called Dwaipayana. My horse lay dead next to the tree. It had succumbed to its injuries. I became anxious as I wondered what had happened at the battlefield where I was rightfully meant to be at that time. Just then, at a distance, I saw a frail figure approaching. When it got closer, I realised that it was

Sanjaya, my father's charioteer. When he saw me, he broke down and wept profusely.

He said, "O Prince, I come from the battlefield. So happy is my heart to know that you still live and yet it cannot bear to see you thus." So saying, he once again broke down.

I said, "Steady yourself, Sanjaya, and tell me everything that happened. No news can be heavy enough to shake me now."

Sanjaya said, "O Prince, in your absence, it was decided that being the foremost of the experienced warriors on our side, the Lord of Madra would be the ideal hero to lead our army. He was appointed the Supreme Commander by Kripacharya with all the ceremonial rituals. Our heroes fought bravely during the day's battle and so long as Shalya led from the front, we still had a semblance of hope. Then Yudhishthira himself came forward and took on Shalya and a great battle ensued. Today, Yudhishthira showed the world that when overtaken by wrath, he is no less than his brothers in battle. A well-aimed javelin from him pierced Shalya's armour causing him to fall lifeless on the battleground. Bheema sought out Prince Sudarshana for battle and killed him with his bare hands. Sahadeva dispatched the King of Gandhara and his son Uluka to the heavens in battle. Arjuna finally eliminated Susharma and the remaining Samsaptakas. The rest of our army has been routed. Only Ashwatthama, Acharya Kripa and Kritavarma remain amongst the chariot warriors, but they have taken flight at the fall of Shalya and are nowhere to be seen. I was repairing towards Hastinapur to update His Majesty on the war when Dhrishtadyumna and Satyaki captured me. They would have killed me if not for the timely intervention of sage Vyasa who appeared there in the nick of time. On his instruction, they set me free. The Kaunteyas and their entire army are on the hunt for you. Please escape at the earliest."

"Escape? Sanjaya, who do I escape from? I have no fear of the Kaunteyas even if they approach me led by Indra himself. Death is the least of my fears, for a glorious death in battle is the most welcomed friend for a Kshatriya. But if I get away with my life now, how would I escape my conscience? How would I escape the curse of the kith and kin of all those who died for me in this battle? How would I face my mother who has lost her ninety-nine sons for my cause? What answer would I have for my sister Dushala when she asks me if the death of her lord meant anything to me at all? How would I face my King after deserting Hastinapur on the battlefield? I will fight the Kaunteyas till the very end. The only way that I can square up with all those heroes who died for me is by either winning the war or paying with my life. So please return to Hastinapur. Tell my father that I seek his final blessings for glory. Tell him to grieve not for the loss of his sons, for each one of them has their place reserved in the highest heavens because they did not turn their backs on the battle. Tell my mother that I was fortunate to have been born to her. The obstinacy that I showed by refusing to come out of her womb in time was the root cause for everything that followed, and unfortunately that obstinacy stayed with me as my second nature. Tell her that I seek her forgiveness for all the grief I have given her. Tell Bhanumati that I have no face to show her for I could not protect our only son. Tell her that her lord fought like a hero and never compromised on his pride. This is not how it was supposed to end. Perhaps, Lord Hari has a different plan. Tell her that I shall be waiting for her in the other world. Now return to Hastinapur, while I prepare for my final battle."

Just then, we saw three chariots approaching us. As they got nearer, we realised that they were Ashwatthama, Kripacharya and Kritavarma. They were relieved to see me. They discussed at length about the day's battle with me. Kripacharya said, "O Prince, more shocking than the fall of Shalya was the news of his treachery that we learnt about from our spies in Yudhishthira's camp. When Shalya fell, all the heroes gathered around him to pay their last respects. However, Nakula and Sahadeva refused to pay their respects as they never forgave their maternal uncle for joining our camp. Yudhishthira admonished them by saying that Shalya's contribution towards their cause far outweighed everyone else's. Before the war, when Shalya had informed Yudhishthira that he was bound by the word he gave you to fight on our side, the clever Yudhishthira had extracted in return a promise from him that as a charioteer, he would do his best to dampen and demoralise Radheya's spirit and enthusiasm in the war. Shalya had kept his promise by constantly deriding Radheya through insulting words and putting him down in comparison to Arjuna. He did his best to dent Radheya's confidence. When Radheya invited Shalya to take up the reins of his chariot, little did he know that he had invited his own death, for Shalya deliberately sank the chariot wheel into the wet earth offering Arjuna the opportunity to kill Radheya. Our spies heard this truth directly from Yudhishthira's mouth as he disclosed it to the twins. Had we known about this unforgivable act of treachery yesterday, we would have killed Shalya instead of honouring him as our Supreme Commander."

To everyone's surprise, I took this information calmly. "Dear Acharya, no such information shocks or surprises me now. I have become immune to such news of betrayal for I have reached far beyond that," I said, with a smirk directed at fate. "I have realised that this war is solely my war...and even if I am betrayed by everyone in my life, I will take it to its very end...for no matter what...I shall never betray myself."

Ashwatthama said, "O Lord, why do you speak thus? All is not lost. You still have us with you. You are not alone. Together, we will take on the Kaunteyas and their forces. Their forces have also reduced in great numbers. I will use all the divine missiles in my arsenal if need be. We just need your approval. Appoint one of us as your commander and we will take the war forward."

I smiled at Ashwatthama and said, "Ashwatthama, you are now the hope of Hastinapur. In your hands rests its destiny. I appoint you as our Supreme Commander." I turned to Kripacharya and asked him to conduct the rituals then and there and appoint Ashwatthama as the new Supreme Commander. The Acharya did the needful and sprinkled water over the head of his nephew, making him the new Supreme Commander.

Ashwatthama then said, "Come, O Prince, let us seek the enemy. Today, you will see what I am capable of. We will attack them right now."

I said, "The evening is approaching. I am fatigued and my body burns from the wounds I have suffered. I am also burning from the inside with rage. I need to cool myself in the waters of this lake and rest. We shall resume the battle, tomorrow. Go today and come back refreshed, tomorrow, with a plan."

The three of them looked at each other and agreed. They took Sanjaya along with them and left while I stayed there all by myself.

I selected a spot on the icy lake where the ice was thin. I stamped on it hard and the surface cracked as the crystal clear waters sparkled inside. I undressed and immersed myself in it, just leaving my face above the ice-cold water. My training in Hatha Yoga served me well to bear the coldness of the water. I closed my eyes and stayed that way for what seemed like eternity in the peaceful silence except for the sound of the birds from the adjoining woods.

Then from a distance came the rumbling sound of chariot wheels and horses. It increased as it approached nearer. I heard a voice calling out, "O coward Duryodhana, did you think that we would not have found you? You are the sole cause for this holocaust. We would have smoked you out even from the netherworld if you had sought refuge there. Do you think you can escape us by hiding in this lake after all this? Your obstinacy has brought ruin to the race of Bharata. Now please don't bring it to disgrace by hiding in the waters. Come out and fight like a true Kshatriya."

I opened my eyes. It was Yudhishthira. At the shore of the lake stood the Kaunteyas with Vaasudeva and all the remaining heroes of their army including Shikhandi, Dhrishtadyumna, Satyaki, the sons of Draupadi, along with my brother Yuyutsu. I remained silent.

Then, Bheema taunted, "Come out, O Great Hero. This is your chance to make true all those threats that you made to us through that wretch, Uluka."

I said, "O Kaunteyas, know that I am not hiding from you cowards. I have immersed myself in this lake to cool myself from the heat of the rage that fills up my entire being. My war has lost its purpose, for all those with whom I cherished to share my victory have left me. Today, I have no interest in the kingdom. You may keep it for yourself as the spoils of your ill-earned victory. But fight all of you I will tomorrow, for today I am exhausted, wounded and in need of rest. So would be all of you. At the break of dawn tomorrow, we shall fight refreshed and I promise you that it will be a fight to the finish."

"Ha, Duryodhana, you touch me with your concern," said Yudhishthira, sarcastically, "but we are all sufficiently rested and refreshed. Stop making excuses. Come out and fight. Do not bring dishonour to your race. Your cowardice puts us to shame. It is because of you that our Grandsire today rests on his bed of arrows. It is because of you that our preceptor whom we all revered has left us. It is because of you that the great Radheya whom we knew not as our own brother was slain by us. It is you who separated our Uncle Shalya from us and made us cause his death. Now when you have lost everything in this war and have nothing to offer us anymore other than your own life, your magnanimity in offering us the kingdom that was never yours to begin with is a joke. I seek no charity from you. However, I am willing to be charitable to you and spare you your life if you seek my pardon even at this moment."

Yudhishthira's taunting words had their effect on me. I rose from the lake. I came out of the water and stood proud in front of the Kaunteyas without a thread of clothing on me. That was my way of showing the 'Emperor' how beyond caring I was for him. The entire host of heroes who stood there were embarrassed, all except Vaasudeva who watched the drama silently with a light grin on his face. Yudhishthira ordered one of the soldiers to hand me my robe. I draped it around me and said in a roaring voice, "O Emperor, here I am, alone, unarmed and ready to fight all of you if you come at me one at a time."

Yudhishthira said, "Ha, Duryodhana, need I remind you of the fate Abhimanyu met at your hands just five days ago? He was a mere sixteen-year-old boy who stood similarly unarmed and alone surrounded by you great heroes. Where did your sense of fair fighting go then? Why is it that suddenly you are reminded of it now?"

I said, "That sixteen-year-old boy was a chariot warrior. He was killing my men in hundreds using the methods of Gandharva warfare much against the ethics of fair fighting amongst Kshatriyas. Therefore, the Acharya had no choice but to order a combined attack on him. Besides, when someone breaks into a Chakravyuha, he should expect to be surrounded from all sides. He should be adept at coming out of the vyuha as much as he is at breaking into it. Unfortunately for you, it wasn't up to him. Do I need to remind you that half-knowledge is more dangerous than ignorance? Your accusing me in this regard is most inappropriate. I would rather say that it was you who killed him by irresponsibly letting him alone into the Chakravyuha."

There was silence. I looked at Arjuna and Vaasudeva and they were silent too. The grin on Vaasudeva's face was missing now. Arjuna's eyes were moist as he turned to Yudhishthira for an answer. From the look on the others' faces I could make out that they grudgingly agreed with me. After some embarrassing moments of silence, Yudhishthira said, "Very well, Duryodhana, I shall give you a fair chance even now. I am truly happy to learn that you are not a coward. Choose any one of us for single combat with a weapon of your choice. If you win, you shall be the Lord of the Earth. Hastinapur along with Indraprastha shall be yours. This is my promise."

There was a murmur across as nobody seemed happy with Yudhishthira's offer. Vaasudeva was furious as he shook his head in disgust. He admonished Yudhishthira in the full hearing of everyone, "Once a gambler, always a gambler. Surely, the Kaunteyas are not destined to enjoy sovereignty. How could you, Yudhishthira, in such foolishness throw away everything thus, when victory is finally within your grasp? Do the lives of all those heroes who died for you in this war mean nothing at all to you? You know very well that there is nobody amongst you brothers except Bheema who can take Duryodhana on in a mace fight. Yet abandoning better judgement, you indulge in such a reckless offer. We know that this wicked man Duryodhana would stoop to any level, as he has no shame. If he picks anyone other than Bheema for a mace fight, you can all be prepared to return to the forest along with Draupadi."

I knew why Vaasudeva rebuked Yudhishthira thus in the full hearing of everybody when he could have done that privately. He was appealing to my sense of pride and ensuring that I chose Bheema for combat. But there was no need for that.

I said, "O Yudhishthira, I now realise why the sages refer to you as 'Ajatashatru'. You are indeed incapable of having enemies. Let any one of you approach me for combat. I am ready to take on anyone including this Vaasudeva. And I will choose the mace for my weapon. However, I have left it back in my camp along with my armour and headgear. If you could send someone to fetch them for me, we could commence the combat."

Yudhishthira sent Sahadeva to fetch my mace and my gear. Bheema stepped forward to take me on. While we waited for Sahadeva's return, at a distance, against the evening sun, we saw the silhouette of a tall figure riding towards us in his chariot. As he came closer, the majestic figure of Balarama, draped in blue silk raiment became clear. My heart filled with euphoria as I saw him. The sight of my Guru felt like the much-needed balm for my lonely heart. I rushed to him and fell at his feet. He lifted and embraced me. The others too greeted him and paid their respects. Vaasudeva, however, did not seem too happy to see his brother there.

Balarama was always favourably disposed towards me and would have supported me in the war had his brother Vaasudeva not been on the Kaunteyas' side. He refused to take part in the war and embarked on a pilgrimage to holy spots across the land of Bharata. He was at the last leg of the pilgrimage at the holy spot called Samantapanchaka, which was very close to the battlefield of Kurukshetra when Sage Narada updated him about the war. When he was informed by Narada that the final battle between his students Bheema and myself was about to commence, he rushed to Dwaipayana.

Sahadeva returned with my mace and my gear. Both Bheema and I then sought the permission of Balarama to begin the combat. Balarama said, "O heroes, both of you are dear to me and I have dedicated myself equally to training both of you. You, Duryodhana, are more skilled and quick on the feet whereas Bheema is stronger and more powerful in his strike. I would like to see both of you fight in such a way that you do not bring shame but pride to your preceptor. Fight hard but fight fair and fight for everlasting glory."

Turning to Yudhishthira, he said, "O Yudhishthira, the earth here is not firm enough and conducive to have a mace fight. The mace fight should be held either in an arena or on earth that can take the heavy blows of the mace. Let us go to the shore of the nearby Samantapanchaka Lake. The ground there is firm enough to withstand the fight. Besides, it is a holy spot rendered auspicious by the holy Bhargava himself. One who dies there is assured of his place in heavens."

Yudhishthira agreed to this proposal. We all moved towards Samantapanchaka Lake for the final battle.

58

Bheema was a formidable opponent. His mace was one-and-a-half times heavier than mine and so was his reach. However, he was no match for me in agility. Sparks flew as our maces clashed and the noise reverberated like thunder in the thin, cold air, causing birds to fly from their branches in fear. Bheema was always a savage fighter who depended on brute strength. With him, it was always brawn and seldom brain. It was important to stay away from his reach. Every time he charged at me like a mad bull, I waited till the last moment before skilfully avoiding his strike. My plan was to first tire him down and then make my move. He made several unsuccessful attempts to strike me. My strategy was working and soon fatigue was overtaking him. I then began my offence as I repeatedly struck him landing several quick blows on his body, sending him reeling on the ground time and again. He was too slow to out-manoeuvre my blows. My moves earned the admiration of the heroes who watched the duel with bated breath. Humiliated, Bheema once again rushed at me. Stepping aside, I swung my mace hard, causing him to go crashing yet again. He fell near where Vaasudeva and Arjuna sat. Vaasudeva said, "Arise, O Hero, you have an oath to fulfil. Remember the assembly hall. Make good of that oath you undertook at the assembly hall that day."

Bheema rose up with great difficulty. He looked at me and his chest began to heave. He turned around and looked at Vaasudeva and Arjuna again. Vaasudeva once again said to Bheema, "Do not hesitate, the time has arrived...fulfil your oath like a true Kshatriya."

As Vaasudeva said this, Arjuna slapped his right thigh twice and said, "Yes, Brother...the time has come to fulfil your oath."

Once again, Bheema charged at me. I jumped out of his way in the air to avoid the lateral swing of his mace. While in the air, came that blow, smashing with fury, my upper thighs. I came crashing to the ground. My thighs were broken and dislocated from my hip. I lay wiggling like an injured serpent. My headgear rolled off my head. Bheema rushed towards me and kicked away my headgear. He then placed his foot on my head, repeatedly kicking it. He roared, "Ha, wretch, I have been dreaming of this blessed day. This is for all the hardship that you put us through the last thirteen years. This is for the humiliation that you subjected Draupadi to on that accursed day in the assembly hall. Let the world know that I have kept my oath. I had sworn at the assembly hall that day, that I shall break your thighs in battle...those thighs that you invited Draupadi to sit on. Look at those thighs now if you can lift your head." So saying, he lifted my head with his foot and dropped it down.

Yudhishthira called out, "Stop that at once, Bheema. That's enough. It is not right to treat a fallen man thus even if he is your enemy. Desist from this dishonourable and deplorable act. It is not the approved way of the Kshatriyas."

The heroes present there were struck with horror and disgust.

Then I heard a loud roar. It was Balarama, "Bheema, you are the scum of the Kshatriya race. By striking Duryodhana below the navel, you have transgressed the rules of mace fighting and brought dishonour not only to your teacher but also to the entire Kshatriya race. Shame on you and shame on all these heroes here who witness this sinful act of yours and bear with it. But not me. Today, you shall suffer my wrath. I will send you to the abode of Yama this very moment." So saying, he rushed with his mace in fury towards Bheema. Just as he was to strike, he was held back by Vaasudeva who grabbed him from behind and encircled him with his strong arms.

He said, "Stop, Dear Brother. Desist from this rash act. There is no doubt that Bheema is as good as dead if you resolve to kill him. But before that, let me remind you that all Bheema did was fulfil the oath that he took at the assembly hall when this wicked Duryodhana exposed his thigh to Draupadi and asked her to come and sit on it. Would any man, leave alone a Kshatriya hero like Bheema, endure such an insult to his wife? You would have approved if he had broken Duryodhana's thighs then and there. But the Kaunteyas endured this insult and more for thirteen years. Duryodhana forced the war upon the Kaunteyas. He closed all doors for peace. Many rules were broken many times in this war by both the sides. Now all that matters is winning. Besides all this, Bheema breaking Duryodhana's thighs was not something done entirely of his own free will. There was also a hand of destiny in this. Sage Maitreya had cursed Duryodhana that Bheema would break his thighs in battle. Who would know better than you that the words of the sages never go false? So, please desist from this anger and forgive Bheema. He is not to be blamed for what happened. Duryodhana brought this upon himself."

Balarama said, "Vaasudeva, you will find ways to justify anything the Kaunteyas do, for you are blinded by your partiality towards them. But not me. I curse this Bheema that he will never be remembered with respect for his valour due to this heinous sin he has committed in the very presence of his teacher. As for Duryodhana, I shall always take pride in that he was my student and undoubtedly the best I ever had. No matter how harshly history will remember and judge him, the legacy of his valour shall redeem his name."

Balarama looked at me for one last time as I lay in a pool of blood, gasping for breath. His eyes were moist as he looked at me with pity...and pride. He wiped his eyes with the corner of his blue silk attire, turned and left without looking back.

The Kaunteyas looked crestfallen after Balarama's tirade. Vaasudeva tried to cheer them up. He said, "O heroes, why this sadness on your faces? If it is because of what my brother said, you should not pay much importance to that. A cup of wine is all it takes for him to forget his anger. This is your moment of glory to celebrate and rejoice. O Yudhishthira, you are now the Lord of this Earth. You have earned a well-deserved victory. Be cheerful."

Yudhishthira said, "O Vaasudeva, it is true that we fought a just war that was imposed upon us by this man lying here. He may have been singularly responsible for all the lives lost in this battle and deserving of nothing less than death. But Bheema, placing his foot on his head and repeatedly kicking it is something that I can never approve of. That was no way to treat a fallen enemy, even if he was the gravest sinner on earth."

Vaasudeva said, "Bheema was just venting the fury that he held inside him for all these years. Don't begrudge him that, although I agree that he could have refrained from placing his foot on a fallen enemy's head. It was not an act befitting a Kshatriya."

All this while, I was listening to the conversation. With great effort, I lifted my head and lashed out, "Ha, Vaasudeva, you have no business to be talking of the Kshatriyas' code of conduct. Born to a slave of Kamsa and brought up among cowherds, you mingle with us royal princes as if you are one of us. If this war had been fought by abiding the rules, the story would have been different and I would be standing as the victor. But it is your involvement that polluted what would have been a fairly fought war between Kshatriyas for justice. By disclosing Radheya's true identity to him and weakening his resolve in the battle, you dealt me the first blow. It was you who prompted Yudhishthira to seek the Grandsire's counsel on how to defeat him and again it was you who was behind the disgraceful attack on the Grandsire, using Shikhandi as a human shield. You prompted Arjuna to attack that great chariot warrior Bhurishravas from behind when he was engaged in combat with Satyaki. You were behind the lie that Yudhishthira spoke to hasten the end of our preceptor. It was you who prompted Arjuna to kill Jayadratha after the sun had set, when he was caught off guard. You instigated Arjuna to perpetrate that most shameful act of slaying Radheya when he was on the ground engaged in pulling his chariot wheel. Do you think I did not notice you and Arjuna prompting Bheema to strike me on my thighs, forgetting all rules of mace fighting? After all this, what moral ground do you have to speak on the Kshatriya's code of conduct? I have lived a full life. I have nothing to regret. I have celebrated my life with my friends and dear ones. I have chastised and subdued my foes. My friends loved me and my foes feared me. I have given alms to the needy and gifted the learned and deserving Brahmins. I have studied the Vedas. I have appeased the deities and performed the highest sacrifices. I have collected tributes from my allies. I have governed well and my subjects have felt no want. I have never sinned, for no act can be deemed a sin if performed with a clear conscience, devoid of guilt. I have always walked with my head held high with pride and without any regrets. Why shouldn't Bheema place his foot on my head when very soon the birds of prey will be pecking on it? I am beyond caring, for soon I shall be received in those regions in the highest of heavens meant for those killed in battle while these Kaunteyas will continue with their wretched lives after inheriting the barren earth bereft of all its lustre."

I stopped my tirade and closed my eyes. A gentle breeze swept across as I felt a shower of fragrant flowers on me. I slowly opened my eyes, I saw up there the Suras, the Gandharvas, the Vasus, the Ashwinis, the Adityas, the Maruts... the entire host of celestials assembled together in the skies as they showered me with a rain of flowers. I closed my eyes again. Perhaps, I was hallucinating in pain. The Kaunteyas remained silent but I knew that the truth in my words had made them all feel small.

Then, Vaasudeva responded assertively, "O Fallen Prince, know that I had promised Draupadi in the Kamyaka Forest that her humiliation would be avenged. The hills may hide and the oceans may dry up but my words would never go false.

Today, my words have come true. But you have brought this tragedy upon yourself. You refused to listen to me or to the wise counsel of your elders and your mother. You are now suffering the consequences. Why blame others?" Turning to Yudhishthira, he said, "Let us leave him to his destiny. Tradition demands that the night of victory must be celebrated in the enemy's camp. So, let us proceed."

I lay there alone, laid to waste. Soon after they had left, I felt long shadows approach me. It was Ashwatthama, Kripacharya and Kritavarma. They came and sat around me. They wept at my plight. They had been hiding behind a tree and watching everything. Ashwatthama washed my face with water from the lake. He held my head in his lap, silent tears running down his face.

I addressed them, "It's all over now, O heroes. I release you all from your obligations to me. Thank you for everything. You have Duryodhana's gratitude. Proceed to some place where you will be safe and live your lives to the full. We shall meet next in the other world."

Ashwatthama said, "O Prince, don't speak thus. We shall abandon neither you nor this war. We have brought your chariot. We will take you to some place safe. This war is not over yet. It will be over with the death of the Kaunteyas. This is my promise to you even now."

I said, "I am too weak and in pain to move from here. You may all proceed. May the three-eyed Mahadeva bless you in your mission. I shall remain here waiting for the good news."

The three of them took leave and I lay there alone clinging to the last thread of hope for victory as the rim of the sun slowly descended on the western hills.

Epilogue

He smiles compassionately as he wipes the dew from my face. I look at him knowing not what to expect. He says, "Know, O great hero, that I harboured no hatred against you. You have always been dear to me. But your unjustified hatred for the Kaunteyas distanced me from you. Know that it is my life's pledge to never abandon truth. This war was important to establish truth and justice, and you were on the wrong side of it. It was never personal."

I hold his hand and ask him, "I've heard Grandsire say that you are Hari, the Lord of the Universe, in the human form. How true is that, O Vaasudeva? I desire to know. Enlighten me, for these are my last moments on earth."

He says, "O Duryodhana, the world knows me as the Son of Devaki, born in the house of Vrishnis. But I will disclose to you the truth for you are dear to me. Know me to be the pervading essence of all creations. The wise know me to be the Source, the Path and the Destination. I am the object of every sacrifice and worship. I hold this universe together with my power. Know that I am the truth and I am the science behind the truth. To know me is to realise me. Today, I shall grant you the vision to behold that which the sages spend several lifetimes for."

He expands, filling up the skies. I see the sun, the moon, the stars, the planets and the galaxies all merge into his form.

I see the Adityas, the Rudras, Daityas, Danavas, Gandharvas, Kinnaras, Nagas...integrated together in his blinding effulgence that spreads to all quarters. I see Hari and I see Hara come together in him. I see the whole of creation in him. I am exhilarated as the hair on my body stand on end. I ask, "Who are you...so wonderful to behold? Are you the Creator himself? Please be kind and reveal to me your true identity."

He says in a voice that reverberates in all quarters, "I am the cause for the sun rising in the east. I am the cause for the stars shining in the night. I am the cause for the flowers blossoming in the spring. I am the cause for the rivers flowing to the ocean. I am the cause for every breath you take. I am that silent witness to the actions of man's free will and I am the dispenser of its fruits. I am that which maintains the universal order. I am the nourisher, I am the nourished and I am the nourishment. I am the all-consuming time and the all-pervading space. There is no end to my description. Know that I am the light of truth shining in the innermost recess of your heart. I AM...and there is no other!"

The overwhelming effulgence blinds me. I shut my eyes as peace slowly engulfs me in the silent stillness of time.

I feel a sprinkle of cold water on my face.

"Wake up, my Lord, wake up! I have brought you glad tidings. The Kaunteyas are no more in this world. We have rid the world of them."

The words ring in my ears like auspicious chimes of the temple bells.

I open my eyes and see a figure in front of me encompassed by a dark aura. But the shining jewel on the forehead is a giveaway...yes, it is you, Ashwatthma. You have finally arrived. He says to my joy, "We entered their tents in stealth and murdered the Kaunteyas...all of them, in their sleep, and along with them the Panchalas, too. We then set fire to their tents. We made sure that no one escaped. We have won the war for you, My Prince. You are now the Lord of the Earth."

Bravo, Ashwatthama! You have accomplished for me what no one else could...not even my Radheya. You have delivered victory to me. Great is your achievement. May you be blessed. You have given me the moment that I've lived for all my life. My body feels light and my soul liberated. O Death, hasten hither to me for I fear not your embrace, I fear not your darkness...for Ashwatthama has placed me securely...in... *THE FAVOURABLE ARMS OF HISTORY.*